Table of Contents

MW01593010

PLANT BASED DIET
MEAL PLAN COOKBOOK

500

Quick & Easy Everyday Recipes
for Busy People on A Plant-Based Diet
21-Day Plant-Based Meal Plan

JENNIFER BOLTON

Copyright

Changing to a plant-based diet is one of the most important decisions you can make to improve your health, boost energy levels, and also prevent chronic diseases. Science shows that eating more healthily helps you to live longer, can also help the environment and reduce the risk of getting sick.

Plant-based diets are really popular nowadays, and you might have heard about some of its advantages. In the long run, this diet can help you not only with your health but also your energy and make some changes that can completely change your life. You can easily find the basics of a plant-based diet in this book, it includes what you should eat, what to avoid, the benefits it has, and some recipes for beginners like you to start this new lifestyle.

This book is also beneficial for those people who have wondered about the plant-based diet but had absolutely no idea where to start. This plant-based diet cookbook is looking forward to helping people make changes in their life, starting with their diet. Nothing in will ever stop you once you start your weight loss journey.

If you want to start a plant-based diet but don't know exactly where to start, don't worry! This book is just for you. Here you can find everything so you can make this change easy and also enjoy it. Here you can find the answers to your questions, advice, and some techniques that you may need.

Some good news is that a plant-based diet makes your body stronger, so it can resist many types of chronic diseases. Some effects of these diseases can be limited or controlled, while others can be completely eliminated. Now it's your time to change your life!

Weight loss is based on a nutrient-dense diet, and it's all that is needed to achieve your goals. So if you have been trying to lose weight, now is the time to make that difference! Read patiently and carefully every section of this cookbook, and you'll understand what it is essential to know about this plant-based diet. You'll find it really interesting.

The caloric density of plant-based unprocessed foods is lower, this means that the portions you eat can be larger and it will be a lot easier to lose the weight as you are consuming more food.

Once people start changing and moving to a plant-based diet, they have more motivation to eat healthy as they feel great and are capable of doing so many things.

This cookbook gives you the opportunity to nourish yourself in a simple, affordable, and delicious way. Start cooking with these plant-based recipes today as making this change could save your life!

With this cookbook, you will enjoy simple and delicious plant-based diet meals that you will love and eat again!

How a Plant-Based Diet Can Boost Your Health

Did you know that a Whole-Food, Plant-Based diet can significantly boost your health? Here is how.

Scientist proves that many chronic diseases can be reduced, reversed, or controlled by eating whole-foods and having a plant-based diet. Studies show that this type of diet can reduce the risk of type 2 diabetes, heart disease, certain types of cancer, and other important illnesses. Other benefits are more significant fitness results, more energy, less inflammation, and better health outcomes after deciding to make this change.

Whole-food, Plant-based diet

This diet is based on the following:

-   Whole food: natural foods are not very or heavily processed. It means minimally refined or unrefined ingredients

-   Plant-based: these are the food that comes from plants and has no anima ingredients (milk, honey, meat, eggs)

By eating natural, no processed foods that don't come from animals, you can meet your nutritional needs.

You'll love these foods!

Here are some of the most critical food categories that you'll enjoy in this diet:

-   Vegetables: a lot of veggies that include avocados, spinach, lettuce, peppers, peas, corn, kale, etc.
-   Whole grains: starches such as cereals and grains, quinoa, brown rice, whole wheat, oats, and other foods that are in their whole form.
-   Fruits: this includes bananas, citrus fruits, apples, grapes, berries, etc.
-   Legumes: includes beans of any type, also lentils, pulses, etc.
-   Tubers: these can be potatoes, carrots, sweet potatoes, parsnips, beets, etc.

Seeds, tofu, nuts, whole grain flour, and breads are other foods that you can enjoy! These foods should be eaten in moderation as they are more calorie-dense and can make you gain weight.

What are the benefits?

Science proves that having a plant-based diet brings different benefits; these include:

-   Managing weight efficiently: this diet helps to lose weight and keep it off without having to count calories; people who follow this diet tend to be leaner.
-   Prevents diseases: chronic diseases such as heart disease and diabetes can be prevented or even reversed with this diet.
-   Lighter environmental footprint: the plant-based diet helps to improve the environment as it reduces the stress in it.

Welcome to the plant-based diet lifestyle. Enjoy!

What to Eat and What to avoid

All recipes call for 100% plant foods: vegetables, fruits, whole grains, legumes, nuts and seeds, and contain no animal-derived ingredients: meat (beef, pork, fowl, fish, or seafood), eggs, honey, or dairy products cow's milk, cream, butter, cheese, or yogurt).

When you switch to a plant-based diet, all meals are center around plant-based foods.

Foods like eggs, dairy, meat, seafood, and poultry could be used as a complement to a plant-based meal, not as the main food.

A Whole-Foods, Plant-Based Shopping List:

-   Fruits: Citrus fruits, berries, peaches, pears, pineapple, bananas, etc.
-   Vegetables: Spinach, tomatoes, kale, peppers, broccoli, cauliflower, carrots, asparagus, etc.
-   Starchy vegetables: Sweet potatoes, potatoes, butternut squash, etc.
-   Whole grains: Rolled oats, quinoa, Brown rice, farro, brown rice pasta, barley, etc.
-   Healthy fats: Olive oil, avocados, coconut oil, unsweetened coconut, etc.
-   Legumes: Chickpeas, lentils, peas, peanuts, black beans, etc.
-   Seeds, nuts, and nut butters: Cashews, macadamia, almonds, nuts, sunflower seeds, natural peanut butter, pumpkin seeds, tahini, etc.
-   Unsweetened plant-based milks: almond milk, cashew milk, Coconut milk, etc.
-   Spices, herbs and seasonings: Rosemary, turmeric, basil, curry, black pepper, salt, etc.
-   Condiments: Nutritional yeast, soy sauce, salsa, mustard, vinegar, lemon juice, etc.
-   Plant-based protein: Tempeh, plant-based protein sources, Tofu, or powders with no added sugar or artificial ingredients.
-   Beverages: Sparkling water, Coffee, tea, etc.

AVOID THIS FOODS

-   Meat: Seafood, red meat, fish, poultry, processed meat.
-   Dairy: Butter, half and half, yogurt, milk, cheese, cream, buttermilk.
-   Eggs: Chicken, duck, quail, ostrich.
-   Plant Fragments (these oftentimes include Plant-based replacement foods): Margarine, Added Fats, oils*
*Oil, including olive oil, is 100% fat, nutrient-poor, and calorically-dense. Oil injures the innermost lining of the artery, the endothelium, and that injury is the gateway to vascular disease. For people with known heart disease, even adding a little oil can have a negative impact on heart health.
-   Refined Sugar: White sugar, beet sugar, brown rice syrup, barley malt, cane juice crystals, cane sugar, brown sugar, corn syrup, confectioner's sugar, fructose.
-   Refined Grains: White rice, quick-cook oats, white flour.
-   Protein Isolates: Pea protein isolate, Soy protein isolate, seitan.
-   Beverages: Fruit juice (even 100% pure fruit juice), Soda, sports drinks, energy drinks.

21-DAYS MEAL PLAN

DAY: 1
Breakfast: Fruity Granola (15)
Lunch: Pesto & White Bean Pasta (101)
Dinner: Golden Harvest Soup (44)

DAY:2
Breakfast: Pumpkin Steel-Cut Oats (15)
Lunch: Green Pea Risotto (83) And Caramelized Onion And Beet Salad (143)
Dinner: Minty Beet and Sweet Potato Soup (45)

DAY:3
Breakfast: Chocolate Quinoa Breakfast Bowl (16)
Lunch: Grilled Portobello with Mashed Potatoes and Green Beans (112)
Dinner: Weeknight Chickpea Tomato Soup (40)

DAY:4
Breakfast: Muesli and Berries Bowl (17)
Lunch: Italian Lentils (96)
Dinner: Tomato Orzo Soup (81)

DAY:5
Breakfast: Cinnamon And Spice Overnight Oats (18)
Lunch: Roasted Cauliflower Tacos (114)
Dinner: Creamy Avocado-Dressed Kale Salad (151)

DAY:6
Breakfast: Baked Banana French Toast with Raspberry Syrup (18)
Lunch: White Bean Burgers (109)
Dinner: Minty Beet and Sweet Potato Soup (45)

DAY:7
Breakfast: Sunshine Muffins (20)
Lunch: Loaded Black Bean Pizza (92)
Dinner: Creamy Butternut Squash Soup (54)

DAY:8
Breakfast: Smoothie Breakfast Bowl (21)
Lunch: Spanish Rice And Beans (103)
Dinner: Tabbouleh Salad (148)

DAY:9
Breakfast: Savory Pancakes (22)
Lunch: Curried Mango Chickpea Wrap (91)
Dinner: Cream of Mushroom Soup (58)

DAY:10
Breakfast: Tropi-Kale Breeze (23)
Lunch: Lemony Lentil And Rice Soup (80)
Dinner: Glazed Curried Carrots (120)

DAY:11
Breakfast: Blueberry Oatmeal Breakfast Bars (25)
Lunch: GGB Bowl (103)
Dinner: Hot & Sour Tofu Soup (59)

DAY:12
Breakfast: Banana Bread Rice Pudding (31)
Lunch: Ratatouille (Pressure cooker) (122)
Dinner: Rainbow Quinoa Salad (155)

DAY:13
Breakfast: Orange French Toast (26)
Lunch: Lemon and Thyme Couscous (98)
Dinner: Tempeh And Vegetable Stir-Fry (135)

DAY:14
Breakfast: Oatmeal Raisin Breakfast Cookie (26)
Lunch: Sushi-Style Quinoa (125)
Dinner: Eggplant Parmesan (138)

DAY:15
Breakfast: Chocolate Quinoa Breakfast Bowl (16)
Lunch: Lentil Spinach Curry (108)
Dinner: Apple-Sunflower Spinach Salad (158)

DAY:16
Breakfast: Quinoa Applesauce Muffins (28)
Lunch: Vegetable and Barley Stew (Pressure Cooker) (52)
Dinner: Moroccan Aubergine Salad (51)

DAY:17
Breakfast: Pumpkin Pancakes (28)
Lunch: Mindful Mushroom Stroganoff (137)
Dinner: Spaghetti Squash Primavera (136)

DAY:18
Breakfast: Warm Quinoa Breakfast Bowl (31)
Lunch: Balsamic Black Beans (100)
Dinner: Red Peppers and Kale (139)

DAY:19
Breakfast: Maple-Pecan Waffles(23)
Lunch: Brown Rice and Lentils (110)
Dinner: Not-Tuna Salad (146)

DAY:20
Breakfast: Breakfast Parfaits (33)
Lunch: Maple Dijon Burgers (124)
Dinner: Caesar Salad (165)

DAY:21
Breakfast: Spiced Orange Breakfast Couscous (33)
Lunch: Maple-Bourbon Acorn Squash (135)
Dinner: Warm Vegetable "Salad" (142)

Fruity Granola
PREP: 15 MINUTES • COOK TIME: 45 MINUTES • TOTAL:60 MINUTES • SERVES: 5

Ingredients
2 cups rolled oats

¾ cup whole-wheat flour

1 tablespoon ground cinnamon

1 teaspoon ground ginger (optional)

½ cup sunflower seeds, or walnuts, chopped

½ cup almonds, chopped

½ cup pumpkin seeds

½ cup unsweetened shredded coconut

1¼ cups pure fruit juice (cranberry, apple, or something similar)

½ cup raisins, or dried cranberries

½ cup goji berries (optional)

Directions
Preparing the Ingredients.
1. Preheat the oven to 350°F.

    Mix together the oats, flour, cinnamon, ginger, sunflower seeds, almonds, pumpkin seeds, and coconut in a large bowl.

    Sprinkle the juice over the mixture, and stir until it's just moistened. You might need a bit more or a bit less liquid, depending on how much your oats and flour absorb.

    Spread the granola on a large baking sheet (the more spread out it is the better), and put it in the oven. After about 15 minutes, use a spatula to turn the granola so that the middle gets dried out. Let the granola bake until it's as crunchy as you want it, about 30 minutes more.

    Take the granola out of the oven and stir in the raisins and goji berries (if using). Store leftovers in an airtight container for up to 2 weeks.
2. Serve with non-dairy milk and fresh fruit, use as a topper for morning porridge or a smoothie bowl to add a bit of crunch, or make a granola parfait by layering with non-dairy yogurt or puréed banana.

Per Serving (½ cup) Calories: 398; Protein: 11g; Total fat: 25g; Carbohydrates: 39g; Fiber: 8g

Pumpkin Steel-Cut Oats
PREP: 2 MINUTES • COOK TIME: 35 MINUTES • TOTAL:37 MINUTES• SERVES: 4

Ingredients
3 cups water

1 cup steel-cut oats

½ cup canned pumpkin purée

¼ cup pumpkin seeds (pepitas)

2 tablespoons maple syrup

Pinch salt

Directions
Preparing the Ingredients.
1. In a large saucepan, bring the water to a boil.

    Add the oats, stir, and reduce the heat to low. Simmer until the oats are soft, 20 to 30 minutes, continuing to stir occasionally.

    Stir in the pumpkin purée and continue cooking on low for 3 to 5 minutes longer. Stir in the pumpkin seeds and maple syrup, and season with the salt.
2. Divide the oatmeal into 4 single-serving containers. Let cool before sealing the lids.

Place the airtight containers in the refrigerator for 5 days or freeze for up to 3 months. To thaw, refrigerate overnight. Reheat in the microwave for 2½ minutes or in a skillet over medium-high heat for 6 to 8 minutes.

Per Serving: Calories:121; Protein: 4g; Total fat: 5g; Carbohydrates: 17g; Fiber: 2g

Granola
PREP: 5 MINUTES • COOK TIME: 15 MINUTES • TOTAL: 20 MINUTES • SERVES: about 8 cups

Ingredients
51/2 cups old-fashioned oats
11/2 cups slivered almonds
1/2 cup shelled sunflower seeds
1 cup golden raisins
1 cup shredded unsweetened coconut

1 cup pure maple syrup
1/2 teaspoon ground cinnamon
1/4 teaspoon ground allspice
Pinch salt

Directions
1. Preheat the oven to 325°F. Spread the oats, almonds, and sunflower seeds in a 9 x 13-inch baking pan and place in the oven for 10 minutes.
   Remove from the oven and reduce the temperature to 300°F. Add the raisins, coconut, maple syrup, cinnamon, allspice, and salt and stir to combine.
2. Return the pan to the oven and bake for 15 minutes, or until the mixture is crisp and dry. Be careful not to burn.
3. Remove from oven and let cool completely, 30 minutes. Transfer to an airtight container and store in the refrigerator where it will keep for several weeks.

Chocolate Quinoa Breakfast Bowl
PREP: 5 MINUTES • COOK TIME: 30 MINUTES • TOTAL:35 MINUTES• SERVES: 2

Ingredients
1 cup quinoa
1 teaspoon ground cinnamon
1 cup non-dairy milk
1 cup water
1 large banana
2 to 3 tablespoons unsweetened cocoa powder, or carob

1 to 2 tablespoons almond butter, or other nut or seed butter
1 tablespoon ground flaxseed, or chia or hemp seeds
2 tablespoons walnuts
¼ cup raspberries

Directions
Preparing the Ingredients.
1. Put the quinoa, cinnamon, milk, and water in a medium pot. Bring to a boil over high heat, then turn down low and simmer, covered, for 25 to 30 minutes.
   While the quinoa is simmering, purée or mash the banana in a medium bowl and stir in the cocoa powder, almond butter, and flaxseed.
2. To serve, spoon 1 cup cooked quinoa into a bowl, top with half the pudding and half the walnuts and raspberries.

Per Serving: Calories: 392; Protein: 12g; Total fat: 19g; Saturated fat: 1g; Carbohydrates: 49g; Fiber: 10g

Savory Oatmeal Porridge

PREP: 2 MINUTES • COOK TIME: 25 MINUTES • TOTAL:27 MINUTES• SERVES: 4

Ingredients
2½ cups vegetable broth
2½ cups unsweetened almond milk or other plant-based milk
½ cup steel-cut oats
1 tablespoon farro

½ cup slivered almonds
¼ cup nutritional yeast
2 cups old-fashioned rolled oats
½ teaspoon salt (optional)

Directions
Preparing the Ingredients.
1. In a large saucepan or pot, bring the broth and almond milk to a boil. Add the oats, farro, almond slivers, and nutritional yeast. Cook over medium-high heat for 20 minutes, stirring occasionally.
2. Add the rolled oats and cook for another 5 minutes, until creamy. Stir in the salt (if using).
   Divide into 4 single-serving containers.
   Let cool before sealing the lids. Place the airtight containers in the refrigerator for 5 days or freeze for up to 3 months. To thaw, refrigerate overnight. Reheat in the microwave for 2½ minutes or in a skillet over medium-high heat for 6 to 8 minutes.

Per Serving: Calories: 208; Protein: 14g; Total fat: 8g; Saturated fat: 1g; Carbohydrates: 22g; Fiber: 7g

Muesli and Berries Bowl

PREP: 10 MINUTES • COOK TIME: 0 MINUTES • TOTAL:10 MINUTES• SERVES: 5

Ingredients
FOR THE MUESLI
1 cup rolled oats
1 cup spelt flakes, or quinoa flakes, or more rolled oats
2 cups puffed cereal
¼ cup sunflower seeds
¼ cup almonds
¼ cup raisins
¼ cup dried cranberries
¼ cup chopped dried figs

¼ cup unsweetened shredded coconut
¼ cup non-dairy chocolate chips
1 to 3 teaspoons ground cinnamon
FOR THE BOWL
½ cup non-dairy milk, or unsweetened applesauce
¾ cup muesli
½ cup berries

Directions
Preparing the Ingredients.
1. Put the muesli ingredients in a container or bag and shake.
   Combine the muesli and bowl ingredients in a bowl or to-go container.
2. *Substitutions:* Try chopped Brazil nuts, peanuts, dried cranberries, dried blueberries, dried mango, or whatever inspires you. Ginger and cardamom are interesting flavors if you want to branch out on spices.

Per Serving: Calories: 441; Protein: 10g; Total fat: 20g; Carbohydrates: 63g; Fiber: 13g

Breakfast Casserole
PREP: 15 MINUTES • COOK TIME: 0 MINUTES • TOTAL: 15 MINUTES • SERVES: 6 servings

Ingredients
1 cup quick-cooking grits
1/2 cup shredded vegan Cheddar cheese
2 tablespoons vegan margarine

1 cup cooked and chopped tempeh bacon or vegan sausage
1 cup fresh or frozen corn kernels

Directions
1. Preheat the oven to 375°F. Lightly oil a 9 x 13-inch baking pan and set aside.
2. In a large saucepan, combine the soy milk and broth and bring to a boil over high heat. Add salt to taste (depending on the saltiness of your broth) and stir in the grits. Reduce the heat to low and cook, stirring occasionally, until the grits are thickened but not stiff. Turn off the heat and stir in the cheese, margarine, tempeh bacon, and corn.
3. Scrape the mixture into the prepared baking pan. Spread evenly, smooth the top, and bake until slightly puffed and golden brown, about 45 minutes. Serve immediately.

Cinnamon And Spice Overnight Oats
PREP: 10 MINUTES • OVERNIGHT TO SOAK• SERVES: 5

Ingredients
2½ cups old-fashioned rolled oats
5 tablespoons pumpkin seeds (pepitas)
5 tablespoons chopped pecans
5 cups unsweetened plant-based milk
2½ teaspoons maple syrup or agave syrup

½ to 1 teaspoon salt
½ to 1 teaspoon ground cinnamon
½ to 1 teaspoon ground ginger
Fresh fruit (optional)

Directions
Preparing the Ingredients.
1. Line up 5 wide-mouth pint jars. In each jar, combine ½ cup of oats, 1 tablespoon of pumpkin seeds, 1 tablespoon of pecans, 1 cup of plant-based milk, ½ teaspoon of maple syrup, 1 pinch of salt, 1 pinch of cinnamon, and 1 pinch of ginger.
2. Stir the ingredients in each jar. Close the jars tightly with lids. To serve, top with fresh fruit (if using). Place the airtight jars in the refrigerator at least overnight before eating and for up to 5 days.

Per Serving: Calories:177; Protein: 6g; Total fat: 9g; Carbohydrates: 19g; Fiber: 4g

Baked Banana French Toast with Raspberry Syrup
PREP: 10 MINUTES • COOK TIME: 30 MINUTES • TOTAL: 40 MINUTES• SERVES: 8 SLICES

Ingredients
FOR THE FRENCH TOAST
1 banana
1 cup coconut milk
1 teaspoon pure vanilla extract
¼ teaspoon ground nutmeg
½ teaspoon ground cinnamon
1½ teaspoons arrowroot powder
Pinch sea salt

8 slices whole-grain bread
FOR THE RASPBERRY SYRUP
1 cup fresh or frozen raspberries, or other berries
2 tablespoons water, or pure fruit juice
1 to 2 tablespoons maple syrup, or coconut sugar (optional)

Directions
1. **Preparing the Ingredients.**

   Preheat the oven to 350°F.

   In a shallow bowl, purée or mash the banana well. Mix in the coconut milk, vanilla, nutmeg, cinnamon, arrowroot, and salt.

   Dip the slices of bread in the banana mixture, and then lay them out in a 13-by-9-inch baking dish. They should cover the bottom of the dish and can overlap a bit but shouldn't be stacked on top of each other. Pour any leftover banana mixture over the bread, and put the dish in the oven.

   Bake about 30 minutes, or until the tops are lightly browned.

   Serve topped with raspberry syrup.

2. **To Make the Raspberry Syrup**

   Heat the raspberries in a small pot with the water and the maple syrup (if using) on medium heat. Leave to simmer, stirring occasionally and breaking up the berries, for 15 to 20 minutes, until the liquid has reduced.

   Leftover raspberry syrup makes a great topping for simple oatmeal as a quick and delicious breakfast, or as a drizzle on top of whole-grain toast smeared with natural peanut butter.

Per Serving: Calories: 166; Protein: 5g; Total fat: 7g; Saturated fat: 1g; Carbohydrates: 23g;

Great Green Smoothie
PREP: 5 MINUTES • COOK TIME: 0 MINUTES • TOTAL: 5 MINUTES• SERVES: 4

Ingredients
4 bananas, peeled

4 cups hulled strawberries

4 cups spinach

4 cups plant-based milk

Directions
Preparing the Ingredients.
1. Open 4 quart-size, freezer-safe bags. In each, layer in the following order: 1 banana (halved or sliced), 1 cup of strawberries, and 1 cup of spinach. Seal and place in the freezer.

   To serve, take a frozen bag of Great Green Smoothie ingredients and transfer to a blender. Add 1 cup of plant-based milk, and blend until smooth. Place freezer bags in the freezer for up to 2 months.

Per Serving: Calories: 173; Protein: 4g; Total fat: 2g; Carbohydrates: 40g; Fiber: 7g

Breakfast Bulgur With Pears And Pecans
PREP: 5 MINUTES • COOK TIME: 15 MINUTES • TOTAL: 20 MINUTES • SERVES: 4 servings

Ingredients
2 cups water

1/2 teaspoon salt

1 cup medium bulgur

1 tablespoon vegan margarine

2 ripe pears, peeled, cored, and chopped

1/4 cup chopped pecans

Directions
1. In a large saucepan, bring the water to a boil over high heat. Add the salt and stir in the bulgur. Reduce heat to low, cover, and simmer until the bulgur is tender and liquid has absorbed, about 15 minutes.

2. Remove from the heat and stir in the margarine, pears, and pecans. Cover and let sit for 12 to 15 minutes more before serving.

Sunshine Muffins
PREP: 15 MINUTES • COOK TIME: 30 MINUTES • TOTAL: 45 MINUTES• SERVES: 6

Ingredients
1 teaspoon coconut oil, for greasing muffin tins (optional)
2 tablespoons almond butter, or sunflower seed butter
¼ cup non-dairy milk
1 orange, peeled
1 carrot, coarsely chopped
2 tablespoons chopped dried apricots, or other dried fruit
3 tablespoons molasses
2 tablespoons ground flaxseed
1 teaspoon apple cider vinegar
1 teaspoon pure vanilla extract
½ teaspoon ground cinnamon
½ teaspoon ground ginger (optional)
¼ teaspoon ground nutmeg (optional)
¼ teaspoon allspice (optional)
¾ cup rolled oats, or whole-wheat flour
1 teaspoon baking powder
½ teaspoon baking soda
MIX-INS (OPTIONAL)
½ cup rolled oats
2 tablespoons raisins, or other chopped dried fruit
2 tablespoons sunflower seeds

Directions
Preparing the Ingredients.
1. Preheat the oven to 350°F.
   Prepare a 6-cup muffin tin by rubbing the insides of the cups with coconut oil or using silicone or paper muffin cups.
   Purée the nut butter, milk, orange, carrot, apricots, molasses, flaxseed, vinegar, vanilla, cinnamon, ginger, nutmeg, and allspice in a food processor or blender until somewhat smooth.
2. Grind the oats in a clean coffee grinder until they're the consistency of flour (or use whole-grain flour). In a large bowl, mix the oats with the baking powder and baking soda. Mix the wet ingredients into the dry ingredients until just combined. Fold in the mix-ins (if using). Spoon about ¼ cup batter into each muffin cup and bake for 30 minutes, or until a toothpick inserted into the center comes out clean.
   The orange creates a very moist base, so the muffins may take longer than 30 minutes, depending on how heavy your muffin tin is. Store the muffins in the fridge or freezer, because they are so moist. If you plan to keep them frozen, you can easily double the batch for a full dozen.

Per Serving: Calories: 287; Protein: 8g; Total fat: 12g; Carbohydrates: 41g; Fiber: 6g

Breakfast Bran Muffins
PREP: 10 MINUTES • COOK TIME: 20 MINUTES • TOTAL: 30 MINUTES • SERVES: 12 muffins

Ingredients
3 cups bran flakes cereal
11/2 cups. Whole-wheat flour
1/2 cup raisins
3 teaspoons baking powder
1/2 teaspoon ground cinnamon
1/2 teaspoon salt
1/3 cup brown sugar
¾ cup fresh orange juice

Directions
1. Preheat the oven to 400°F. Lightly oil a 12-cup muffin tin or line it with paper liners and set aside.

2. In a large bowl, combine the bran flakes, flour, raisins, baking powder, cinnamon, and salt.
3. In a medium bowl, combine the sugar, orange juice, and oil and mix until blended. Pour the wet Ingredients into the dry Ingredients and mix until just moistened.
4. Fill the cups about two-thirds full. Bake until golden brown and a toothpick inserted into a muffin comes out clean, about 20 minutes. Serve warm.

Smoothie Breakfast Bowl
PREP: 10 MINUTES • COOK TIME: 0 MINUTES • TOTAL:10 MINUTES• SERVES: 4

Ingredients
4 bananas, peeled
1 cup dragon fruit or fruit of choice
1 cup Baked Granola
2 cups fresh berries

½ cup slivered almonds
4 cups plant-based milk

Directions
Preparing the Ingredients.
1. Open 4 quart-size, freezer-safe bags, and layer in the following order: 1 banana (halved or sliced) and ¼ cup dragon fruit. Into 4 small jelly jars, layer in the following order: ¼ cup granola, ½ cup berries, and 2 tablespoons slivered almonds.
2. To serve, take a frozen bag of bananas and dragon fruit and transfer to a blender. Add 1 cup of plant-based milk, and blend until smooth. Pour into a bowl. Add the contents of 1 jar of granola, berries, and almonds over the top of the smoothie, and serve with a spoon. Place the freezer bags in the freezer for up to 2 months. Store the jars of berries, granola, and nuts in the refrigerator for up to 1 week.

Per Serving: Calories: 384; Protein: 6g; Total fat: 5g; Carbohydrates: 57g; Fiber: 8g

Pink Panther Smoothie
PREP: 5 MINUTES • COOK TIME: 0 MINUTES • TOTAL:5 MINUTES• SERVES: 3 CUPS

Ingredients
1 cup strawberries
1 cup chopped melon (any kind)
1 cup cranberries, or raspberries
1 tablespoon chia seeds
½ cup coconut milk, or other non-dairy milk

1 cup water
(OPTIONAL)
1 teaspoon goji berries
2 tablespoons fresh mint, chopped

Directions
Preparing the Ingredients.
1. Purée everything in a blender until smooth, adding more water (or coconut milk) if needed.
2. Add bonus boosters, as desired. Purée until blended. If you don't have (or don't like) coconut, try using sunflower seeds for an immune boost of zinc and selenium.

Per Serving 3 Cups: Calories: 459; Protein: 8g; Total fat: 30g; Carbohydrates: 52g; Fiber: 19g

Mango Madness
PREP: 5 MINUTES • COOK TIME: 0 MINUTES • TOTAL:5 MINUTES• SERVES: 4 CUPS

Ingredients

1 banana
1 cup chopped mango (frozen or fresh)
1 cup chopped peach (frozen or fresh)

1 cup strawberries
1 carrot, peeled and chopped (optional)
1 cup water

Directions

Preparing the Ingredients.

1. Purée everything in a blender until smooth, adding more water if needed.
   If you can't find frozen peaches and fresh ones aren't in season, just use extra mango or strawberries, or try cantaloupe.

Per Serving: Calories: 376; Protein: 5g; Total fat: 2g; Carbohydrates: 95g; Fiber: 14g

Savory Pancakes
PREP: 10 MINUTES • COOK TIME: 15 MINUTES • TOTAL: 25 MINUTES• SERVES: 4

Ingredients

1 cup whole-wheat flour
1 teaspoon garlic salt
1 teaspoon onion powder
½ teaspoon baking soda
¼ teaspoon salt
1 cup lightly pressed, crumbled soft or firm tofu
⅓ cup unsweetened plant-based milk

¼ cup lemon juice (about 2 small lemons)
2 tablespoons extra-virgin olive oil
½ cup finely chopped mushrooms
½ cup finely chopped onion
2 cups tightly packed greens (arugula, spinach, or baby kale work great)
Nonstick cooking spray

Directions

Preparing the Ingredients.

1. In a large bowl, combine the flour, garlic salt, onion powder, baking soda, and salt. Mix well. In a blender, combine the tofu, plant-based milk, lemon juice, and olive oil. Purée on high speed for 30 seconds.
2. Pour the contents of the blender into the bowl of dry ingredients and whisk until combined well. Fold in the mushrooms, onion, and greens.
3. Spray a large skillet or griddle pan with nonstick cooking spray and set over medium-high heat. Reduce the heat to medium and add ½ cup of batter per pancake. Cook on both sides for about 3 minutes, or until set. After flipping, press down on the cooked side of the pancake with a spatula to flatten out the pancake. Repeat until the batter is gone.
4. Divide the cooked pancakes among 4 single-serving containers. Let cool before sealing the lids.
5. Place the airtight storage containers in the refrigerator for up to 4 days. To reheat, microwave for 1½ to 2 minutes. To freeze, place the pancakes on a parchment paper–lined baking sheet in a single layer. If there's more than one layer, place another piece of parchment paper over the pancakes and place the second layer on top. Place the baking sheet in the freezer for 2 to 4 hours. Transfer the frozen pancakes to a freezer-safe bag (cut the parchment paper and place a small piece between each pancake). To thaw, refrigerate overnight. Preheat an oven or toaster oven to 350ºF. Place the pancakes on a parchment paper–lined baking sheet and bake for 10 to 15 minutes, or stack the pancakes on a plate and microwave for 2 to 3 minutes.

Per Serving: Calories: 246; Protein: 10g; Total fat: 11g; Carbohydrates: 30g; Fiber: 3g

Maple-Pecan Waffles

PREP: 10 MINUTES • COOK TIME: 5 MINUTES • TOTAL: 15 MINUTES • SERVES: 4 servings

Ingredients

1¾ cups whole-wheat flour
1/3 cup coarsely ground pecans
1 tablespoon baking powder
1/2 teaspoon salt

11/2 cups soy milk
3 tablespoons pure maple syrup
3 tablespoons vegan margarine, melted

Directions

1. Lightly oil the waffle iron and preheat it. Preheat the oven to 225°F.
   In a large bowl, combine the flour, pecans, baking powder, and salt. Set aside.
   In a medium bowl, whisk together the soy milk, maple syrup, and margarine. Add the wet Ingredients to the dry Ingredients and blend with a few swift strokes, mixing until just combined.
2. Ladle 1/2 to 1 cup of the batter (depending on the Directions with your waffle iron) onto the hot waffle iron. Cook until done, 3 to 5 minutes for most waffle irons. Transfer the cooked waffles to a heatproof platter and keep warm in the oven while cooking the rest of the waffles.

Lemon-Kissed Blueberry Waffles

PREP: 10 MINUTES • COOK TIME: 5 MINUTES • TOTAL: 15 MINUTES • SERVES: 4 servings

Ingredients

11/2 cups whole-heat flour
1/2 cup old-fashioned oats
1/4 cup sugar
3 teaspoons baking powder
1/2 teaspoon salt
1 teaspoon ground cinnamon

2 cups soy milk
1 tablespoon fresh lemon juice
1 teaspoon lemon zest
1/4 cup vegan margarine, melted
1/2 cup fresh blueberries

Directions

1. Lightly oil the waffle iron and preheat it. Preheat the oven to 225°F.
2. In a large bowl, combine the flour, oats, sugar, baking powder, salt, and cinnamon. Set aside.
3. In a separate large bowl, whisk together the soy milk, lemon juice, lemon zest, and margarine. Add the wet Ingredients to the dry Ingredients and blend with a few swift strokes, mixing until just combined. Fold in the blueberries.
4. Ladle 1/2 to 1 cup of the batter (depending on the Directions with your waffle iron) onto the hot waffle iron. Cook until done, 3 to 5 minutes for most waffle irons. Transfer the cooked waffles to a heatproof platter and keep warm in the oven while cooking the rest.

Tropi-Kale Breeze

PREP: 5 MINUTES • COOK TIME: 0MINUTES • TOTAL:5 MINUTES• SERVES: 4

Ingredients

1 cup chopped pineapple (frozen or fresh)
1 cup chopped mango (frozen or fresh)
½ to 1 cup chopped kale
½ avocado

½ cup coconut milk
1 cup water, or coconut water
1 teaspoon matcha green tea powder (optional)

Directions

Preparing the Ingredients.
1. Purée everything in a blender until smooth, adding more water (or coconut milk) if needed.

Per Serving: Calories: 566; Protein: 8g; Total fat: 36g; Saturated fat: 1g; Carbohydrates: 66g; Fiber: 12g

Tofu-Spinach Scramble
PREP: 20 MINUTES • COOK TIME: 15 MINUTES • TOTAL:35 MINUTES• SERVES: 5

Ingredients
1 (14-ounce) package water-packed extra-firm tofu
1 teaspoon extra-virgin olive oil or ¼ cup vegetable broth
1 small yellow onion, diced
3 teaspoons minced garlic (about 3 cloves)
3 large celery stalks, chopped

2 large carrots, peeled (optional) and chopped
1 teaspoon chili powder
½ teaspoon ground cumin
½ teaspoon ground turmeric
½ teaspoon salt (optional)
¼ teaspoon freshly ground black pepper
5 cups loosely packed spinach

Directions
Preparing the Ingredients.
1. Press and drain the tofu by placing it, wrapped in a paper towel, on a plate in the sink. Place a cutting board over the tofu, then set a heavy pot, can, or cookbook on the cutting board. Remove after 10 minutes. (Alternatively, use a tofu press.)
   In a medium bowl, crumble the tofu with your hands or a potato masher. Set aside.
   In a large skillet over medium-high heat, heat the olive oil. Add the onion, garlic, celery, and carrots, and sauté for 5 minutes, until the onion is softened.
   Add the crumbled tofu, chili powder, cumin, turmeric, salt (if using), and pepper, and continue cooking for 7 to 8 more minutes, stirring frequently, until the tofu begins to brown.
   Add the spinach and mix well. Cover and reduce the heat to medium. Steam the spinach for 3 minutes.
2. Divide evenly among 5 single-serving containers. Let cool before sealing the lids.
   Place the airtight containers in the refrigerator for 5 days or freeze for up to 1 month. To thaw, refrigerate overnight. Reheat in the microwave for 2½ minutes or in a skillet over medium-high heat for 6 to 8 minutes.

Per Serving: Calories: 170; Protein: 7g; Total fat: 9g; Carbohydrates: 9g; Fiber: 3g

Chai Chia Smoothie
PREP: 5 MINUTES • COOK TIME: 0MINUTES • TOTAL:5 MINUTES• SERVES: 3

Ingredients
1 banana
½ cup coconut milk
1 cup water
1 cup alfalfa sprouts (optional)
1 to 2 soft Medjool dates, pitted

1 tablespoon chia seeds, or ground flax or hemp hearts
¼ teaspoon ground cinnamon
Pinch ground cardamom
1 tablespoon grated fresh ginger, or ¼ teaspoon ground ginger

Directions
Preparing the Ingredients.
Purée everything in a blender until smooth, adding more water (or coconut milk) if needed.

Although dates are super sweet, they don't cause a large blood sugar spike. They're great to boost sweetness while also boosting your intake of fiber and potassium.
Per Serving (3 cups)

Per Serving: Calories: 477; Protein: 7g; Total fat: 29g; Carbohydrates: 57g; Fiber: 14g

Broiled Grapefruit with Cinnamon Pitas
PREP: 10 MINUTES • COOK TIME: 15 MINUTES • TOTAL:25 MINUTES• SERVES: 5

Ingredients
2 whole-wheat pitas, cut into wedges
2 tablespoons coconut oil, melted
1 tablespoon ground cinnamon

2 tablespoons brown sugar
1 grapefruit, halved
2 tablespoons pure maple syrup or agave

Directions
Preparing the Ingredients.
Preheat the oven to 375°F.
1. Line a baking sheet with parchment paper.
Spread pita wedges in a single layer on a baking sheet and brush with melted coconut oil.
2. In a small bowl, combine the cinnamon and brown sugar and sprinkle over the pita wedges.
Bake in preheated oven until the wedges are crisp, about 8 minutes. Transfer the pita wedges to a plate and set aside.
3. Turn the oven to broil. Place the grapefruit halves on the baking sheet. Drizzle the maple syrup over the top of the grapefruit, if using. Broil until the syrup bubbles and begins to crystallize, 3 to 5 minutes. Serve immediately.

Blueberry Oatmeal   Breakfast Bars
PREP: 10 MINUTES • COOK TIME: 40 MINUTES • TOTAL:50 MINUTES• SERVES: 12

Ingredients
2 cups uncooked rolled oats
2 cups all-purpose flour
1½ cups dark-brown sugar
1½ teaspoons baking soda
½ teaspoon sea salt

½ teaspoon ground cinnamon
1 cup vegan butter, melted
4 cups blueberries, fresh or frozen
¼ cup organic cane sugar
2 tablespoons cornstarch

Directions
Preparing the Ingredients.
Preheat the oven to 375°F. Lightly grease a 9-by-13-inch baking dish.
1. In a large bowl, combine the oats, flour, sugar, baking soda, salt, and cinnamon. Add the butter and mix until well incorporated and crumbly.
2. In a separate large bowl, combine the blueberries, cane sugar, and cornstarch, mixing until the blueberries are evenly coated.
3. Press 3 cups of the oatmeal mixture into the prepared baking pan. Spread the blueberry mixture on top and crumble the remaining oatmeal mixture over the blueberries.
Bake for 40 minutes.

Remove from the oven and let cool completely before cutting into bars.

Chocolate PB Smoothie
PREP: 5 MINUTES • COOK TIME: 0 MINUTES • TOTAL:5 MINUTES• SERVES: 4

Ingredients
1 banana

¼ cup rolled oats, or 1 scoop plant protein powder

1 tablespoon flaxseed, or chia seeds

1 tablespoon unsweetened cocoa powder

1 tablespoon peanut butter, or almond or sunflower seed butter

1 tablespoon maple syrup (optional)

1 cup alfalfa sprouts, or spinach, chopped (optional)

½ cup non-dairy milk (optional)

1 cup water

OPTIONAL

1 teaspoon maca powder

1 teaspoon cocoa nibs

Directions
Preparing the Ingredients.

Purée everything in a blender until smooth, adding more water (or non-dairy milk) if needed. Add bonus boosters, as desired. Purée until blended.

Per Serving: Calories: 474; Protein: 13g; Total fat: 16g; Carbohydrates: 79g; Fiber: 18g

Orange French Toast
PREP: 15 MINUTES • COOK TIME: 10 MINUTES • TOTAL: 25 MINUTES• SERVES: 4

Ingredients
3 very ripe bananas

1 cup unsweetened nondairy milk

zest and juice of 1 orange

1 teaspoon ground cinnamon

¼ teaspoon grated nutmeg

4 slices french bread

1 tablespoon coconut oil

Directions
Preparing the Ingredients.

1. In a blender, combine the bananas, almond milk, orange juice and zest, cinnamon, and nutmeg and blend until smooth. Pour the mixture into a 9-by-13-inch baking dish. Soak the bread in the mixture for 5 minutes on each side.
2. While the bread soaks, heat a griddle or sauté pan over medium-high heat. Melt the coconut oil in the pan and swirl to coat. Cook the bread slices until golden brown on both sides, about 5 minutes each. Serve immediately.

Oatmeal Raisin Breakfast Cookie
PREP: 5 MINUTES • COOK TIME: 15 MINUTES • TOTAL:20 MINUTES• SERVES: 2 COOKIES

Ingredients
½ cup rolled oats

1 tablespoon whole-wheat flour

½ teaspoon baking powder

1 to 2 tablespoons brown sugar

½ teaspoon pumpkin pie spice or ground cinnamon (optional)
¼ cup unsweetened applesauce, plus more as needed

2 tablespoons raisins, dried cranberries, or vegan chocolate chips

Directions
Preparing the Ingredients.

1. In a medium bowl, stir together the oats, flour, baking powder, sugar, and pumpkin pie spice (if using). Stir in the applesauce until thoroughly combined. Add another 1 to 2 tablespoons of applesauce if the mixture looks too dry (this will depend on the type of oats used).
2. Shape the mixture into 2 cookies. Put them on a microwave-safe plate and heat on high power for 90 seconds. Alternatively, bake on a small tray in a 350°F oven or toaster oven for 15 minutes. Let cool slightly before eating.

Per Serving (2 cookies): Calories: 175; Protein: 74g; Total fat: 2g; Saturated fat:0g; Carbohydrates: 39g; Fiber: 4g

Berry Beetsicle Smoothie
PREP: 3 MINUTES • COOK TIME: 0MINUTES • TOTAL:3 MINUTES• SERVES: 1

Ingredients
½ cup peeled and diced beets
½ cup frozen raspberries
1 frozen banana

1 tablespoon maple syrup
1 cup unsweetened soy or almond milk

Directions

Preparing the Ingredients.
Combine all the ingredients in a blender and blend until smooth.

Blueberry Oat Muffins
PREP: 10 MINUTES • COOK TIME: 20 MINUTES • TOTAL:30 MINUTES• SERVES: 12 MUFINS

Ingredients
2 tablespoons coconut oil or vegan margarine, melted, plus more for preparing the muffin tin
1 cup quick-cooking oats or instant oats
1 cup boiling water
½ cup nondairy milk
¼ cup ground flaxseed
1 teaspoon vanilla extract

1 teaspoon apple cider vinegar
1½ cups whole-wheat flour
½ cup brown sugar
2 teaspoons baking soda
Pinch salt
1 cup blueberries

Directions
Preparing the Ingredients.
Preheat the oven to 400°F.

1. Coat a muffin tin with coconut oil, line with paper muffin cups, or use a nonstick tin.
2. In a large bowl, combine the oats and boiling water. Stir so the oats soften. Add the coconut oil, milk, flaxseed, vanilla, and vinegar and stir to combine. Add the flour, sugar, baking soda, and salt. Stir until

just combined. Gently fold in the blueberries. Scoop the muffin mixture into the prepared tin, about ⅓ cup for each muffin.
3. Bake for 20 to 25 minutes, until slightly browned on top and springy to the touch. Let cool for about 10 minutes. Run a dinner knife around the inside of each cup to loosen, then tilt the muffins on their sides in the muffin wells so air gets underneath. These keep in an airtight container in the refrigerator for up to 1 week or in the freezer indefinitely.

Per Serving (1muffin): Calories: 174; Protein: 5g; Total fat: 3g; Saturated fat:2g; Carbohydrates: 33g; Fiber: 4g

Quinoa Applesauce Muffins
PREP: 10 MINUTES • COOK TIME: 15 MINUTES • TOTAL:25 MINUTES• SERVES: 5

Ingredients
2 tablespoons coconut oil or margarine, melted, plus more for coating the muffin tin
¼ cup ground flaxseed
½ cup water
2 cups unsweetened applesauce
½ cup brown sugar

1 teaspoon apple cider vinegar
2½ cups whole-wheat flour
1½ cups cooked quinoa
2 teaspoons baking soda
Pinch salt
½ cup dried cranberries or raisins

Directions
Preparing the Ingredients.
1. Preheat the oven to 400°F.
2. Coat a muffin tin with coconut oil, line with paper muffin cups, or use a nonstick tin. In a large bowl, stir together the flaxseed and water. Add the applesauce, sugar, coconut oil, and vinegar. Stir to combine. Add the flour, quinoa, baking soda, and salt, stirring until just combined. Gently fold in the cranberries without stirring too much. Scoop the muffin mixture into the prepared tin, about ⅓ cup for each muffin.
3. Bake for 15 to 20 minutes, until slightly browned on top and springy to the touch. Let cool for about 10 minutes. Run a dinner knife around the inside of each cup to loosen, then tilt the muffins on their sides in the muffin wells so air gets underneath. These keep in an airtight container in the refrigerator for up to 1 week or in the freezer indefinitely.

Per Serving(1muffin): Calories: 387; Protein: 7g; Total fat: 5g; Saturated fat: 2g; Carbohydrates: 57g; Fiber: 8g

Pumpkin Pancakes
PREP: 15 MINUTES • COOK TIME: 15 MINUTES • TOTAL:30 MINUTES• SERVES: 4

Ingredients
2 cups unsweetened almond milk
1 teaspoon apple cider vinegar
2½ cups whole-wheat flour
2 tablespoons baking powder
½ teaspoon baking soda
1 teaspoon sea salt

1 teaspoon pumpkin pie spice or ½ teaspoon ground -cinnamon plus ¼ teaspoon grated -nutmeg plus ¼ teaspoon ground allspice
½ cup canned pumpkin purée
1 cup water
1 tablespoon coconut oil

Directions

Preparing the Ingredients.
1. In a small bowl, combine the almond milk and apple cider vinegar. Set aside.
2. In a large bowl, whisk together the flour, baking powder, baking soda, salt, and pumpkin pie spice. In another large bowl, combine the almond milk mixture, pumpkin purée, and water, whisking to mix well. Add the wet ingredients to the dry ingredients and fold together until the dry -ingredients are just moistened. You will still have a few streaks of flour in the bowl.
3. In a nonstick pan or griddle over medium-high heat, melt the coconut oil and swirl to coat. Pour the batter into the pan ¼ cup at a time and cook until the pancakes are browned, about 5 minutes per side. Serve immediately.

Green Breakfast Smoothie
PREP: 10 MINUTES • COOK TIME: 0 MINUTES • TOTAL: 10 MINUTES • SERVES: 2

Ingredients
½ banana, sliced
2 Cups Spinach or other greens, such as kale
1 Cup sliced berries of your choosing, fresh or frozen

1 orange, peeled and cut into segments
1 cup unsweetened nondairy milk
1 cup ice

Directions
Preparing the Ingredients. In a blender, combine all the ingredients.
Starting with the blender on low speed, begin blending the smoothie, gradually increasing blender speed until smooth. Serve immediately.

Blueberry Lemonade Smoothie
PREP: 5 MINUTES • COOK TIME: 0 MINUTES • TOTAL: 5 MINUTES • SERVES: 1

Ingredients
1 cup roughly chopped kale
¾ cup frozen blueberries

1 cup unsweetened soy or almond milk
Juice of 1 lemon
1 tablespoon maple syrup

Directions
Preparing the Ingredients.
Combine all the ingredients in a blender and blend until smooth. Enjoy immediately.

Berry Protein Smoothie
PREP: 5 MINUTES • COOK TIME: 0 MINUTES • TOTAL:5 MINUTES • SERVES: 1

Ingredients
1 banana
1 cup fresh or frozen berries
¾ cup water or nondairy milk, plus more as needed
1 scoop plant-based protein powder, 3 ounces silken tofu, ¼ cup rolled oats, or ½ cup cooked quinoa

Additions
1 tablespoon ground flaxseed or chia seeds
1 handful fresh spinach or lettuce, or 1 chunk cucumber
coconut water to replace some of the liquid

Directions
Preparing the Ingredients
1. In a blender, combine the banana, berries, water, and your choice of protein.
2. Add any addition ingredients as desired. Purée until smooth and creamy, about 50 seconds. Add a bit more water if you like a thinner smoothie.

Per Serving: Calories: 332; Protein: 7g; Total fat: 5g; Saturated fat: 1g; Carbohydrates: 72g; Fiber: 11g

Blueberry and Chia Smoothie
PREP: 10 MINUTES • COOK TIME: 0 MINUTES • TOTAL: 10 MINUTES • SERVES: 2

Ingredients
2 tablespoons chia seeds
2 cups unsweetened nondairy milk
2 cups blueberries, fresh or frozen

2 tablespoons pure maple syrup or agave
2 tablespoons cocoa powder

Directions
Preparing the Ingredients
1. Soak the chia seeds in the almond milk for 5 minutes.
2. In a blender, combine the soaked chia seeds, almond milk, blueberries, maple syrup, and cocoa powder and blend until smooth. Serve immediately.

Green Kickstart Smoothie
PREP: 5 MINUTES • COOK TIME: 0 MINUTES • TOTAL: 5 MINUTES • SERVES: 1

Ingredients
½ avocado or 1 banana
½ cup chopped cucumber, peeled if desired
1 handful fresh spinach or chopped lettuce
1 pear or apple, peeled and cored, or 1 cup unsweetened applesauce
2 tablespoons freshly squeezed lime juice

1 cup water or nondairy milk, plus more as needed
Additions
½-inch piece peeled fresh ginger
1 tablespoon ground flaxseed or chia seeds
½ cup soy yogurt or 3 ounces silken tofu
 coconut water to replace some of the liquid

2 tablespoons chopped fresh mint or ½ cup chopped mango

Directions
Preparing the Ingredients
1. In a blender, combine the avocado, cucumber, spinach, pear, lime juice, and water.
2. Add any Additions ingredients as desired. Purée until smooth and creamy, about 50 seconds. Add a bit more water if you like a thinner smoothie.

Per Serving: Calories: 263; Protein: 4g; Total fat: 14g; Saturated fat: 2g; Carbohydrates: 36g; Fiber: 10g

Warm Maple and Cinnamon Quinoa
PREP: 5 MINUTES • COOK TIME: 15 MINUTES • TOTAL: 20 MINUTES • SERVES: 4

Ingredients
1 cup unsweetened nondairy milk

1 cup water

1 cup quinoa, rinsed
1 teaspoon cinnamon

¼ cup chopped pecans or other nuts or seeds, such as chia, sunflower seeds, or almonds
2 tablespoons pure maple syrup or agave

Directions
Preparing the Ingredients
1. In a medium saucepan over medium-high heat, bring the almond milk, water, and quinoa to a boil. Lower the heat to medium-low and cover. Simmer until the liquid is mostly absorbed and the quinoa softens, about 15 minutes.
2. Turn off the heat and allow to sit, covered, for 5 minutes. Stir in the cinnamon, pecans, and syrup. Serve hot.

Warm Quinoa Breakfast Bowl
PREP: 5 MINUTES • COOK TIME: 0 MINUTES • TOTAL: 5 MINUTES • SERVES: 4

Ingredients
3 cups freshly cooked quinoa
1⅓ cups unsweetened soy or almond milk
2 bananas, sliced
1 cup raspberries

1 cup blueberries
½ cup chopped raw walnuts
¼ cup maple syrup

Directions
Preparing the Ingredients
Divide the ingredients among 4 bowls, starting with a base of ¾ cup quinoa, ⅓ cup milk, ½ banana, ¼ cup raspberries, ¼ cup blueberries, and 2 tablespoons walnuts.
Drizzle 1 tablespoon of maple syrup over the top of each bowl.

Banana Bread Rice Pudding
PREP: 5 MINUTES • COOK TIME: 50 MINUTES • TOTAL: 55 MINUTES • SERVES: 4

Ingredients
1 cup brown rice
1½ cups water
1½ cups nondairy milk
3 tablespoons sugar (omit if using a sweetened nondairy milk)

2 teaspoons pumpkin pie spice or ground cinnamon
2 bananas
3 tablespoons chopped walnuts or sunflower seeds (optional)

Directions
Preparing the Ingredients
1. In a medium pot, combine the rice, water, milk, sugar, and pumpkin pie spice. Bring to a boil over high heat, turn the heat to low, and cover the pot. Simmer, stirring occasionally, until the rice is soft and the liquid is absorbed. White rice takes about 20 minutes; brown rice takes about 50 minutes.
2. Smash the bananas and stir them into the cooked rice. Serve topped with walnuts (if using). Leftovers will keep refrigerated in an airtight container for up to 5 days.

Per Serving: Calories: 479; Protein: 9g; Total fat: 13g; Saturated fat: 1g; Carbohydrates: 86g; Fiber: 7g

Apple and Cinnamon Oatmeal

Ingredients

1¼ cups apple cider
1 apple, peeled, cored, and chopped
⅔ cup rolled oats

1 teaspoon ground cinnamon
1 tablespoon pure maple syrup or agave (optional)

Directions

Preparing the Ingredients.

1. In a medium saucepan, bring the apple cider to a boil over medium-high heat. Stir in the apple, oats, and cinnamon.
2. Bring the cereal to a boil and turn down heat to low. Simmer until the oatmeal thickens, 3 to 4 minutes. Spoon into two bowls and sweeten with maple syrup, if using. Serve hot.

Mango Key Lime Pie Smoothie
PREP: 5 MINUTES • COOK TIME: 0 MINUTES • TOTAL: 5 MINUTES • SERVES: 1

Ingredients

¼ avocado
1 cup baby spinach
½ cup frozen mango chunks

1 cup unsweetened soy or almond milk
Juice of 1 lime (preferably a Key lime).
1 tablespoon maple syrup

Directions

Preparing the Ingredients.

1. Combine all the ingredients in a blender and blend until smooth. Enjoy immediately.

Spiced Cranberry-Almond Granola
PREP: 10 MINUTES • COOK TIME: 35 MINUTES • TOTAL: 45 MINUTES• SERVES: 8

Ingredients

½ cup coconut oil or vegan margarine, melted
½ cup maple syrup or Simple Syrup
1 teaspoon vanilla extract (optional)
2 to 3 teaspoons pumpkin pie spice
4 cups rolled oats
⅓ cup whole-wheat flour

¼ cup ground flaxseed
½ cup sunflower seeds
½ cup slivered almonds
½ cup unsweetened shredded coconut
½ cup dried cranberries
½ cup dried apricots, chopped

Directions

Preparing the Ingredients.

Preheat the oven to 350°F.

1. In a small bowl, stir together the coconut oil, maple syrup, and vanilla. Stir in the pumpkin pie spice. On a large rimmed baking sheet, combine the oats, flour, flaxseed, sunflower seeds, almonds, and coconut. Toss to mix.
2. Drizzle the coconut oil–syrup mixture over the oat mixture and toss to combine. Sprinkle with cold water, as needed, to fully moisten. Press the granola onto the baking sheet so it sticks together. Bake for 30 minutes.
3. Remove from the oven and break the granola into chunks. Stir in the cranberries and apricots. Bake for 5 minutes more. Cool and store in airtight bags or containers for up to 2 weeks.

Per Serving (½ cup) Calories: 354; Protein: 7g; Total fat: 21g; Saturated fat: 11g; Carbohydrates: 40g; Fiber: 7g

Spiced Orange Breakfast Couscous
PREP: 10 MINUTES • COOK TIME: 10 MINUTES • TOTAL:20 MINUTES • SERVES: 4

Ingredients
3 cups orange juice
1½ cups couscous
1 teaspoon ground cinnamon

¼ teaspoon ground cloves
½ cup dried fruit, such as raisins or apricots
½ cup chopped almonds or other nuts or seeds

Directions
Preparing the Ingredients.
1. In a small saucepan, bring the orange juice to a boil. Add the couscous, cinnamon, and cloves and remove from heat. Cover the pan with a lid and allow to sit until the -couscous softens, about 5 minutes.
2. Fluff the couscous with a fork and stir in the dried fruit and nuts. Serve -immediately.

Breakfast Parfaits
PREP: 15 MINUTES • COOK TIME: 0 MINUTES • TOTAL: 15 MINUTES • SERVES: 2

Ingredients
one 14-ounce can coconut milk, refrigerated overnight
1 cup granola

½ cup walnuts
1 cup sliced strawberries or other seasonal berries

Directions
1. Pour off the canned coconut-milk liquid and retain the solids.
2. In two parfait glasses, layer the coconut-milk solids, granola, walnuts, and -strawberries. Serve immediately.

Sweet Potato and Kale Hash
PREP: 10 MINUTES • COOK TIME: 15 MINUTES • TOTAL: 25 MINUTES • SERVES: 2

Ingredients
1 sweet potato
2 tablespoons olive oil
½ onion, chopped
1 carrot, peeled and chopped
2 garlic cloves, minced

½ teaspoon dried thyme
1 cup chopped kale
sea salt
freshly ground black pepper

Directions
Preparing the Ingredients.
1. Prick the sweet potato with a fork and microwave on high until soft, about 5 minutes. Remove from the microwave and cut into ¼-inch cubes.
2. In a large nonstick sauté pan, heat the olive oil over medium-high heat. Add the onion and carrot and cook until softened, about 5 minutes. Add the garlic and thyme and cook until the garlic is fragrant, about 30 seconds.
3. Add the sweet potatoes and cook until the potatoes begin to brown, about 7 -minutes. Add the kale and cook just until it wilts, 1 to 2 minutes. Season with salt and pepper. Serve immediately.

Indian Red Split Lentil Soup
PREP: 5 MINUTES • COOK TIME: 50 MINUTES • TOTAL: 55 MINUTES • SERVES: 4

Ingredients
1 cup red split lentils
2 cups water
1 teaspoon curry powder plus 1 tablespoon, divided, or 5 coriander seeds (optional)
1 teaspoon coconut oil, or 1 tablespoon water or vegetable broth
1 red onion, diced
1 tablespoon minced fresh ginger
2 cups peeled and cubed sweet potato

1 cup sliced zucchini
Freshly ground black pepper
Sea salt
3 to 4 cups vegetable stock, or water
1 to 2 teaspoons toasted sesame oil
1 bunch spinach, chopped
Toasted sesame seeds

Directions
Preparing the Ingredients.
1. Put the lentils in a large pot with 2 cups water, and 1 teaspoon of the curry powder. Bring the lentils to a boil, then reduce the heat and simmer, covered, for about 10 minutes, until the lentils are soft.
2. Meanwhile, heat a large pot over medium heat. Add the coconut oil and sauté the onion and ginger until soft, about 5 minutes. Add the sweet potato and leave it on the heat about 10 minutes to soften slightly, then add the zucchini and cook until it starts to look shiny, about 5 minutes. Add the remaining 1 tablespoon curry powder, pepper, and salt, and stir the vegetables to coat.
3. Add the vegetable stock, bring to a boil, then turn down to simmer and cover. Let the vegetables slowly cook for 20 to 30 minutes, or until the sweet potato is tender.
   Add the fully cooked lentils to the soup. Add another pinch salt, the toasted sesame oil, and the spinach. Stir, allowing the spinach to wilt before removing the pot from the heat.
   Serve garnished with toasted sesame seeds.

Per Serving: Calories: 319; Protein: 16g; Total fat: 8g; Carbohydrates: 50g; Fiber: 10g

Light Vegetable Broth
PREP: 10 MINUTES • COOK TIME:1 HOUR 30 MINUTES •• SERVES: about 6 cups

Ingredients
1 tablespoon olive oil
2 medium onions, quartered
2 medium carrots, chopped
1 celery rib, chopped
2 garlic cloves, unpeeled and crushed
8 cups water

2 teaspoons soy sauce
1/3 cup coarsely chopped fresh parsley
1 bay leaf
1 teaspoon salt
1/2 teaspoon black peppercorns

Directions
1. In a large stockpot, heat the oil over medium heat. Add the onions, carrots, celery, and garlic. Cover and cook until softened, about 10 minutes. Stir in the water, soy sauce, parsley, bay leaf, salt, and peppercorns. Bring to a boil and then reduce heat to low and simmer, uncovered, for 11/2 hours.
2. Set aside to cool, then strain through a fine-mesh sieve into a large bowl or pot, pressing against the solids with the back of a spoon to release all the liquid. Discard solids. Cool broth completely, then portion into tightly covered containers and refrigerate for up to 4 days or freeze for up to 3 months.

Roasted Vegetable Broth
PREP: 5 MINUTES • COOK TIME: 1HOUR 30 MINUTES • • SERVES: about 6 cups

Ingredients
1 large onion, thickly sliced
2 large carrots, chopped
1 celery rib, chopped
1 large potato, unpeeled and chopped
3 garlic cloves, unpeeled and crushed
2 tablespoons olive oil

Salt and freshly ground black pepper
8 cups water
1/2 cup coarsely chopped fresh parsley
2 bay leaves
1/2 teaspoon black peppercorns
1 tablespoon soy sauce

Directions
1. Preheat the oven to 425°F. In a lightly oiled 9 x 13-inch baking pan, place the onion, carrots, celery, potato, and garlic. Drizzle with the oil and sprinkle with salt and pepper to taste. Roast the vegetables until they are slightly browned, turning once, about 30 minutes total. Set aside for 10 minutes to cool slightly.
2. Place the roasted vegetables in a large stockpot. Add the water, parsley, bay leaves, peppercorns, soy sauce, and salt to taste. Bring to a boil and then reduce heat to low and simmer, uncovered, until the broth has reduced slightly and is a deep golden color, about 1 hour.
3. Set aside to cool, then strain through a fine-mesh sieve into a large bowl or pot, pressing against the solids with the back of a spoon to release all the liquid. Discard solids. Cool broth completely, then portion into tightly covered containers and refrigerate for up to 4 days or freeze for up to 3 months.

Root Vegetable Broth
PREP: 5 MINUTES • COOK TIME:1 HOUR 38 MINUTES • • SERVES: about 6 cups

Ingredients
1 tablespoon olive oil
1 large onion, coarsely chopped
2 medium carrots, coarsely chopped
2 medium parsnips, coarsely chopped
1 medium turnip, coarsely chopped
8 cups water

1 medium white potato, unpeeled and quartered
3 garlic cloves, unpeeled and crushed
¾ cup coarsely chopped fresh parsley
2 bay leaves
1/2 teaspoon black peppercorns
1 teaspoon salt

Directions
1. In a large stockpot, heat the oil over medium heat. Add the onion, carrots, parsnips, and turnip. Cover and cook until softened, about 8 minutes. Stir in the water. Add the potato, garlic, parsley, bay leaves, peppercorns, and salt. Bring to a boil and then reduce heat to low and simmer, uncovered, for 11/2 hours.
2. Set aside to cool, then strain through a fine-mesh sieve into a large bowl or pot, pressing against the solids with the back of a spoon to release all the liquid. Discard solids. Cool broth completely, then portion into tightly covered containers and refrigerate for up to 4 days or freeze for up to 3 months.

Mushroom Vegetable Broth
PREP: 5 MINUTES • COOK TIME:1 HOUR 37 MINUTES • • SERVES: about 6 cups

Ingredients
1 tablespoon olive oil

1 medium onion, unpeeled and quartered

1 medium carrot, coarsely chopped
1 celery rib with leaves, coarsely chopped
8 ounces white mushrooms, lightly rinsed, patted dry, and coarsely chopped
5 dried shiitake or porcini mushrooms, soaked in 2 cups hot water, drained, soaking liquid strained and reserved

3 garlic cloves, unpeeled and crushed
1/2 cup coarsely chopped fresh parsley
2 bay leaves
1/2 teaspoon black peppercorns
1 teaspoon salt
5 cups water

Directions

1. In a large stockpot, heat the oil over medium heat. Add the onion, carrot, celery, and white mushrooms. Cover and cook until softened, about 7 minutes. Stir in the softened dried mushrooms and the reserved soaking liquid, along with the garlic, parsley, bay leaves, peppercorns, salt, and water. Bring to a boil and then reduce heat to low and simmer, uncovered, for 11/2 hours.
2. Set aside to cool, then strain through a fine-mesh sieve into a large bowl or pot, pressing against the solids with the back of a spoon to release all the liquid. Discard solids. Cool broth completely, then portion into tightly covered containers and refrigerate for up to 4 days or freeze for up to 3 months.

Jamaican Red Bean Stew
PREP: 10 MINUTES • COOK TIME: 40 MINUTES • TOTAL: 50 MINUTES • SERVES: 4 servings

Ingredients
1 tablespoon olive oil
1 medium yellow onion, chopped
2 large carrots, cut into 1/4-inch slices
2 garlic cloves, minced
1 large sweet potato, peeled and cut into 1/4-inch dice
1/4 teaspoon crushed red pepper
3 cups cooked or 2 (15.5-ounce) cans dark red kidney beans, drained and rinsed

1 (14.5-ounce) can diced tomatoes, drained
1 teaspoon hot or mild curry powder
1 teaspoon dried thyme
1/4 teaspoon ground allspice
1/2 teaspoon salt
1/4 teaspoon freshly ground black pepper
1/2 cup water
1 (13.5-ounce) can unsweetened coconut milk

Directions

1. In a large saucepan, heat the oil over medium heat. Add the onion and carrots, cover, and cook until softened, 5 minutes.
2. Add the garlic, sweet potato, and crushed red pepper. Stir in the kidney beans, tomatoes, curry powder, thyme, allspice, salt, and black pepper.
3. Stir in the water, cover, and simmer until the vegetables are tender, about 30 minutes. Stir in the coconut milk and simmer, uncovered, for 10 minutes to blend flavors and thicken the sauce. If a thicker sauce is desired, puree some of the vegetables with an immersion blender. Serve immediately.

Greens And Beans Soup
PREP: 15 MINUTES • COOK TIME: 0 MINUTES • TOTAL: 15 MINUTES • SERVES: 4 servings

Ingredients
1 tablespoon olive oil
1 medium onion, chopped
3 large garlic cloves, minced

11/2 cups cooked or 1 (15.5-ounce) can cannellini beans, drained and rinsed
11/2 cups cooked or 1 (15.5-ounce) can dark red kidney beans, drained and rinsed

5 cups vegetable broth or store-bought, or water
1/4 teaspoon crushed red pepper
Salt and freshly ground black pepper

3 cups coarsely chopped stemmed Swiss chard
3 cups coarsely chopped stemmed kale

Directions

1. In a large soup pot, heat the oil over medium heat. Add the onion, cover, and cook until softened, about 5 minutes. Add the garlic and cook, uncovered, 1 minute.
2. Stir in the beans, broth, crushed red pepper, and salt and black pepper to taste and bring to a boil. Reduce heat to a simmer, uncovered, and stir in the greens. Continue to cook until the greens are tender, 15 to 20 minutes. Serve hot.

Hearty Chili
PREP: 10 MINUTES • COOK TIME: 15 MINUTES • TOTAL: 25 MINUTES • SERVES: 4

Ingredients
1 onion, diced
2 to 3 garlic cloves, minced
1 teaspoon olive oil, or 1 to 2 tablespoons water, vegetable broth, or red wine
1 (28-ounce) can tomatoes
¼ cup tomato paste, or crushed tomatoes

1 (14-ounce) can kidney beans, rinsed and drained, or 1½ cups cooked
2 to 3 teaspoons chili powder
¼ teaspoon sea salt
¼ cup fresh cilantro, or parsley leaves

Directions
Preparing the Ingredients.

1. In a large pot, sauté the onion and garlic in the oil, about 5 minutes. Once they're soft, add the tomatoes, tomato paste, beans, and chili powder. Season with the salt.
2. Let simmer for at least 10 minutes, or as long as you like. The flavors will get better the longer it simmers, and it's even better as leftovers.
   Garnish with cilantro and serve.
   Per Serving: Calories: 160; Protein: 8g; Total fat: 3g; Saturated fat: 11g; Carbohydrates: 29g; Fiber: 7g

Golden Beet Soup With A Twist
PREP: 5 MINUTES • COOK TIME: 50 MINUTES • TOTAL: 55 MINUTES • SERVES: 6 servings

Ingredients
2 tablespoons olive oil
1 medium yellow onion, finely chopped
1 medium carrot, finely chopped
4 medium golden beets, peeled and diced
1 small yellow bell pepper, chopped
1 medium Yukon Gold potato, diced

5 cups vegetable broth, homemade (see Light Vegetable Broth) or store-bought, or water
1 teaspoon dried thyme
Salt and freshly ground black pepper
1 tablespoon fresh lemon juice
2 tablespoons minced fresh dillweed or 11/2 teaspoons dried, for garnish

Directions

1. In a large soup pot, heat the oil over medium heat. Add the onion and carrot. Cover and cook until softened, 5 minutes. Add the beets, bell pepper, and potato and cook, uncovered, stirring, for 1 minute. Stir in the broth, sugar, and thyme and season with salt and black pepper to taste. Cook until the vegetables are tender, about 45 minutes.

2. Serve hot or, alternately, set aside to cool, then refrigerate until chilled. Just before serving, stir in the lemon juice and garnish with the dill.

Asian-Inspired Chili
PREP: 15 MINUTES • COOK TIME: 20 MINUTES • TOTAL: 35 MINUTES • SERVES: 4

Ingredients

1 teaspoon sesame oil or 2 teaspoons vegetable broth or water
1 cup diced onion
3 teaspoons minced garlic (about 3 cloves)
1 cup chopped carrots
2 cups shredded green or napa cabbage
1 (14.5-ounce) can small red beans or adzuki beans, drained and rinsed

1 (14.5-ounce) fire-roasted diced tomatoes
2 cups vegetable broth
2 tablespoons red miso paste or tomato paste
2 tablespoons hot water
1 tablespoon hot sauce
2 teaspoons to 1 tablespoon tamari or soy sauce (optional)

Directions

Preparing the Ingredients.

1. In a large pot, over medium-high heat, heat the sesame oil. Add the onion, garlic, and carrot. Sauté for 5 minutes, until the onions are translucent. Add the cabbage, beans, tomatoes, and broth, and stir well. Bring to a boil.
2. Cover, reduce the heat to low, and simmer for 15 minutes.
   In a measuring cup, whisk the miso paste and hot water. Set aside.
   After 15 minutes, remove the chili from the stove, add the miso mixture and hot sauce, and stir well. Taste before determining how much tamari to add (if using).
3. Divide the chili evenly among 4 single-serving containers or large glass jars. Let cool before sealing the lids.
   Place the containers in the refrigerator for up to 5 days or freeze for up to 3 months. To thaw, refrigerate overnight. Reheat in the microwave for 2 to 3 minutes.

Per Serving: Calories: 177; Protein: 9g; Total fat: 2g; Carbohydrates: 33g; Fiber: 191g

Weeknight Chickpea Tomato Soup
PREP: 10 MINUTES • COOK TIME: 20 MINUTES • TOTAL: 30 MINUTES • SERVES: 2

Ingredients

1 to 2 teaspoons olive oil, or vegetable broth
½ cup chopped onion
3 garlic cloves, minced
1 cup mushrooms, chopped
⅛ to ¼ teaspoon sea salt, divided
1 tablespoon dried basil
½ tablespoon dried oregano

1 to 2 tablespoons balsamic vinegar, or red wine
1 (19-ounce) can diced tomatoes
1 (14-ounce) can chickpeas, drained and rinsed, or 1½ cups cooked
2 cups water
1 to 2 cups chopped kale

Directions

Preparing the Ingredients.

1. In a large pot, warm the olive oil and sauté the onion, garlic, and mushrooms with a pinch salt until softened, 7 to 8 minutes. Add the basil and oregano and stir to mix. Then add the vinegar to deglaze the

pan, using a wooden spoon to scrape all the browned, savory bits up from the bottom. Add the tomatoes and chickpeas. Stir to combine, adding enough water to get the consistency you want. Add the kale and the remaining salt. Cover and simmer for 5 to 15 minutes, until the kale is as soft as you like it.

2. This is delicious topped with a tablespoon of toasted walnuts and a sprinkle of nutritional yeast, or the Cheesy Sprinkle.

Per Serving: Calories: 343; Protein: 17g; Total fat: 9g; Carbohydrates: 61g; Fiber: 15g

---

Shiitake Mushroom Soup With Sake
PREP: 5 MINUTES • COOK TIME: 20 MINUTES • TOTAL: 25 MINUTES • SERVES: 4 servings

Ingredients

1 tablespoon canola or grapeseed oil
2 leeks, white parts only, well rinsed and chopped
2 celery ribs with leaves, chopped
8 ounces fresh shiitake mushrooms, lightly rinsed, patted dry, stemmed, and sliced
3 tablespoons sake

2 tablespoons soy sauce
6 cups vegetable broth, homemade (see Light Vegetable Broth) or store-bought, or water
Salt and freshly ground black pepper
2 tablespoons minced fresh parsley

Directions

1. In a large soup pot, heat the oil over medium heat. Add the leeks and celery. Cover and cook until softened, about 5 minutes.
2. Stir in the mushrooms, sake, soy sauce, and broth and season with salt and pepper to taste. Bring to a boil, then reduce heat to low and simmer, uncovered, until the mushrooms are tender, about 15 minutes. Stir in the parsley, taste, adjusting seasonings if necessary, and serve.

Potato And Kale Soup
PREP: 5 MINUTES • COOK TIME: 50 MINUTES • TOTAL: 55 MINUTES • SERVES: 4 servings

Ingredients

1 tablespoon olive oil
1 medium onion, chopped
2 garlic cloves, minced
6 cups vegetable broth, homemade (see Light Vegetable Broth) or store-bought, or water
2 large russet potatoes, peeled and cut into 1/2-inch dice

1/2 teaspoon dried oregano
1/4 teaspoon crushed red pepper
1 bay leaf
Salt
4 cups chopped stemmed kale
11/2 cups cooked or 1 (15.5-ounce) can Great Northern beans, drained and rinsed

Directions

1. In a large pot, heat the oil over medium heat. Add the onion and garlic, cover, and cook until softened, about 5 minutes. Add the broth, potatoes, oregano, crushed red pepper, bay leaf, and salt to taste, and bring to a boil. Reduce heat to low and simmer, uncovered, for 30 minutes.
2. Stir in the kale and the beans and cook until the vegetables are tender, 15 to 20 minutes longer. Remove, discard the bay leaf, and serve.

Coconut Watercress Soup
PREP: 10 MINUTES • COOK TIME: 20 MINUTES • TOTAL: 30 MINUTES • SERVES: 4

Ingredients

1 teaspoon coconut oil
1 onion, diced
2 cups fresh or frozen peas
4 cups water, or vegetable stock
1 cup fresh watercress, chopped

1 tablespoon fresh mint, chopped
Pinch sea salt
Pinch freshly ground black pepper
¾ cup coconut milk

Directions

Preparing the Ingredients.
1. Melt the coconut oil in a large pot over medium-high heat. Add the onion and cook until soft, about 5 minutes, then add the peas and the water. Bring to a boil, then lower the heat and add the watercress, mint, salt, and pepper.
   Cover and simmer for 5 minutes. Stir in the coconut milk, and purée the soup until smooth in a blender or with an immersion blender.
2. Try this soup with any other fresh, leafy green—anything from spinach to collard greens to arugula to Swiss chard.

Per Serving: Calories: 178; Protein: 6g; Total fat: 10g; Carbohydrates: 18g; Fiber: 5g

Roasted Red Pepper and Butternut Squash Soup
PREP: 10 MINUTES • COOK TIME: 45 MINUTES • TOTAL: 55 MINUTES • SERVES: 6

Ingredients
1 small butternut squash
1 tablespoon olive oil
1 teaspoon sea salt
2 red bell peppers
1 yellow onion
1 head garlic
2 cups water, or vegetable broth

Zest and juice of 1 lime
1 to 2 tablespoons tahini
Pinch cayenne pepper
½ teaspoon ground coriander
½ teaspoon ground cumin
Toasted squash seeds (optional)

Directions
Preparing the Ingredients.
1. Preheat the oven to 350°F.
2. Prepare the squash for roasting by cutting it in half lengthwise, scooping out the seeds, and poking some holes in the flesh with a fork. Reserve the seeds if desired.
   Rub a small amount of oil over the flesh and skin, then rub with a bit of sea salt and put the halves skin-side down in a large baking dish. Put it in the oven while you prepare the rest of the vegetables.
   Prepare the peppers the exact same way, except they do not need to be poked.
   Slice the onion in half and rub oil on the exposed faces. Slice the top off the head of garlic and rub oil on the exposed flesh.
3. After the squash has cooked for 20 minutes, add the peppers, onion, and garlic, and roast for another 20 minutes. Optionally, you can toast the squash seeds by putting them in the oven in a separate baking dish 10 to 15 minutes before the vegetables are finished.
   Keep a close eye on them. When the vegetables are cooked, take them out and let them cool before handling them. The squash will be very soft when poked with a fork.
   Scoop the flesh out of the squash skin into a large pot (if you have an immersion blender) or into a blender.

Chop the pepper roughly, remove the onion skin and chop the onion roughly, and squeeze the garlic cloves out of the head, all into the pot or blender. Add the water, the lime zest and juice, and the tahini. Purée the soup, adding more water if you like, to your desired consistency. Season with the salt, cayenne, coriander, and cumin. Serve garnished with toasted squash seeds (if using).

Per Serving: Calories: 156; Protein: 4g; Total fat: 7g; Saturated fat: 11g; Carbohydrates: 22g; Fiber: 5g

Mushroom Medley Soup
PREP: 5 MINUTES • COOK TIME: 40 MINUTES • TOTAL: 45 MINUTES • SERVES: 4 to 6 servings

Ingredients
1 tablespoon olive oil
1 medium onion, chopped
1 large carrot, chopped
1 celery rib, chopped
8 ounces fresh shiitake mushrooms, lightly rinsed, patted dry, stemmed and cut into 1/4-inch slices
8 ounces cremini mushrooms, lightly rinsed, patted dry, and quartered

8 ounces white mushrooms, lightly rinsed, patted dry, and quartered
6 cups vegetable broth, mushroom broth, homemade
1/4 cup chopped fresh parsley
1 teaspoon minced fresh thyme or 1/2 teaspoon dried
Salt and freshly ground black pepper

Directions
1. In a large pot, heat the oil over medium heat. Add the onion, carrot, and celery. Cover and cook until softened, about 10 minutes. Stir in all the mushrooms and broth, and bring to boil.
2. Reduce heat to low, add the parsley and thyme, and season with salt and pepper to taste. Simmer, uncovered, until the vegetables are tender, about 30 minutes. Serve hot.

Black Bean, Pumpkin, and Kale Chili (pressure cooker)
PREP: 8 MINUTES • PRESSURE: 10 MINUTES • TOTAL: 30 MINUTES • PRESSURE LEVEL: HIGH • RELEASE: NATURAL• SERVES 4-5

Ingredients
¾ cup dried black beans, soaked in water overnight
1 (28-ounce) can crushed tomatoes
2 cups chopped pumpkin
2 to 3 cups water or unsalted vegetable broth

2 tablespoons chili powder
1 teaspoon onion powder
½ teaspoon garlic powder
2 to 3 cups finely shredded kale
½ teaspoon salt

Directions
1. **Preparing the Ingredients.** Drain the black beans, then put them in your electric pressure cooker's cooking pot. Add the tomatoes, pumpkin, water (2 cups for thick chili, 3 cups if you like it a bit more soupy), chili powder, onion powder, and garlic powder.
2. **High pressure for 10 minutes.** Close and lock the lid and ensure the pressure valve is sealed, then select High Pressure and set the time for 10 minutes.
3. **Pressure Release.** Once the cook time is complete, let the pressure release naturally, about 20 minutes. Once all the pressure has released, carefully unlock and remove the lid. Stir in the kale to wilt. Stir in the salt.

Per Serving: Calories: 209; Protein: 13g; Total fat: 2g; Carbohydrates: 75g; Fiber: 13g

Golden Harvest Soup
PREP: 5 MINUTES • COOK TIME: 45 MINUTES • TOTAL: 50 MINUTES • SERVES: 4 to 6 servings

Ingredients

2 tablespoons olive oil
1 medium yellow onion, finely chopped
2 medium carrots, chopped
1 medium sweet potato, peeled and chopped
1 medium yellow bell pepper, chopped
2 garlic cloves, minced
4 large ripe yellow tomatoes, chopped
6 cups vegetable broth, homemade (see Light Vegetable Broth) or store-bought, or water

1 bay leaf
1 teaspoon fresh savory or 1/2 teaspoon dried
Salt
Ground cayenne
11/2 cups cooked or 1 (15.5-ounce) can chickpeas, drained and rinsed
1/3 cup ditalini or other small soup pasta
1/4 teaspoon turmeric

Directions

1. In a large pot, heat the oil over medium heat. Add the onion, carrots, sweet potato, bell pepper, and garlic. Cover and cook until softened, about 10 minutes. Stir in the tomatoes, broth, bay leaf, savory, and salt and cayenne to taste. Bring to a boil, reduce heat, and simmer, uncovered, 30 minutes. Add the chickpeas and simmer another 15 minutes.
2. In a medium saucepan of boiling salted water, cook the ditalini and turmeric, stirring occasionally, until pasta is al dente, about 5 minutes. Drain well and stir into the soup. Remove and discard bay leaf before serving. Ladle soup into bowls and serve.

Creamy Pumpkin and Toasted Walnut Soup
PREP: 15 MINUTES • COOK TIME: 30 MINUTES • TOTAL: 45 MINUTES • SERVES: 4

Ingredients

1 small pie pumpkin, peeled, seeded, and chopped (about 6 cups)
1 teaspoon olive oil
¼ teaspoon sea salt
1 onion, diced
4 cups water, or vegetable stock

2 to 3 teaspoons ground sage
2 to 3 tablespoons nutritional yeast
1 cup non-dairy milk, or 1 tablespoon nut or seed butter plus 1 cup water or stock
¼ cup toasted walnuts
Freshly ground black pepper

Directions

Preparing the Ingredients.

1. Place a large saucepan on medium and sauté the pumpkin in the oil, seasoning with the salt, until slightly softened, about 10 minutes. Add the onion to the pot and sauté until slightly softened, about 5 minutes. Add the water and bring to a boil. Then turn down to a simmer, cover, and cook 15 to 20 minutes, until the pumpkin is tender when pierced with a fork. Stir in the sage, nutritional yeast, and non-dairy milk.
2. Then purée the soup with an immersion blender or in a regular blender until smooth. Garnish with toasted walnuts and pepper.

Per Serving: Calories: 236; Protein: 10g; Total fat: 12g; Carbohydrates: 29g; Fiber: 8g

Miso Noodle Soup
PREP: 10 MINUTES • COOK TIME: 15 MINUTES • TOTAL: 25 MINUTES • SERVES: 4

Ingredients
7 ounces soba noodles (use 100% buckwheat for gluten-free)
4 cups water
4 tablespoons miso

1 cup adzuki beans (cooked or canned), drained and rinsed
2 tablespoons fresh cilantro, or basil, finely chopped
2 scallions, thinly sliced

Directions
Preparing the Ingredients.
1. Bring a large pot of water to a boil, then add the soba noodles. Stir them occasionally; they'll take about 5 minutes to cook. Meanwhile, prepare the rest of the soup by warming the water in a separate pot to just below boiling, then remove it from heat. Stir the miso into the water until it has dissolved. Once the soba noodles are cooked, drain them and rinse with hot water.
2. Add the cooked noodles, adzuki beans, cilantro, and scallions to the miso broth and serve.

Per Serving: Calories: 102; Protein: 11g; Total fat: 1g; Saturated fat: 11g; Carbohydrates: 18g; Fiber: 5g

Versatile Vegetable Soup
PREP: 5 MINUTES • COOK TIME: 50 MINUTES • TOTAL: 55 MINUTES • SERVES: 4 to 6 servings

Ingredients
1 tablespoon olive oil
2 medium carrots, chopped
1 large onion, chopped
1 celery rib, chopped
2 garlic cloves, minced
2 cups chopped cabbage
1/2 medium red bell pepper, chopped
4 small red-skinned potatoes, unpeeled and quartered

6 cups vegetable broth, homemade (see Light Vegetable Broth) or store-bought, or water
11/2 cups cooked or 1 (15.5-ounce) can chickpeas, drained and rinsed
Salt and freshly ground black pepper
1/2 cup fresh or frozen green peas, thawed
2 tablespoons chopped fresh parsley

Directions
1. In large soup pot, heat the oil over medium heat. Add the carrots, onion, celery, and garlic. Cover and cook until softened, about 5 minutes. Add the cabbage, bell pepper, potatoes, and broth. Bring to a boil, then reduce heat to low.
2. Add the chickpeas and salt and pepper to taste. Simmer, uncovered, until the vegetables are tender, about 45 minutes. About 5 minutes before serving, stir in the peas. Add the parsley, taste, adjusting seasonings if necessary, and serve.

Minty Beet and Sweet Potato Soup
PREP: 10 MINUTES • COOK TIME: 30 MINUTES • TOTAL: 40 MINUTES • SERVES: 6

Ingredients
5 cups water, or salt-free vegetable broth (if salted, omit the sea salt below)

1 to 2 teaspoons olive oil, or vegetable broth
1 cup chopped onion

3 garlic cloves, minced
1 tablespoon thyme, fresh or dried
1 to 2 teaspoons paprika
2 cups peeled and chopped beets
2 cups peeled and chopped sweet potato
2 cups peeled and chopped parsnips½ teaspoon sea salt

1 cup fresh mint, chopped
½ avocado, or 2 tablespoons nut or seed butter (optional)
2 tablespoons balsamic vinegar (optional)
2 tablespoons pumpkin seeds

Directions
Preparing the Ingredients.
1. In large pot, boil the water. In another large pot, warm the olive oil and sauté the onion and garlic until softened, about 5 minutes.
   Add the thyme, paprika, beets, sweet potato, and parsnips, along with the boiling water and salt.
   Cover and leave to gently boil for about 30 minutes, or until the vegetables are soft.
   Set aside a little mint for a garnish and add the rest, along with the avocado (if using).
   Stir until well combined.
2. Transfer the soup to a blender or use an immersion blender to purée, adding the balsamic vinegar (if using).
   Serve topped with fresh mint and pumpkin seeds—and maybe chunks of the other half of the avocado, if you used it. This soup is perfect to make in big batches and keep in single-serving containers in the freezer for quick weeknight meals.

Per Serving: Calories: 156; Protein: 4g; Total fat: 4g; Carbohydrates: 31g; Fiber: 7g

Leek and Potato Soup (Pressure Cooker)
PREP: 15 MINUTES • PRESSURE: 7 MINUTES • TOTAL: 45 MINUTES • PRESSURE LEVEL: HIGH • RELEASE: NATURAL• SERVES 4-6

Ingredients
3 leeks (white and light green parts only), chopped
1 white or yellow onion, chopped
3 or 4 garlic cloves, minced
1 tablespoon olive oil
6 medium russet potatoes, scrubbed or peeled and roughly chopped (6 to 7 cups)

½ (13.5-ounce) can coconut milk (about ¾ cup)
4 cups water or unsalted vegetable broth
½ teaspoon salt, plus more as needed
1 teaspoon garlic powder (optional)
Freshly ground black pepper

Directions
1. **Preparing the Ingredients.** On your electric pressure cooker, select Sauté. Add the leeks, onion, garlic, and olive oil. Cook for 4 to 5 minutes, stirring occasionally, until the leek and onion are softened. Add the potatoes, coconut milk, water, and salt. Cancel Sauté.
2. **High pressure for 7 minutes.** Close and lock the lid and ensure the pressure valve is sealed, then select High Pressure and set the time for 7 minutes.
3. **Pressure Release.** Once the cook time is complete, let the pressure release naturally, about 20 minutes. Once all the pressure has released, carefully unlock and remove the lid. Let cool for a few minutes and then purée the soup—either use an immersion blender right in the pot or transfer the soup (in batches, if necessary) to a countertop blender. Taste and season with the garlic powder (if using), salt, and pepper.

Per Serving: Calories: 274; Protein: 5g; Total fat: 10g; Carbohydrates: 75g; Fiber: 4g

Split Pea Soup (Pressure Cooker)

PREP: 10 MINUTES • PRESSURE: 10 MINUTES • TOTAL: 45 MINUTES • PRESSURE LEVEL: HIGH • RELEASE: NATURAL• SERVES 6

Ingredients

3 or 4 carrots, scrubbed or peeled and chopped
1 large yellow onion, chopped
1 cup dried split green peas
3 cups water or unsalted vegetable broth
1 tablespoon tamari or soy sauce
2 to 3 teaspoons dried thyme or 1 teaspoon ground thyme

1 teaspoon onion powder
½ teaspoon garlic powder
Pinch freshly ground black pepper
¼ cup chopped sun-dried tomatoes or chopped pitted black olives
Salt

Directions

1. **Preparing the Ingredients.** In your electric pressure cooking pot, combine the carrots, onion, split peas, water, tamari, thyme, onion powder, garlic powder, and pepper.
2. **High pressure for 10 minutes**. Close and lock the lid and ensure the pressure valve is sealed, then select High Pressure and set the time for 10 minutes.
3. **Pressure Release.** Once the cook time is complete, let the pressure release naturally, about 20 minutes. Once all the pressure has released, carefully unlock and remove the lid. Let cool for a few minutes and then purée the soup—either use an immersion blender right in the pot or transfer the soup (in batches, if necessary) to a countertop blender.
   Stir in the nutritional yeast (if using) and sun-dried tomatoes. Taste and season with salt.

Per Serving: Calories: 182; Protein: 12g; Total fat: 1g; Saturated fat: 11g; Carbohydrates: 26g; Fiber: 12g

Zesty Black Bean Soup

PREP: 10 MINUTES • COOK TIME: 25 MINUTES • TOTAL: 35 MINUTES • SERVES: 2

Ingredients

1 teaspoon olive oil
1 onion, chopped
6 garlic cloves, minced
1 teaspoon chili powder
½ teaspoon ground cinnamon or pumpkin pie spice
½ to 1 teaspoon salt

1 (15-ounce) can black beans, drained and rinsed
1 (28-ounce) can crushed or diced tomatoes, undrained
3 cups water
3 celery stalks, chopped
2 cups chopped collard greens
2 tablespoons freshly squeezed lime juice

Directions

Preparing the Ingredients.

1. Heat the olive oil in a large soup pot over medium heat.
   Add the onion and garlic, and sauté for about 5 minutes, until soft.
   Stir in the chili powder, cinnamon, and salt, then add the beans, tomatoes with their juices, and water.
   Bring to a boil and turn the heat to low.
   Simmer the soup for 10 to 15 minutes.
2. Using a hand blender, purée the soup, or let it cool slightly before transferring it to a countertop blender to purée. Stir in the celery and greens, and cover the pot. Let the soup cook for 10 minutes more or longer if you want softer greens. Stir in the lime juice just before serving.
   Leftovers will keep in an airtight container for up to 1 week in the refrigerator or up to 1 month in the freezer.

Per Serving (2 cups) Calories: 209; Protein: 12g; Total fat: 3g; Saturated fat: 0g; Carbohydrates: 38g; Fiber: 13g

Roasted Tomato Soup
PREP: 10 MINUTES • COOK TIME: 50 MINUTES • TOTAL: 60 MINUTES • SERVES: 4 servings

Ingredients
2 pounds ripe tomatoes, cored and halved
2 large garlic cloves, crushed
3 tablespoons olive oil
1 tablespoon balsamic vinegar
Salt and freshly ground black pepper

1/2 cup chopped red onion
2 cups light vegetable broth, homemade (see Light Vegetable Broth) or store-bought, or water
1/2 cup lightly packed fresh basil leaves

Directions
1. Preheat the oven to 450°F. In a large bowl, combine the tomatoes, garlic, 2 tablespoons of the oil, vinegar, and salt and pepper to taste. Spread the tomato mixture into a 9 x 13-inch baking pan and roast until the tomatoes begin to darken, about 30 minutes. Remove from the oven and set aside.
2. In a large soup pot, heat the remaining 1 tablespoon of oil over medium heat. Add the onion, cover, and cook until very soft, about 10 minutes, stirring occasionally. Add the roasted tomatoes and broth and bring to a boil. Reduce heat to low and simmer, uncovered, for 10 minutes. Remove from the heat, add the basil, and season with salt and pepper to taste. Puree the soup in the pot with an immersion blender or in a blender or food processor, in batches if necessary, and return to the pot. Reheat over medium heat, if necessary. To serve this soup chilled, refrigerate it for at least 1 hour before serving.

Hearty Split Lentil Soup
PREP: 10 MINUTES • COOK TIME: 20 MINUTES • TOTAL: 30 MINUTES • SERVES: 3

Ingredients
1 teaspoon olive oil
2 carrots, peeled and chopped
1 onion, diced
2 garlic cloves, minced
1 tablespoon dried herbs

1 to 2 tablespoons apple cider vinegar
5 cups water or Vegetable Broth
1 cup dried split red lentils
¼ teaspoon salt
2 tablespoons nutritional yeast (optional)

Directions
Preparing the Ingredients.
1. Heat the olive oil in a large soup pot over medium heat.
   Add the carrots, onion, and garlic, and sauté for about 5 minutes, until the vegetables are softened. Add the dried herbs and vinegar, and let it sizzle and deglaze the bottom of the pot. Stir in the water and lentils. Bring the soup to a boil, then reduce the heat to low. Simmer for about 15 minutes, until the lentils are very soft and creamy. Stir in the salt and nutritional yeast (if using).
2. Using a hand blender, purée the soup until smooth, or let it cool slightly before transferring to a countertop blender to purée. Leftovers will keep in an airtight container for up to 1 week in the refrigerator or up to 1 month in the freezer.

Per Serving (about 2 cups) Calories: 457; Protein: 31g; Total fat: 5g; Saturated fat: 1g; Carbohydrates: 76g; Fiber: 16g

Matzo Ball Soup
PREP: 5 MINUTES • COOK TIME: 40 MINUTES • TOTAL: 45 MINUTES • SERVES: 4 servings

Ingredients

1 tablespoon olive oil
1 small onion, finely chopped
1 medium carrot, chopped
1 celery rib, chopped
3 green onions, chopped
6 cups vegetable broth, homemade (see Light Vegetable Broth) or store-bought, or water

2 tablespoons minced fresh parsley
1 teaspoon fresh or dried dillweed
1/2 teaspoon salt, or more if needed
1/4 teaspoon freshly ground black pepper
Matzo Balls (recipe follows)

Directions

1. In a large soup pot, heat the oil over medium heat. Add the onion, carrot, and celery. Cover and cook until softened, about 5 minutes. Add the green onions and cook 3 minutes longer. Stir in the broth, parsley, dill, salt, and pepper. You may need to add additional salt, depending on the saltiness of your broth. Bring to a boil, then reduce heat to low and simmer, uncovered, until the vegetables are tender, about 30 minutes.
2. When ready to serve, place 3 of the matzo balls into each soup bowl and ladle the soup on top. Serve immediately.

Matzo Balls

PREP: 15 MINUTES • COOK TIME: 0 MINUTES • TOTAL: 15 MINUTES • SERVES: about 12 matzo balls

Ingredients

1 cup matzo meal
1/2 teaspoon onion powder
1/2 teaspoon salt
1/4 teaspoon freshly ground black pepper
1 cup crumbled drained firm tofu

1/3 cup vegetable broth, homemade (see Light Vegetable Broth) or store-bought, or water
2 tablespoons fresh minced dillweed
2 tablespoons chopped fresh parsley
1/4 cup olive oil

Directions

1. In a medium bowl, combine the matzo meal, onion powder, salt, and pepper. Set aside.
2. In a food processor, combine the tofu, broth, dill, parsley, and oil and puree. Stir the tofu mixture into the matzo mixture and blend well. Cover the bowl and refrigerate for 1 hour or overnight.
3. Preheat the oven to 375°F. Lightly oil a baking sheet and set aside. Divide the matzo mixture into 12 equal portions. Use your hands to form the mixture into tightly packed balls and arrange on the oiled baking sheet. Cover tightly with foil and bake for about 30 minutes. Set aside to cool. Serve warm.

Four-Bean Chili

PREP: 10 MINUTES • COOK TIME: 15 MINUTES•TOTAL: 25 MINUTES • SERVES: 6

Ingredients

2 tablespoons olive oil
1 onion, chopped
4 garlic cloves, minced
one 15-ounce can black beans, drained and rinsed
one 15-ounce can kidney beans, drained and rinsed
one 15-ounce can pinto beans, drained and rinsed

one 15-ounce can white beans, drained and rinsed
two 15-ounce cans ro-tel roasted tomatoes and peppers
2 cups vegetable stock
3 tablespoons chili powder
1 teaspoon sea salt

Directions

Preparing the Ingredients.

1. In a large pot, heat the olive oil over medium-high heat until it shimmers.
2. Add the onion and cook until it softens, about 5 minutes. Add the garlic and cook until it is fragrant, about 30 seconds. Add the beans, tomatoes and peppers, vegetable stock, chili powder, and salt. Cook, stirring occasionally, until heated through, about 10 minutes. Serve immediately.

Miso Soup
PREP: 5 MINUTES • COOK TIME: 10 MINUTES • TOTAL: 15 MINUTES • SERVES: 4 servings

Ingredients

5 cups water
2 tablespoons soy sauce, or to taste
4 white mushrooms, lightly rinsed, patted dry, and cut into 1/4-inch slices

1/4 cup chopped green onions
3 tablespoons mellow white miso paste
6 ounces extra-firm tofu, cut into small dice

Directions

1. In a large soup pot, bring the water and soy sauce to a boil. Add the mushrooms and green onions. Reduce the heat to low and simmer for 5 minutes to soften the vegetables.
2. Place 1/2 cup of the hot soup into a small bowl and add the miso paste, blending well. Stir the blended miso into the soup and simmer for 2 minutes. Do not boil. Add the tofu and adjust the seasonings, adding a little more miso paste or soy sauce if needed, and serve.

Moroccan Aubergine Salad
PREP: 30 MINUTES • COOK TIME: 15 MINUTES • TOTAL: 45 MINUTES • SERVES: 2

Ingredients

1 teaspoon olive oil
1 eggplant, diced
½ teaspoon ground cumin
½ teaspoon ground ginger
¼ teaspoon turmeric
¼ teaspoon ground nutmeg
Pinch sea salt

1 lemon, half zested and juiced, half cut into wedges
2 tablespoons capers
1 tablespoon chopped green olives
1 garlic clove, pressed
Handful fresh mint, finely chopped
2 cups spinach, chopped

Directions

Preparing the Ingredients.

1. Heat the oil in a large skillet on medium heat, then sauté the eggplant. Once it has softened slightly, about 5 minutes, stir in the cumin, ginger, turmeric, nutmeg, and salt.
   Cook until the eggplant is very soft, about 10 minutes.
   Add the lemon zest and juice, capers, olives, garlic, and mint.
   Sauté for another minute or two, to blend the flavors.
   Put a handful of spinach on each plate, and spoon the eggplant mixture on top.
   Serve with a wedge of lemon, to squeeze the fresh juice over the greens.

2. To tenderize the eggplant and reduce some of its naturally occurring bitter taste, you can sweat the eggplant by salting it. After dicing the eggplant, sprinkle it with salt and let it sit in a colander for about 30 minutes. Rinse the eggplant to remove the salt, then continue with the recipe as written.

Per Serving. Calories: 97; Protein: 4g; Total fat: 4g; Carbohydrates: 16; Fiber: 8g

Tuscan Tomato And Bread Soup
PREP: 5 MINUTES • COOK TIME: 50 MINUTES • TOTAL: 55 MINUTES • SERVES: 4 servings

Ingredients
4 cups cubed Italian bread
1/4 cup olive oil
4 garlic cloves, minced
1 (28-ounce) can crushed tomatoes
2 fresh ripe tomatoes, cut into 1/2-inch dice

4 cups vegetable broth or water
2 tablespoons minced fresh parsley
Salt and freshly ground black pepper
Torn fresh basil leaves, for garnish

Directions
1. Preheat the oven to 400°F. Spread the bread cubes on a baking sheet and bake until lightly toasted, about 20 minutes, stirring once about halfway through.
2. In a large soup pot over medium heat, heat 2 tablespoons of the oil. Add the garlic and cook until softened, about 1 minute. Stir in the canned and fresh tomatoes, broth, parsley, and salt and pepper to taste. Bring to a boil, then reduce heat to low and simmer for 30 minutes.
3. Divide the toasted bread among 4 bowls and ladle the soup over the bread. The bread should absorb most of the liquid in the soup. Garnish with basil leaves, drizzle with the remaining 2 tablespoons oil, and serve.

Vegetable and Barley Stew (Pressure Cooker)
PREP: 15 MINUTES • PRESSURE: 20 MINUTES • TOTAL: 45 MINUTES • PRESSURE LEVEL: HIGH • RELEASE: QUICK• SERVES: 6

Ingredients
2 or 3 parsnips, peeled and chopped
2 cups chopped peeled sweet potato, russet potato, winter squash, or pumpkin
1 large yellow onion, chopped
1 cup pearl barley
1 (28-ounce) can diced tomatoes

4 cups water or unsalted vegetable broth
2 to 3 teaspoons dried mixed herbs or 1 teaspoon dried basil plus 1 teaspoon dried oregano
Salt
Freshly ground black pepper

Directions

1. **Preparing the Ingredients.** In your electric pressure cooking pot, combine the parsnips, sweet potato, onion, barley, tomatoes with their juice, water, and herbs.
2. **High pressure for 20 minutes.** Lock the lid and ensure the pressure valve is sealed, then select High Pressure and set the time for 20 minutes.
3. **Pressure Release.** Once the cook time is complete, quick release the pressure. Once all the pressure has released, carefully unlock and remove the lid. Taste and season with salt and pepper.

Per Serving. Calories: 300; Protein: 9g; Total fat: 2g; Carbohydrates: 16; Fiber: 14g

Garden Vegetable Stew
PREP: 5 MINUTES • COOK TIME: 60 MINUTES • TOTAL: 65 MINUTES • SERVES: 4 servings

Ingredients

2 tablespoons olive oil
1 medium red onion, chopped
1 medium carrot, cut into 1/4-inch slices
1/2 cup dry white wine
3 medium new potatoes, unpeeled and cut into 1-inch pieces
1 medium red bell pepper, cut into 1/2-inch dice
11/2 cups vegetable broth
2 medium zucchini, trimmed, halved lengthwise, and cut into 1/2-inch slices

1 medium yellow summer squash, trimmed, halved lengthwise, and cut into 1/2-inch slices
1 pound ripe plum tomatoes, chopped
Salt and freshly ground black pepper
2 cups fresh corn kernels
1 cup fresh peas
1/4 cup fresh basil
1/4 cup chopped fresh parsley
1 tablespoon minced fresh savory or 1 teaspoon dried

Directions

1. In a large saucepan, heat the oil over medium heat. Add the onion and carrot, cover, and cook until softened, 7 minutes. Add the wine and cook, uncovered, for 5 minutes. Stir in the potatoes, bell pepper, and broth and bring to a boil. Reduce the heat to medium and simmer for 15 minutes.
2. Add the zucchini, yellow squash, and tomatoes. Season with salt and black pepper to taste, cover, and simmer until the vegetables are tender, 20 to 30 minutes. Stir in the corn, peas, basil, parsley, and savory. Taste, adjusting seasonings if necessary. Simmer to blend flavors, about 10 minutes more. Serve immediately.

Moroccan Vermicelli Vegetable Soup
PREP: 5 MINUTES • COOK TIME: 35 MINUTES • TOTAL: 40 MINUTES • SERVES: 4 to 6 servings

Ingredients

1 tablespoon olive oil
1 small onion, chopped
1 large carrot, chopped
1 celery rib, chopped
3 small zucchini, cut into 1/4-inch dice
1 (28-ounce) can diced tomatoes, drained
2 tablespoons tomato paste
11/2 cups cooked or 1 (15.5-ounce) can chickpeas, drained and rinsed

2 teaspoons smoked paprika
1 teaspoon ground cumin
1 teaspoon za'atar spice (optional)
1/4 teaspoon ground cayenne
6 cups vegetable broth, homemade (see Light Vegetable Broth) or store-bought, or water
Salt
4 ounces vermicelli
2 tablespoons minced fresh cilantro, for garnish

Directions

1. In a large soup pot, heat the oil over medium heat. Add the onion, carrot, and celery. Cover and cook until softened, about 5 minutes. Stir in the zucchini, tomatoes, tomato paste, chickpeas, paprika, cumin, za'atar, and cayenne. Add the broth and salt to taste. Bring to a boil, then reduce heat to low and simmer, uncovered, until the vegetables are tender, about 30 minutes.
2. Shortly before serving, stir in the vermicelli and cook until the noodles are tender, about 5 minutes. Ladle the soup into bowls, garnish with cilantro, and serve.

Mediterranean Vegetable Stew
PREP: 5 MINUTES • COOK TIME: 45 MINUTES • TOTAL: 50 MINUTES • SERVES: 4 servings

Ingredients

1 tablespoon olive oil
1 medium yellow onion, chopped
1 medium carrot, chopped
3 garlic cloves, minced
1 medium red bell pepper, cut into 1/2-inch dice

1 medium fennel bulb, quartered and cut into 1/4-inch slices
1 medium zucchini, chopped
1 (14.5-ounce) can diced tomatoes, undrained
1 cup vegetable broth

Freshly ground black pepper
8 ounces white or porcini mushrooms, lightly rinsed, patted dry, and sliced
3 cups fresh baby spinach

1 1/2 cups cooked or 1 (15.5-ounce) can cannellini beans, drained and rinsed
1/2 teaspoon dried basil
1/2 teaspoon dried marjoram
2 tablespoons minced fresh parsley

Directions

1. In a large saucepan, heat the oil over medium heat. Add the onion, carrot, garlic, and bell pepper. Cover and cook until softened, 7 minutes.
   Add the fennel, zucchini, tomatoes, and broth. Bring to a boil, then reduce heat to low. Season with salt and black pepper to taste, cover, and simmer until the vegetables are tender, about 30 minutes.
2. Stir in the mushrooms, spinach, beans, basil, marjoram, and parsley. Taste, adjusting seasonings if necessary. Simmer 10 minutes more. Serve immediately.

Indonesian Vegetable Stew
PREP: 5 MINUTES • COOK TIME: 55 MINUTES • TOTAL: 60 MINUTES • SERVES: 4 to 6 servings

Ingredients

2 tablespoons canola or grapeseed oil
1 yellow onion, chopped
3 garlic cloves, minced
1 or 2 fresh hot chiles, seeded and minced
1 tablespoon grated fresh ginger
1 large russet potato, cut into 1/2-inch dice
1 medium eggplant, peeled and cut into 1/2-inch dice
8 ounces green beans, cut into 1-inch pieces
2 cups small cauliflower florets
1 1/2 cups vegetable broth

1 (14.5-ounce) can crushed tomatoes
2 tablespoons soy sauce
1/2 teaspoon ground turmeric
1 (13.5-ounce) can unsweetened coconut milk
1 tablespoon tamarind paste
1 tablespoon light brown sugar
Salt and freshly ground black pepper
2 tablespoons fresh lime juice
3 tablespoons minced fresh cilantro
2 tablespoons minced scallions, for garnish

Directions

1. Heat the oil in a large pot over medium heat. Add the onion, garlic, chile, and ginger. Cover and cook until softened, about 7 minutes.
2. Add the potato, eggplant, green beans, cauliflower, broth, tomatoes, soy sauce, and turmeric. Cover and cook until the vegetables are tender, stirring occasionally, about 45 minutes.
3. Uncover, reduce heat to low, and add the coconut milk, tamarind paste, sugar, and salt and pepper to taste. The amount of salt needed depends on the saltiness of your broth. Simmer uncovered, until the sauce thickens, stirring occasionally, about 10 minutes. Stir in the lime juice. Serve hot, sprinkled with cilantro and scallions, if using.

Moroccan Vegetable Stew
PREP: 5 MINUTES • COOK TIME: 35 MINUTES • TOTAL: 40 MINUTES • SERVES: 4 servings

Ingredients

1 tablespoon olive oil
2 medium yellow onions, chopped
2 medium carrots, cut into 1/2-inch dice
1/2 teaspoon ground cumin
1/2 teaspoon ground cinnamon or allspice

1/2 teaspoon ground ginger
1/2 teaspoon sweet or smoked paprika
1/2 teaspoon saffron or turmeric
1 (14.5-ounce) can diced tomatoes, undrained

8 ounces green beans, trimmed and cut into 1-inch pieces

2 cups peeled, seeded, and diced winter squash

1 large russet or other baking potato, peeled and cut into 1/2-inch dice

11/2 cups vegetable broth

11/2 cups cooked or 1 (15.5-ounce) can chickpeas, drained and rinsed

¾ cup frozen peas

1/2 cup pitted dried plums (prunes)

1 teaspoon lemon zest

Salt and freshly ground black pepper

1/2 cup pitted green olives

1 tablespoon minced fresh cilantro or parsley, for garnish

1/2 cup toasted slivered almonds, for garnish

Directions

1. In a large saucepan, heat the oil over medium heat. Add the onions and carrots, cover, and cook for 5 minutes. Stir in the cumin, cinnamon, ginger, paprika, and saffron. Cook, uncovered, stirring, for 30 seconds. Add the tomatoes, green beans, squash, potato, and broth and bring to a boil. Reduce heat to low, cover, and simmer until the vegetables are tender, about 20 minutes.
2. Add the chickpeas, peas, dried plums, and lemon zest. Season with salt and pepper to taste. Stir in the olives and simmer, uncovered, until the flavors are blended, about 10 minutes. Sprinkle with cilantro and almonds and serve immediately.

Creamy Butternut Squash Soup
PREP: 10 MINUTES • COOK TIME: 20 MINUTES • TOTAL: 30 MINUTES • SERVES: 5

Ingredients

1 butternut squash (roughly 2 pounds), peeled, seeded, and cut into ½-inch cubes

1 red bell pepper, seeded and chopped

1 large onion, chopped

3 garlic cloves, minced

4 cups low-sodium vegetable broth

Juice of ½ lemon

2 tablespoons maple syrup

¾ teaspoon salt

¾ teaspoon black pepper

Directions

Preparing the Ingredients.

1. In a large stockpot, combine the squash, bell pepper, onion, garlic, and broth.
   Mix well to combine, cover, and bring to a boil.
   Reduce to a simmer and cook, covered, for 15 minutes, or until the squash is fork-tender. Add the lemon juice, maple syrup, salt, and pepper and stir well to combine.
2. Carefully transfer the soup to a blender. Remove the plug from the blender lid to allow steam to escape, hold a towel firmly over the hole in the lid, and blend until smooth.
   Start on the lowest speed possible and increase gradually until the soup is completely smooth. Depending on your blender capacity, this might have to be done in two batches. (If you have an immersion blender, it would work great here.) Gently reheat over a low heat to serve.

Sweet Potato and Peanut Stew (Pressure Cooker)
PREP: 15 MINUTES • PRESSURE: 6 MINUTES • TOTAL: 30 MINUTES • PRESSURE LEVEL: HIGH • RELEASE: QUICK • SERVES: 4

Ingredients

2 onions, diced

2 tablespoons olive oil or coconut oil

2 large sweet potatoes, peeled and chopped (about 4 cups)

⅓ cup chunky peanut butter
1 teaspoon smoked paprika
¼ teaspoon red pepper flakes or ⅛ teaspoon cayenne

2 cups water or unsalted vegetable broth
¼ teaspoon salt, plus more as needed
1 to 2 cups finely chopped fresh spinach or kale
Freshly ground black pepper

Directions

1. **Preparing the Ingredients.** On your electric pressure cooker select Sauté. Add the onions and olive oil and cook for 4 to 5 minutes, stirring occasionally, until the onion is softened. Stir in the sweet potatoes, peanut butter, paprika, red pepper flakes, water, and salt. Stir to mix the peanut butter into the water a bit, but don't worry too much, as it will melt when heated. Cancel Sauté.
2. **High pressure for 6 minutes.** Close and lock the lid and ensure the pressure valve is sealed, then select High Pressure and set the time for 6 minutes.
3. **Pressure Release.** Once the cook time is complete, quick release the pressure. Once all the pressure has released, carefully unlock and remove the lid. Stir in the spinach to wilt. Taste and season with more salt and pepper.

Per Serving. Calories: 350; Protein: 10g; Total fat: 18g; Carbohydrates: 16; Fiber: 8g

Beans-And-Rice Soup With Collards
PREP: 5 MINUTES • COOK TIME: 50 MINUTES • TOTAL: 55 MINUTES • SERVES: 4 to 6 servings

Ingredients

6 cups coarsely chopped stemmed collard greens
2 tablespoons olive oil
1 medium onion, chopped
2 garlic cloves, minced
3 cups cooked or 2 (15.5-ounce) cans black-eyed peas, drained and rinsed

5 cups vegetable broth, homemade (see Light Vegetable Broth) or store-bought, or water
Salt and freshly ground black pepper
1/2 cup long-grain brown rice
Tabasco sauce, for serving

Directions

1. In a pot of boiling salted water, cook the collards until tender, about 20 minutes. Drain and set aside.
2. In a large soup pot, heat the oil over medium heat. Add the onion and garlic, cover, and cook until softened, about 5 minutes. Stir in the black-eyed peas, broth, cooked collards, and salt and pepper to taste. Bring to a boil, then reduce heat to low, add the rice, and simmer, uncovered, until the rice is cooked, about 30 minutes. Serve with Tabasco sauce.

Chickpea Noodle Soup
PREP: 10 MINUTES • COOK TIME: 10 MINUTES • TOTAL: 20 MINUTES • SERVES: 7

Ingredients

2 carrots, peeled and chopped
4 celery stalks, chopped
6 cups Vegetable Broth or store-bought vegetable broth
7 to 8 cups water
8 ounces spaghetti or thin brown rice noodles, broken (2 cups)

1 (15-ounce) can chickpeas, drained and rinsed, or 1½ cups cooked chickpeas
1 teaspoon dried herbs
¼ to ½ teaspoon salt
Freshly ground black pepper

Directions

Preparing the Ingredients.

1. In a large soup pot, combine the carrots, celery, vegetable broth, and water. Bring to a boil over medium heat, then add the spaghetti, chickpeas, dried herbs, ¼ teaspoon salt (or ½ teaspoon if your broth is unsalted), and a few grinds of pepper.
2. Cook for 8 to 10 minutes, until the noodles are soft.
    Leftovers will keep in an airtight container in the refrigerator for up to 1 week or in the freezer for up to 1 month.

Golden Carrot and Cauliflower Soup (Pressure Cooker)
PREP: 15 MINUTES • PRESSURE: 7 MINUTES • TOTAL: 50 MINUTES • PRESSURE LEVEL: HIGH • RELEASE: NATURAL • SERVES: 4

Ingredients
1 onion, chopped

1 tablespoon minced peeled fresh ginger or 1 teaspoon ground ginger

1 teaspoon olive oil

5 or 6 carrots, scrubbed or peeled and chopped

1 head cauliflower, chopped into florets

½ (13.5-ounce) can coconut milk (about ¾ cup)

3 cups water or unsalted vegetable broth

½ teaspoon ground turmeric

¼ to ½ teaspoon salt, plus more as needed

Freshly ground black pepper

Directions

1. **Preparing the Ingredients.** On your electric pressure cooker, select Sauté. Add the onion, ginger, and olive oil. Cook for 4 to 5 minutes, stirring occasionally, until the onion is softened. Add the carrots, cauliflower, coconut milk, water, turmeric, and salt. Cancel Sauté.
2. **High pressure for 7 minutes.** Close and lock the lid and ensure the pressure valve is sealed, then select High Pressure and set the time for 7 minutes.
3. **Pressure Release.** Once the cook time is complete, let the pressure release naturally, about 20 minutes. Once all the pressure has released, carefully unlock and remove the lid. Let cool for a few minutes and then purée the soup—either use an immersion blender right in the pot or transfer it (in batches, if necessary) to a countertop blender. Taste and season with more salt and pepper, if needed.

Per Serving. Calories: 176; Protein: 4g; Total fat: 11g; Carbohydrates: 16; Fiber: 6g

Potato and Leek Soup
PREP: 10 MINUTES • COOK TIME: 15 MINUTES • TOTAL: 25 MINUTES • SERVES: 4

Ingredients
2 tablespoons olive oil

3 leeks, thinly sliced and thoroughly cleaned

2 cups cubed yukon gold -potatoes (1-inch cubes)

5 cups vegetable stock

1 teaspoon sea salt

½ teaspoon freshly ground black pepper

3 tablespoons chopped fresh chives

Directions
Preparing the Ingredients.

1. In a large pot over medium-high heat, heat the olive oil until it shimmers.
    Add the leeks and cook until they soften, about 5 minutes.
    Add the potatoes, vegetable stock, salt, and pepper and cook until potatoes soften, about 10 minutes.
2. Transfer the soup to a blender or food processor, or use an immersion blender, and purée. Taste and adjust the seasonings. Serve hot, topped with chives.

Creamy Spinach-Stuffed Mushrooms
PREP: 10 MINUTES • COOK TIME: 25 MINUTES • TOTAL: 35 MINUTES • SERVES: 4

Ingredients

1 tablespoon olive oil
1 onion, chopped
3 garlic cloves, minced
1 (14-ounce) block extra-firm tofu, drained and crumbled
1 (5-ounce) package baby spinach

2 teaspoons Italian seasoning
1 teaspoon onion powder
½ teaspoon garlic powder
1 teaspoon sea salt
½ teaspoon black pepper
4 large portobello mushroom caps, stemmed

Directions

Preparing the Ingredients.

1. Preheat the oven to 450°F. Line a baking sheet with parchment paper. In a large skillet, heat the oil over medium heat.
   Add the onion and sauté for 3 minutes, or until soft.
   Add the garlic and sauté for 1 additional minute, or until fragrant. Stir in the crumbled tofu and spinach and cook for 3 minutes, or until the spinach is wilted.
   Add the Italian seasoning, onion powder, garlic powder, salt, and pepper and mix until well combined. Set the mushroom caps on the prepared baking sheet, top-sides down. Divide the tofu mixture among the 4 mushroom caps.
2. Bake for 15 to 20 minutes, until the stuffing has browned slightly.

Farro And White Bean Soup With Italian Parsley
PREP: 5 MINUTES • COOK TIME: 1HOUR 20 MINUTES • TOTAL: 1HOUR 25 MINUTES • SERVES: 6 servings

Ingredients

3 tablespoons olive oil
2 celery ribs, chopped
2 medium carrots, chopped
3 medium shallots, chopped
3 garlic cloves, minced
1 cup farro
6 cups vegetable broth, homemade (see Light Vegetable Broth) or store-bought, or water

1 (14.5-ounce) can diced tomatoes, undrained
2 bay leaves
1 teaspoon salt
1/2 teaspoon freshly ground black pepper
3 cups cooked or 2 (15.5-ounce) cans cannellini or other white beans, drained and rinsed
1/4 cup chopped flat-leaf parsley

Directions

1. In large soup pot, heat 2 tablespoons of the oil over medium heat. Add the celery, carrots, shallots, and garlic. Cover and cook, stirring occasionally, for 5 minutes.
2. Add the farro to the pot along with the broth, tomatoes, bay leaves, salt, and pepper. Bring to a boil, then reduce heat to low and cook, uncovered, until the vegetables and farro are tender, about 1 hour. Add the beans and parsley and simmer 20 minutes longer, adding more broth if the soup becomes too thick. Remove and discard bay leaves before serving.
3. Ladle into bowls, drizzle with the remaining 1 tablespoon oil, and serve.

Cream of Mushroom Soup
PREP: 10 MINUTES • COOK TIME: 20 MINUTES • TOTAL: 30 MINUTES • SERVES: 2

Ingredients

1 to 2 teaspoons olive oil
1 onion, chopped
2 garlic cloves, minced
2 cups chopped mushrooms
Pinch salt
2 tablespoons whole-wheat flour

1 teaspoon dried herbs
4 cups Vegetable Broth, store-bought broth, or water
1½ cups nondairy milk
Pinch freshly ground black pepper

Directions

Preparing the Ingredients.

1. Heat the olive oil in a large soup pot over medium-high heat.
   Add the onion, garlic, mushrooms, and salt. Sauté for about 5 minutes, until softened. Sprinkle the flour over the ingredients in the pot and toss to combine.
   Cook for 1 to 2 minutes more to toast the flour.
   Add the dried herbs, vegetable broth, milk, and pepper.
   Turn the heat to low, and let the broth come to a simmer. (Don't bring to a full boil or the milk may separate.)
   Cook for 10 minutes, until slightly thickened. Leftovers will keep in an airtight container for up to 1 week in the refrigerator or up to 1 month in the freezer.

Per Serving. Calories: 127; Protein: 4g; Total fat: 4g; Saturated fat: 0g; Carbohydrates: 21g; Fiber: 3g

Two-Potato Soup With Rainbow Chard
PREP: 5 MINUTES • COOK TIME: 45 MINUTES • TOTAL: 50 MINUTES • SERVES: 6 servings

Ingredients

2 tablespoons olive oil
1 medium red onion, chopped
1 medium leek, white part only, well rinsed and chopped
2 garlic cloves, minced
6 cups vegetable broth, homemade (see Light Vegetable Broth) or store-bought, or water

1 pound red potatoes, unpeeled and cut into 1/2-inch dice
1 pound sweet potatoes, peeled and cut into 1/2-inch dice
1/4 teaspoon crushed red pepper
Salt and freshly ground black pepper
1 medium bunch rainbow chard, tough stems removed and coarsely chopped

Directions

1. In large soup pot, heat the oil over medium heat. Add the onion, leek, and garlic. Cover and cook until softened, about 5 minutes. Add the broth, potatoes, and crushed red pepper and bring to a boil. Reduce heat to low, season with salt and black pepper to taste, and simmer, uncovered, for 15 minutes.
2. Stir in the chard and cook until the vegetables are tender, about 15 minutes longer and serve.

Hot & Sour Tofu Soup
PREP: 40 MINUTES • COOK TIME: 15 MINUTES • TOTAL: 55MINUTES • SERVES: 3

Ingredients

6 to 7 ounces firm or extra-firm tofu

1 teaspoon olive oil

1 cup sliced mushrooms
1 cup finely chopped cabbage
1 garlic clove, minced
½-inch piece fresh ginger, peeled and minced
Salt
4 cups water or Vegetable Broth
2 tablespoons rice vinegar or apple cider vinegar

2 tablespoons soy sauce
1 teaspoon toasted sesame oil
1 teaspoon sugar
Pinch red pepper flakes
1 scallion, white and light green parts only, chopped

Directions

Preparing the Ingredients.

1. Press your tofu before you start: Put it between several layers of paper towels and place a heavy pan or book (with a waterproof cover or protected with plastic wrap) on top. Let stand for 30 minutes. Discard the paper towels. Cut the tofu into ½-inch cubes.
2. In a large soup pot, heat the olive oil over medium-high heat.

   Add the mushrooms, cabbage, garlic, ginger, and a pinch of salt. Sauté for 7 to 8 minutes, until the vegetables are softened.

   Add the water, vinegar, soy sauce, sesame oil, sugar, red pepper flakes, and tofu.

   Bring to a boil, then turn the heat to low. Simmer the soup for 5 to 10 minutes.

   Serve with the scallion sprinkled on top.

   Leftovers will keep in an airtight container for up to 1 week in the refrigerator or up to 1 month in the freezer.

Per Serving (2 cups) Calories: 161; Protein: 13g; Total fat: 9g; Saturated fat: 1g; Carbohydrates: 10g; Fiber: 3g

Autumn Medley Stew
PREP: 5 MINUTES • COOK TIME: 60 MINUTES • TOTAL: 65 MINUTES • SERVES: 4 to 6 servings

Ingredients

2 tablespoons olive oil
8 ounces seitan, homemade or store-bought, cut in 1-inch cubes
Salt and freshly ground black pepper
1 large yellow onion, chopped
2 garlic cloves, minced
1 large russet potato, peeled and cut into 1/2-inch dice
1 medium carrot, cut into 1/4-inch dice
1 medium parsnip, cut into 1/4-inch dice chopped

1 small butternut squash, peeled, halved, seeded, and cut into 1/2-inch dice
1 small head savoy cabbage, chopped
1 (14.5-ounce) can diced tomatoes, drained
11/2 cups cooked or 1 (15.5-ounce) can chickpeas, drained and rinsed
2 cups vegetable broth,
1/2 cup dry white wine
1/2 teaspoon dried marjoram
1/2 teaspoon dried thyme
1/2 cup crumbled angel hair pasta

Directions

1. In a large skillet, heat 1 tablespoon of the oil over medium-high heat. Add the seitan and cook until browned on all sides, about 5 minutes. Season with salt and pepper to taste and set aside.
2. In a large saucepan, heat the remaining 1 tablespoon oil over medium heat. Add the onion and garlic. Cover and cook for until softened, about 5 minutes. Add the potato, carrot, parsnip, and squash. Cover and cook until softened, about 10 minutes.

3. Stir in the cabbage, tomatoes, chickpeas, broth, wine, marjoram, thyme, and salt and pepper to taste. Bring to a boil, then reduce heat to low. Cover and cook, stirring occasionally, until the vegetables are tender, about 45 minutes.
4. Add the cooked seitan and the pasta and simmer until the pasta is tender and the flavors are blended, about 10 minutes longer. Serve immediately.
   Variation: Leave out the pasta and serve with some warm crusty bread.

Pumpkin-Pear Soup
PREP: 10 MINUTES • COOK TIME: 15 MINUTES • TOTAL: 25 MINUTES • SERVES: 4

Ingredients
1 teaspoon olive oil or coconut oil
1 onion, diced, or 2 teaspoons onion powder
1-inch piece fresh ginger, peeled and diced, or 1 teaspoon ground ginger
1 pear, cored and chopped
Optional spices to take the taste up a notch:
1 teaspoon curry powder
½ teaspoon pumpkin pie spice
½ teaspoon smoked paprika
Pinch red pepper flakes
4 cups water or Vegetable Broth
3 cups canned pumpkin purée
1 to 2 teaspoons salt (less if using salted broth)
Pinch freshly ground black pepper
¼ to ½ cup canned coconut milk (optional)
2 to 4 tablespoons nutritional yeast (optional)

Directions
Preparing the Ingredients.
1. Heat the olive oil in a large pot over medium heat. Add the onion, ginger, and pear and sauté for about 5 minutes, until soft. Sprinkle in any optional spices and stir to combine.
   Add the water, pumpkin, salt, and pepper, and stir until smooth and combined. Cook until just bubbling, about 10 minutes.
2. Stir in the coconut milk (if using) and nutritional yeast (if using), and remove the soup from the heat. Leftovers will keep in an airtight container for up to 1 week in the refrigerator or up to 1 month in the freezer.

Per Serving (2 cups) Calories: 90; Protein: 2g; Total fat: 1g; Saturated fat: 0g; Carbohydrates: 17g; Fiber: 3g

Sweet Potato And Peanut Soup With Baby Spinach
PREP: 5 MINUTES • COOK TIME: 40 MINUTES • TOTAL: 45 MINUTES • SERVES: 4 servings

Ingredients
1 tablespoon olive oil
1 medium onion, chopped
11/2 pounds sweet potatoes, peeled and cut into 1/2-inch dice
6 cups vegetable broth, or water
1/3 cup creamy peanut butter
1/4 teaspoon ground cayenne
1/8 teaspoon ground nutmeg
Salt and freshly ground black pepper
4 cups fresh baby spinach

Directions
1. In a large soup pot, heat the oil over medium heat. Add the onion, cover, and cook until softened, about 5 minutes. Add the sweet potatoes and broth and cook, uncovered, until the potatoes are tender, about 30 minutes.
2. Ladle about a cup of hot broth into a small bowl. Add the peanut butter and stir until smooth. Stir the peanut butter mixture into the soup along with the cayenne, nutmeg, and salt and pepper to taste.

3. About 10 minutes before ready to serve, stir in the spinach, and serve.

Tuscan White Bean Soup
PREP: 10 MINUTES • COOK TIME: 15 MINUTES • TOTAL: 25 MINUTES • SERVES: 4

Ingredients
1 to 2 teaspoons olive oil
1 onion, chopped
4 garlic cloves, minced, or 1 teaspoon garlic powder
2 carrots, peeled and chopped
Salt
1 tablespoon dried herbs
Pinch freshly ground black pepper

Pinch red pepper flakes
4 cups Vegetable Broth or water
2 (15-ounce) cans white beans, such as cannellini, navy, or great northern, drained and rinsed
2 tablespoons freshly squeezed lemon juice
2 cups chopped greens, such as spinach, kale, arugula, or chard

Directions
Preparing the Ingredients.
1. Heat the olive oil in a large soup pot over medium-high heat.
   Add the onion, garlic (if using fresh), carrots, and a pinch of salt.
   Sauté for about 5 minutes, stirring occasionally, until the vegetables are lightly browned. Sprinkle in the dried herbs (plus the garlic powder, if using), black pepper, and red pepper flakes, and toss to combine.
2. Add the vegetable broth, beans, and another pinch of salt, and bring the soup to a low simmer to heat through. If you like, make the broth a bit creamier by puréeing 1 to 2 cups of soup in a countertop blender and returning it to the pot. Alternatively, use a hand blender to purée about one-fourth of the beans in the pot.
3. Stir in the lemon juice and greens, and let the greens wilt into the soup before serving. Leftovers will keep in an airtight container for up to 1 week in the refrigerator or up to 1 month in the freezer.

Per Serving (2 cups) Calories: 145; Protein: 7g; Total fat: 2g; Saturated fat: 0g; Carbohydrates: 26g; Fiber: 6g

Mexican Fideo Soup With Pinto Beans
PREP: 5 MINUTES • COOK TIME: 25 MINUTES • TOTAL: 30 MINUTES • SERVES: 4 servings

Ingredients
3 tablespoons olive oil
1 medium onion, chopped
3 garlic cloves, chopped
8 ounces fideo, vermicelli, or angel hair pasta, broken into 2-inch pieces
1 (14.5-ounce) can crushed tomatoes
11/2 cups cooked or 1 (15.5-ounce) can pinto beans, rinsed and drained

1 (4-ounce) can chopped hot or mild green chiles
1 teaspoon ground cumin
1/2 teaspoon dried oregano
6 cups vegetable broth, homemade (see Light Vegetable Broth) or store-bought, or water
Salt and freshly ground black pepper
1/4 cup chopped fresh cilantro, for garnish

Directions
1. In a large soup pot, heat 1 tablespoon of the oil over medium heat. Add the onion, cover, and cook until soft, about 10 minutes. Stir in the garlic and cook 1 minute longer. Remove the onion mixture with a slotted spoon and set aside.
2. In the same pot, heat the remaining 2 tablespoons of oil over medium heat, add the noodles, and cook until golden, stirring frequently, 5 to 7 minutes. Be careful not to burn the noodles.

3. Stir in the tomatoes, beans, chiles, cumin, oregano, broth, and salt and pepper to taste. Stir in the onion mixture and simmer until the vegetables and noodles are tender, 10 to 15 minutes. Ladle into soup bowls, garnish with cilantro, and serve.

Spinach, Tomato, and Orzo Soup
PREP: 10 MINUTES • COOK TIME: 20 MINUTES • TOTAL: 30 MINUTES • SERVES: 6

Ingredients
1 tablespoon olive oil
1 onion, chopped
4 garlic cloves, minced
1 (14.5-ounce) can diced Italian tomatoes (preferably with oregano and basil)
4 cups low-sodium vegetable broth

4 cups water
1 teaspoon sea salt
1 teaspoon black pepper
1 pound uncooked orzo pasta
1 (5-ounce) package baby spinach

Directions
Preparing the Ingredients
1. Heat the oil in a large stockpot over medium heat. Add the onion and sauté for 3 minutes, or until soft. Add the garlic and sauté for 1 additional minute, or until fragrant. Add the tomatoes with their juice, broth, water, salt, and pepper. Cover the pot and bring to a boil. Reduce the heat to a simmer.
2. Add the orzo and cook, uncovered, for 9 minutes, or until the pasta is tender. Turn off the heat and stir in the spinach until wilted.

Coconut and Curry Soup
PREP: 15 MINUTES • COOK TIME: 15 MINUTES • TOTAL: 30 MINUTES • SERVES: 4

Ingredients
1 tablespoon coconut oil
½ onion, thinly sliced
1 carrot, peeled and julienned
½ cup sliced shiitake mushrooms
3 garlic cloves, minced

one 14-ounce can coconut milk
1 cup vegetable stock
juice from 1 lime, or 2 teaspoons lime juice
½ teaspoon sea salt
2 teaspoons curry powder

Directions
Preparing the Ingredients
1. In a large soup pot, heat the coconut oil over medium-high heat until it shimmers. Add the onion, carrot, and mushrooms and cook until soft, about 7 minutes. Stir in the garlic and cook until it is fragrant, about 30 seconds.
2. Add the coconut milk, vegetable stock, lime juice, salt, and curry powder and heat through. Serve immediately.

Black Bean Soup With A Splash
PREP: 5 MINUTES • COOK TIME: 45 MINUTES • TOTAL: 50 MINUTES • SERVES: 4 to 6 servings

Ingredients
1 tablespoon olive oil
1 medium onion, finely chopped
1 celery rib, finely chopped
2 medium carrots, finely chopped

1 small green bell pepper, finely chopped
2 garlic cloves, minced
4 cups vegetable broth, or water

4 1/2 cups cooked or 3 (15.5-ounce) cans black beans, drained and rinsed
1 teaspoon dried thyme
1 teaspoon salt

1/4 teaspoon ground cayenne
2 tablespoons minced fresh parsley, for garnish
1/3 cup dry sherry

Directions

1. In a large soup pot, heat the oil over medium heat. Add the onion, celery, carrots, bell pepper, and garlic. Cover and cook until tender, stirring occasionally, about 10 minutes. Add the broth, beans, thyme, salt, and cayenne. Bring to a boil, then reduce the heat to low and simmer, uncovered, until the soup has thickened, about 45 minutes.
2. Puree the soup in the pot with an immersion blender or in a blender or food processor, in batches if necessary, and return to the pot. Reheat if necessary.
3. Ladle the soup into bowls and garnish with parsley. Serve accompanied by the sherry.

Cream of Tomato Soup
PREP: 5 MINUTES • COOK TIME: 5 MINUTES • TOTAL: 10 MINUTES • SERVES: 2

Ingredients

1 (28-ounce) can crushed, diced, or whole peeled tomatoes, undrained
1 to 2 teaspoons dried herbs
2 to 3 teaspoons onion powder (optional)

¾ to 1 cup unsweetened nondairy milk
½ teaspoon salt, or to taste
Freshly ground black pepper

Directions

Preparing the Ingredients.
1. Pour the tomatoes and their juices into a large pot and bring them to near-boiling over medium heat.
2. Add the dried herbs, onion powder (if using), milk, salt, and pepper to taste. Stir to combine. If you used diced or whole tomatoes, use a hand blender to purée the soup until smooth. (Alternatively, let the soup cool for a few minutes, then transfer to a countertop blender.) Leftovers will keep in an airtight container for up to 1 week in the refrigerator or up to 1 month in the freezer (though if you want leftovers for this soup, you might want to double the recipe).

Per Serving (2 cups) Calories: 90; Protein: 4g; Total fat: 3g; Saturated fat: 0g; Carbohydrates: 16g; Fiber: 4g

Southern Succotash Stew
PREP: 5 MINUTES • COOK TIME: 60 MINUTES • TOTAL: 65 MINUTES • SERVES: 4 servings

Ingredients

8 ounces tempeh
2 tablespoons olive oil
1 large sweet yellow onion, finely chopped
2 medium russet potatoes, peeled and cut into 1/2-inch dice
2 carrots, cut into 1/4-inch slices
1 (14.5-ounce) can diced tomatoes, drained
1 (16-ounce) package frozen succotash

2 cups vegetable broth or water
2 tablespoons soy sauce
1 teaspoon dry mustard
1/2 teaspoon dried thyme
1/2 teaspoon ground allspice
1/4 teaspoon ground cayenne
Salt and freshly ground black pepper
1/2 teaspoon liquid smoke

Directions

1. In a medium saucepan of simmering water, cook the tempeh for 30 minutes. Drain, pat dry, and cut into 1-inch dice.
2. In a large skillet, heat 1 tablespoon of the oil over medium heat. Add the tempeh and cook until browned on both sides, about 10 minutes. Set aside.
3. In a large saucepan, heat the remaining 1 tablespoon oil over medium heat. Add the onion and cook until softened, 5 minutes. Add the potatoes, carrots, tomatoes, succotash, broth, soy sauce, mustard, sugar, thyme, allspice, and cayenne. Season with salt and pepper to taste. Bring to a boil, then reduce heat to low and add the tempeh. Simmer, covered, until the vegetables are tender, stirring occasionally, about 45 minutes.
4. About 10 minutes before the stew is finished cooking, stir in the liquid smoke. Taste, adjusting seasonings if necessary. Serve immediately.

Quick Thai Coconut Mushroom Soup
PREP: 5 MINUTES • COOK TIME: 10 MINUTES • TOTAL: 15 MINUTES • SERVES: 4

Ingredients
1½ cups low-sodium vegetable broth, divided
2 garlic cloves, minced
1 tablespoon minced fresh ginger
1 (8-ounce) package baby bella or white button mushrooms, stemmed and sliced
1 (13.5-ounce) can full-fat coconut milk

Juice of ½ lemon
Juice of ½ lime
2 tablespoons chopped fresh Thai basil
1 tablespoon chopped fresh cilantro
Fresh cilantro leaves, for garnish (optional)
Lime wedges, for garnish (optional)

Directions
Preparing the Ingredients.
1. Heat ½ cup of broth in a large saucepot over medium-high heat. Sauté the garlic and ginger in the broth for 1 minute, or until fragrant.
2. Add the mushrooms and slowly pour in the remaining 1 cup of broth. Bring to a boil and reduce the heat to a simmer. Add the coconut milk, lemon juice, lime juice, basil, and chopped cilantro.
3. Let simmer for 5 minutes, or until heated through. Garnish with whole cilantro leaves and lime wedges, if desired.

Spicy Black Bean Orzo Soup
PREP: 5 MINUTES • COOK TIME: 50 MINUTES • TOTAL: 55 MINUTES • SERVES: 4 to 6 servings

Ingredients
2 tablespoons olive oil
3 garlic cloves, minced
1 tablespoon chili powder
1 teaspoon dried oregano
41/2 cups cooked or 3 (15.5-ounce) cans black beans, drained and rinsed
1 small jalapeño, seeded and finely chopped (optional)

1/4 cup minced oil-packed sun-dried tomatoes
4 cups vegetable broth, or water
1 cup water
Salt and freshly ground black pepper
1/2 cup orzo
2 tablespoons chopped fresh cilantro, for garnish

Directions
1. In a large soup pot, heat the oil over medium heat. Add the garlic and cook until fragrant, about 1 minute. Stir in the chili powder, oregano, beans, jalapeño, if using, tomatoes, broth, water, and salt and pepper to taste. Simmer for 30 minutes to blend flavors.

2. Puree the soup in the pot with an immersion blender or in a blender or food processor, in batches if necessary, and return to the pot. Cook the soup 15 minutes longer over medium heat. Taste, adjusting seasonings, and add more water if necessary.
3. While the soup is simmering, cook the orzo in a pot of boiling salted water, stirring occasionally, until al dente, about 5 minutes. Drain the orzo and divide it among the soup bowls. Ladle the soup into the bowls, garnish with cilantro, and serve.

Root Vegetable Soup
PREP: 15 MINUTES • COOK TIME: 15 MINUTES • TOTAL: 30 MINUTES • SERVES: 4

Ingredients
2 tablespoons olive oil
1 onion, diced
3 garlic cloves, minced
1 carrot, julienned or grated
1 rutabaga, julienned or grated
1 parsnip, julienned or grated

1 red potato, julienned or grated
5 cups vegetable stock
2 teaspoons dried thyme
sea salt
freshly ground black pepper

Directions
Preparing the Ingredients.
1. In a large soup pot, heat the olive oil over medium-high heat until it shimmers.
2. Add the onion and cook until it softens, about 5 minutes. Add the garlic and cook until it is fragrant, about 30 seconds. Add the carrot, rutabaga, parsnip, potato, vegetable stock, and thyme. Cover and boil until vegetables soften, about 10 minutes.
   Remove from the heat. Using a food processor or blender, purée the soup in batches. Season with salt and pepper. Serve immediately.

Minestrone
PREP: 15 MINUTES • COOK TIME: 15 MINUTES • TOTAL: 30 MINUTES • SERVES: 4

Ingredients
2 tablespoons olive oil
½ onion, diced
1 carrot, peeled and diced
1 stalk celery, diced
4 garlic cloves, minced
5 cups vegetable stock
1 zucchini, diced

one 15-ounce can kidney beans, drained and rinsed
one 15-ounce can chopped tomatoes with liquid, or 2 fresh tomatoes, peeled and chopped
2 teaspoons italian seasoning
sea salt
freshly ground pepper

Directions
Preparing the Ingredients.
1. In a large soup pot, heat the olive oil over medium-high heat until it shimmers.
2. Add the onion, carrot, and celery and cook until vegetables soften, about 5 minutes. Add the garlic and cook until it is fragrant, about 30 seconds. Add the vegetable stock, zucchini, kidney beans, tomatoes, and Italian seasoning. Simmer the soup until the vegetables are soft, about 10 minutes. Season with salt and pepper and serve immediately.

Chickpea, Tomato, And Eggplant Stew
PREP: 5 MINUTES • COOK TIME: 55 MINUTES • TOTAL: 60 MINUTES • SERVES: 4 servings

Ingredients

1 tablespoon olive oil
1 large onion, chopped
1 medium eggplant, peeled and cut into 1/2-inch dice
2 medium carrots, cut into 1/4-inch slices
1 large Yukon Gold potato, peeled and cut into 1/2-inch dice
1 medium red bell pepper, cut into 1-inch dice
3 garlic cloves, minced

2 cups cooked or 1 (15.5-ounce) cans chickpeas, drained and rinsed if canned
1 (28-ounce) can diced tomatoes, undrained
1 tablespoon minced fresh parsley
1/2 teaspoon dried oregano
1/2 teaspoon dried basil
1 tablespoon soy sauce
1/2 cup vegetable broth, or water
Salt and freshly ground black pepper

Directions

1. In a large saucepan, heat the oil over medium heat. Add the onion, eggplant, and carrots, cover, and cook until vegetables begin to soften, about 5 minutes.
2. Reduce heat to low. Add the potato, bell pepper, and garlic and cook, stirring, uncovered, for 5 minutes. Stir in the chickpeas, tomatoes, parsley, oregano, basil, soy sauce, and broth. Season with salt and black pepper to taste. Cover and cook until vegetables are tender, about 45 minutes. Serve immediately.

Tomato Cream Pasta (Pressure Cooker)
PREP: 10 MINUTES • PRESSURE: 4 MINUTES • TOTAL: 25 MINUTES • PRESSURE LEVEL: HIGH • RELEASE: NATURAL• SERVES: 4

Ingredients

1 (28-ounce) can crushed tomatoes
1 tablespoon dried basil
½ teaspoon garlic powder
10 ounces whole-grain pasta
½ teaspoon salt, plus more as needed

1½ cups water or unsalted vegetable broth
1 cup unsweetened nondairy milk or creamer
2 cups chopped fresh spinach (optional)
Freshly ground black pepper

Directions

1. **Preparing the Ingredients.** In your electric pressure cooking pot, combine the tomatoes, basil, garlic powder, pasta, salt, and water.
2. **High pressure for 4 minutes.** Lock the lid and ensure the pressure valve is sealed, then select High Pressure and set the time for 4 minutes.
3. **Pressure Release.** Once the cook time is complete, let the pressure release naturally for 5 minutes, then quick release any remaining pressure. Once all the pressure has released, carefully unlock and remove the lid.
   Stir in the milk and spinach (if using). Taste and season with more salt, if needed, and pepper. On your pressure cooker, select Sauté or Simmer. Let cook for 4 to 5 minutes, until the sauce thickens and the greens wilt.

Per Serving Calories: 321; Protein: 14g; Total fat: 3g; Saturated fat: 0g; Carbohydrates: 16g; Fiber: 9g

Senegalese Soup
PREP: 5 MINUTES • COOK TIME: 40 MINUTES • TOTAL: 45 MINUTES • SERVES: 4 servings

Ingredients

1 tablespoon canola or grapeseed oil
1 medium onion, chopped
1 medium carrot, chopped
1 garlic clove, minced

3 Granny Smith apples, peeled, cored, and chopped
2 tablespoons hot or mild curry powder
2 teaspoons tomato paste

3 cups light vegetable broth, homemade (see Light Vegetable Broth) or store-bought, or water
Salt

1 cup plain unsweetened soy milk
4 teaspoons mango chutney, homemade or store-bought, for garnish

Directions

1. In a large soup pot, heat the oil over medium heat. Add the onion, carrot, and garlic. Cover and cook until softened, about 10 minutes. Add the apples and continue to cook, uncovered, stirring occasionally, until the apples begin to soften, about 5 minutes. Add the curry powder and cook, stirring, 1 minute. Stir in the tomato paste, broth, and salt to taste. Simmer, uncovered, for 30 minutes.
2. Puree the soup in the pot with an immersion blender or in a blender or food processor, in batches if necessary. Pour the soup into a large container, stir in the soy milk, cover, and refrigerate until chilled, about 3 hours.
3. Ladle the soup into bowls, garnish each with a teaspoonful of chutney, and serve.

Three Bean Soup
PREP: 5 MINUTES • COOK TIME: 52 MINUTES • TOTAL: 57 MINUTES • SERVES: 4 to 6 servings

Ingredients

2 tablespoons olive oil
1 medium onion, chopped
1 medium carrot, chopped
1 cup chopped celery
2 garlic cloves, minced
1 (14.5-ounce) can diced tomatoes, drained
11/2 cups cooked or 1 (15.5-ounce) can dark red kidney beans, drained and rinsed
11/2 cups cooked or 1 (15.5-ounce) can black beans, drained and rinsed

11/2 cups cooked or 1 (15.5-ounce) can navy or other white beans, drained and rinsed
4 cups vegetable broth, homemade (see Light Vegetable Broth) or store-bought, or water
1 tablespoon soy sauce
1 teaspoon dried thyme
1 bay leaf
Salt and freshly ground black pepper
2 tablespoons chopped fresh parsley

Directions

1. In a large soup pot, heat the oil over medium heat. Add the onion, carrot, celery, and garlic. Cover and cook until softened, about 7 minutes. Uncover, and stir in the tomatoes, all the beans, and the broth. Add the soy sauce, thyme, and bay leaf and season with salt and pepper to taste. Bring to a boil, then reduce heat to low and simmer until the vegetables are tender, about 45 minutes.
2. Remove the bay leaf and discard before serving. Add the parsley and serve.

Creamy Potato-Cauliflower Soup
PREP: 10 MINUTES • COOK TIME: 25 MINUTES • TOTAL: 35 MINUTES • SERVES: 6

Ingredients

1 teaspoon olive oil
1 onion, chopped
3 cups chopped cauliflower
2 potatoes, scrubbed or peeled and chopped
6 cups water or Vegetable Broth

2 tablespoons dried herbs
Salt
Freshly ground black pepper
1 or 2 scallions, white and light green parts only, sliced

Directions
Preparing the Ingredients.

1. Heat the olive oil in a large soup pot over medium-high heat.
2. Add the onion and cauliflower, and sauté for about 5 minutes, until the vegetables are slightly softened. Add the potatoes, water, and dried herbs, and season to taste with salt and pepper. Bring the soup to a boil, reduce the heat to low, and cover the pot. Simmer for 15 to 20 minutes, until the potatoes are soft.
3. Using a hand blender, purée the soup until smooth. (Alternatively, let it cool slightly, then transfer to a countertop blender.) Stir in the scallions and serve. Leftovers will keep in an airtight container for up to 1 week in the refrigerator or up to 1 month in the freezer.

Per Serving (2 cups) Calories: 80; Protein: 2g; Total fat: 1g; Saturated fat: 0g; Carbohydrates: 17g; Fiber: 3g

Spicy Pinto Bean Soup
PREP: 5 MINUTES • COOK TIME: 25 MINUTES • TOTAL: 30 MINUTES • SERVES: 4 servings

Ingredients

41/2 cups cooked or 3 (15.5-ounce) cans pinto beans, drained and rinsed
1 (14.5-ounce) can crushed tomatoes
1 teaspoon chipotle chile in adobo
2 tablespoons olive oil
1 medium onion, chopped
1/4 cup chopped celery

2 garlic cloves, minced
1/2 teaspoon ground cumin
1/2 teaspoon dried oregano
4 cups vegetable broth, homemade or water
Salt and freshly ground black pepper
2 tablespoons chopped fresh cilantro, for garnish

Directions

1. In a food processor, puree 11/2 cups of the pinto beans with the tomatoes and chipotle. Set aside.
2. In a large soup pot, heat the oil over medium heat. Add the onion, celery, and garlic. Cover and cook until soft, stirring occasionally, about 10 minutes. Stir in the cumin, oregano, broth, pureed bean mixture, and the remaining 3 cups beans. Season with salt and pepper to taste.
3. Bring to a boil and reduce heat to low and simmer, uncovered, stirring occasionally, until the flavors are incorporated and the soup is hot, about 15 minutes. Ladle into bowls, garnish with cilantro, and serve.

Black And Gold Gazpacho
PREP: 15 MINUTES • COOK TIME: 0 MINUTES • TOTAL: 15 MINUTES • SERVES: 4 servings

Ingredients

11/2 pounds ripe yellow tomatoes, chopped
1 large cucumber, peeled, seeded, and chopped
1 large yellow bell pepper, seeded, and chopped
4 green onions, white part only
2 garlic cloves, minced
2 tablespoons olive oil
2 tablespoons white wine vinegar

Salt
Ground cayenne
11/2 cups cooked or 1 (15.5-ounce) can black beans, drained and rinsed
2 tablespoons minced fresh parsley
1 cup toasted croutons (optional)

Directions

1. In a blender or food processor, combine half the tomatoes with the cucumber, bell pepper, green onions, and garlic. Process until smooth. Add the oil and vinegar, season with salt and cayenne to taste, and process until blended.

2. Transfer the soup to a large nonmetallic bowl and stir in the black beans and remaining tomatoes. Cover the bowl and refrigerate for 1 to 2 hours. Taste, adjusting seasonings if necessary.
3. Ladle the soup into bowls, garnish with parsley and croutons, if using, and serve.

Black-Eyed Pea & Sweet Potato Soup
PREP: 10 MINUTES • COOK TIME: 25 MINUTES • TOTAL: 35 MINUTES • SERVES: 4

Ingredients
1 teaspoon olive oil
2 to 3 cups peeled, cubed sweet potato, squash, or pumpkin
½ onion, chopped
1 garlic clove, minced
Salt
2 cups water
1 (15-ounce) can black-eyed peas, drained and rinsed

2 tablespoons freshly squeezed lime juice
1 tablespoon sugar
1 teaspoon smoked or regular paprika
Pinch red pepper flakes or cayenne pepper
3 cups shredded cabbage
1 cup corn kernels, thawed if frozen, drained if canned

Directions
Preparing the Ingredients.
1. Heat the olive oil in a large soup pot over medium-high heat.
2. Add the sweet potato, onion, garlic, and a pinch of salt. Sauté for 3 to 4 minutes, until the onion and garlic are softened. Add the water, black-eyed peas, lime juice, sugar, paprika, red pepper flakes, and salt to taste. Bring to a boil and cook for 15 minutes. Add the cabbage and corn to the pot, stirring to combine, and cook for 5 minutes more, or until the sweet potato is tender.
3. Turn off the heat, let cool for a few minutes, and serve. Leftovers will keep in an airtight container for up to 1 week in the refrigerator or up to 1 month in the freezer.

Per Serving (2 cups) Calories: 224; Protein: 9g; Total fat: 2g; Saturated fat: 0g; Carbohydrates: 46g; Fiber: 10g

Soba And Green Lentil Soup
PREP: 5 MINUTES • COOK TIME: 55 MINUTES • TOTAL: 60 MINUTES • SERVES: 4 to 6 servings

Ingredients
2 tablespoons olive oil
1 medium onion, minced
1 medium carrot, halved lengthwise and sliced diagonally
2 garlic cloves, minced
1 (28-ounce) can crushed tomatoes

1 cup green (French) lentils, picked over, rinsed, and drained
1 teaspoon dried thyme
6 cups vegetable broth, homemade (see Light Vegetable Broth) or store-bought, or water
Salt and freshly ground black pepper
4 ounces soba noodles, broken into thirds

Directions
1. In a large soup pot over medium heat, heat the oil. Add the onion, carrot, and garlic. Cover and cook until softened, about 7 minutes. Uncover and stir in the tomatoes, lentils, thyme, and broth and bring to a boil. Reduce heat to medium, season with salt and pepper to taste, and cover and simmer until the lentils are just tender, about 45 minutes.
2. Stir in the noodles and cook until tender, about 10 minutes longer, and serve.

Black Bean Soup

PREP: 10 MINUTES • COOK TIME: 15 MINUTES • TOTAL: 25 MINUTES • SERVES: 4

Ingredients

2 tablespoons olive oil
1 onion, diced
1 green bell pepper, diced
1 carrot, peeled and diced
4 garlic cloves, minced

two 15-ounce cans black beans, drained and rinsed
2 cups vegetable stock
¼ teaspoon ground cumin
1 teaspoon sea salt
¼ cup chopped cilantro, for garnish

Directions

Preparing the Ingredients.

1. In a large soup pot, heat the olive oil over medium-high heat until it shimmers.
2. Add the onion, bell pepper, and carrot and cook until the vegetables soften, about 5 -minutes. Add garlic and cook until it is fragrant. about 30 seconds. Add the black beans, vegetable stock, cumin, and salt. Cook over medium-high heat, stirring occasionally, for about 10 minutes.
3. Remove from the heat. Using a potato masher, mash the beans lightly, leaving some chunks in the soup. For a smoother soup, process in a blender or food processor. Serve hot, garnished with cilantro.

Creamy Garlic-Spinach Rotini Soup

PREP: 10 MINUTES • COOK TIME: 15 MINUTES • TOTAL: 25 MINUTES • SERVES: 4

Ingredients

1 teaspoon olive oil
1 cup chopped mushrooms
¼ teaspoon plus a pinch salt
4 garlic cloves, minced, or 1 teaspoon garlic powder
2 peeled carrots or ½ red bell pepper, chopped
6 cups Vegetable Broth or water
Pinch freshly ground black pepper

1 cup rotini or gnocchi
¾ cup unsweetened nondairy milk
¼ cup nutritional yeast
2 cups chopped fresh spinach
¼ cup pitted black olives or sun-dried tomatoes, chopped
Herbed Croutons, for topping (optional)

Directions

Preparing the Ingredients.

1. Heat the olive oil in a large soup pot over medium-high heat.
2. Add the mushrooms and a pinch of salt. Sauté for about 4 minutes, until the mushrooms are softened. Add the garlic (if using fresh) and carrots, sauté for 1 minute more. Add the vegetable broth, remaining ¼ teaspoon of salt, and pepper (plus the garlic powder, if using). Bring to a boil and add the pasta. Cook for about 10 minutes, until the pasta is just cooked.
3. Turn off the heat and stir in the milk, nutritional yeast, spinach, and olives. Top with croutons (if using). Leftovers will keep in an airtight container for up to 1 week in the refrigerator or up to 1 month in the freezer.

Per Serving (2 cups) Calories: 207; Protein: 11g; Total fat: 5g; Saturated fat: 1g; Carbohydrates: 34g; Fiber: 7g

Roasted Vegetable Bisque

PREP: 10 MINUTES • COOK TIME: 15 MINUTES • TOTAL: 25 MINUTES • SERVES: 6 servings

Ingredients

1 large onion, coarsely chopped
2 medium carrots, coarsely chopped
1 large russet potato, peeled and cut into 1/2-inch dice
1 medium zucchini, thinly sliced
1 large ripe tomato, quartered
2 garlic cloves, crushed

2 tablespoons olive oil
1/2 teaspoon dried savory
1/2 teaspoon dried thyme
Salt and freshly ground black pepper
4 cups vegetable broth, homemade (see Light Vegetable Broth) or store-bought, or water
1 tablespoon minced fresh parsley, for garnish

Directions

1. Preheat the oven to 400°F. In a lightly oiled 9 x 13-inch baking pan, place the onion, carrots, potato, zucchini, tomato, and garlic. Drizzle with the oil and season with savory, thyme, and salt and pepper to taste. Cover tightly with foil and bake until softened, about 30 minutes. Uncover and bake, stirring once, until vegetables are lightly browned, about 30 minutes more.
2. Transfer the roasted vegetables to a large soup pot, add the broth, and bring to a boil. Reduce the heat to low and simmer, uncovered, for 15 minutes.
3. Puree the soup in the pot with an immersion blender or in a blender or food processor, in batches if necessary, and return to the pot. Heat over medium heat until hot. Taste, adjusting seasonings if necessary.
4. Ladle into bowls, sprinkle with parsley, and serve.

Spicy Gazpacho
PREP: 15 MINUTES • COOK TIME: 0 MINUTES • TOTAL: 15 MINUTES • SERVES: 4

Ingredients

1 tablespoon olive oil
3 cups vegetable juice, such as v8
1 red onion, diced
3 tomatoes, chopped
1 red bell pepper, diced
2 garlic cloves, minced

juice of 1 lemon
2 tablespoons chopped fresh basil
¼ to ½ teaspoon cayenne pepper
sea salt
freshly ground black pepper

Directions
Preparing the Ingredients.

1. In a blender or a food processor, combine the olive oil, vegetable juice, all but ½ cup of the onion, all but ½ cup of the tomato, all but ½ cup of the bell pepper, the garlic, lemon juice, basil, and cayenne. Season with salt and pepper and process until smooth.
2. Stir the reserved ½ cup onion, ½ cup tomatoes, and ½ cup bell pepper into the processed ingredients and refrigerate for 1 hour. Serve chilled.

Mushroom & Wild Rice Stew
PREP: 10 MINUTES • COOK TIME: 50 MINUTES • TOTAL: 60 MINUTES • SERVES: 6

Ingredients

1 to 2 teaspoons olive oil
2 cups chopped mushrooms
½ to 1 teaspoon salt
1 onion, chopped, or 1 teaspoon onion powder
3 or 4 garlic cloves, minced, or ½ teaspoon garlic powder
1 tablespoon dried herbs

¾ cup brown rice
¼ cup wild rice or additional brown rice
3 cups water
3 cups Vegetable Broth or store-bought broth
2 to 4 tablespoons balsamic vinegar (optional)
Freshly ground black pepper
1 cup frozen peas, thawed

1 cup unsweetened nondairy milk (optional)

1 to 2 cups chopped greens, such as spinach, kale, or chard

Directions
Preparing the Ingredients.
1. Heat the olive oil in a large soup pot over medium-high heat.
2. Add the mushrooms and a pinch of salt, and sauté for about 4 minutes, until the mushrooms are softened. Add the onion and garlic (if using fresh), and sauté for 1 to 2 minutes more. Stir in the dried herbs (plus the onion powder and/or garlic powder, if using), white or brown rice, wild rice, water, vegetable broth, vinegar (if using), and salt and pepper to taste. Bring to a boil, turn the heat to low, and cover the pot. Simmer the soup for 15 minutes (for white rice) or 45 minutes (for brown rice). Turn off the heat and stir in the peas, milk (if using), and greens. Let the greens wilt before serving.
3. Leftovers will keep in an airtight container for up to 1 week in the refrigerator or up to 1 month in the freezer.

Per Serving (2 cups) Calories: 201; Protein: 6g; Total fat: 3g; Saturated fat: 0g; Carbohydrates: 44g; Fiber: 4g

Almond Soup With Cardamom
PREP: 5 MINUTES • COOK TIME: 35 MINUTES • TOTAL: 40MINUTES • SERVES: 4 servings

Ingredients
1 tablespoon olive oil
1 medium onion, chopped
1 medium russet potato, chopped
1 medium red bell pepper, chopped
4 cups vegetable broth, homemade or water

1/2 teaspoon ground cardamom
Salt and freshly ground black pepper
1/2 cup almond butter
1/4 cup sliced toasted almonds, for garnish

Directions
1. In a large soup pot, heat the oil over medium heat. Add the onion, potato, and bell pepper. Cover and cook until softened, about 5 minutes. Add the broth, cardamom, and salt and pepper to taste. Bring to a boil, then reduce heat to low and simmer, uncovered, until the vegetables are tender, about 30 minutes.
2. Add the almond butter and puree in the pot with an immersion blender or in a blender or food processor, in batches if necessary, and return to the pot. Reheat over medium heat until hot. Taste, adjusting seasonings if necessary, and add more broth or some soy milk if needed for desired consistency.
3. Ladle the soup into bowls, sprinkle with toasted sliced almonds, and serve.

Easy Corn Chowder
PREP: 15 MINUTES • COOK TIME: 15 MINUTES • TOTAL: 30 MINUTES • SERVES: 4

Ingredients
2 tablespoons olive oil or other vegetable oil, such as coconut oil
1 onion, chopped
1 cup chopped fennel bulb or celery
2 carrots, peeled and chopped
1 red bell pepper, finely chopped

¼ cup all-purpose flour
6 cups vegetable stock
2 cups fresh or canned corn
2 cups cubed red potato
1 cup unsweetened almond milk or other unsweetened nut or grain milk

½ teaspoon sriracha sauce or chili paste (optional)

sea salt
freshly ground black pepper

Directions

Preparing the Ingredients.

1. In a large pot, heat the olive oil over medium-high heat until it shimmers.
   Add the onion, fennel, carrots, and bell pepper and cook, stirring occasionally, until the vegetables soften, about 3 minutes.
   Sprinkle the flour over the vegetables and continue to cook, stirring constantly, for about 2 minutes.
2. Stir in the vegetable stock, using a spoon to scrape any bits of flour or vegetables from the bottom of the pan. Continue stirring until the liquid comes to a boil and the soup begins to thicken. Lower the heat to medium.
   Add the corn, potatoes, almond milk, and Sriracha, if using. Simmer until the potatoes are soft, about 10 minutes. Season with salt and pepper. Serve hot.

Tamarind Chickpea Stew
PREP: 5 MINUTES • COOK TIME: 60 MINUTES • TOTAL: 65 MINUTES • SERVES: 4 servings

Ingredients

1 tablespoon olive oil
1 large onion, chopped
2 medium Yukon Gold potatoes, peeled and cut into 1/4-inch dice
3 cups cooked chickpeas or 2 (15.5-ounce) cans chickpeas, drained and rinsed
1 (28-ounce) can crushed tomatoes
1 (4-ounce) can mild chopped green chiles, drained

2 tablespoons tamarind paste
1/4 cup pure maple syrup
1 cup vegetable broth, homemade or water
2 tablespoons chili powder
1 teaspoon ground coriander
1/2 teaspoon ground cumin
Salt and freshly ground black pepper
1 cup frozen baby peas, thawed

Directions

1. In a large saucepan, heat the oil over medium heat. Add the onion, cover, and cook until softened, about 5 minutes. Add the potatoes, chickpeas, tomatoes, and chiles and simmer, uncovered, for 5 minutes.
2. In a small bowl, combine the tamarind paste, maple syrup, and broth and blend until smooth. Stir the tamarind mixture into the vegetables, along with the chili powder, coriander, cumin, and salt and pepper to taste. Bring to a boil, then reduce the heat to medium and simmer, covered, until the potatoes are tender, about 40 minutes.
3. Taste, adjusting seasonings if necessary, and stir in the peas. Simmer, uncovered, about 10 minutes longer. Serve immediately.

Cream Of Artichoke Soup
PREP: 10 MINUTES • COOK TIME: 20 MINUTES • TOTAL: 30 MINUTES • SERVES: 4 servings

Ingredients

1 tablespoon olive oil
2 medium shallots, chopped
2 (10-ounce) packages frozen artichoke hearts, thawed
3 cups vegetable broth, homemade or water
1 teaspoon fresh lemon juice

Salt
1/3 cup almond butter
1/8 teaspoon ground cayenne
1 cup plain unsweetened soy milk
1 tablespoon snipped fresh chives, for garnish
2 tablespoons sliced toasted almonds, for garnish

Directions

1. In a large soup pot, heat the oil over medium heat. Add the shallots, cover, and cook until softened. Uncover and stir in the artichoke hearts, broth, lemon juice, and salt to taste. Bring to a boil, then reduce heat to low and simmer, uncovered, until the artichokes are tender, about 20 minutes.
2. Add the almond butter and cayenne to the artichoke mixture. Puree in a high-speed blender or food processor, in batches if necessary, and return to the pot. Stir in the soy milk and taste, adjusting seasonings if necessary. Simmer the soup over medium heat until hot, about 5 minutes.
3. Ladle into bowls, sprinkle with chives and almonds, and serve.

Pomegranate-Infused Lentil And Chickpea Stew
PREP: 5 MINUTES • COOK TIME: 55 MINUTES • TOTAL: 60 MINUTES • SERVES: 4 servings

Ingredients

¾ cup brown lentils, picked over, rinsed, and drained
2 tablespoons olive oil
1/2 cup chopped green onions
2 teaspoons minced fresh ginger
¾ cup long-grain brown rice
1/2 cup dried apricots, quartered
1/4 cup golden raisins
1/4 teaspoon ground allspice
1/4 teaspoon ground cumin

1/4 teaspoon ground cayenne
1 teaspoon turmeric
Salt and freshly ground black pepper
1/3 cup pomegranate molasses, homemade or store-bought
3 cups water
11/2 cups cooked or 1 (15.5-ounce) can chickpeas, drained and rinsed
1/4 cup minced fresh cilantro or parsley

Directions

1. Soak the lentils in a medium bowl of hot water for 45 minutes. Drain and set aside.
2. In a large saucepan, heat the oil over medium heat. Add the green onions, ginger, soaked lentils, rice, apricots, raisins, allspice, cumin, cayenne, turmeric, and salt and pepper to taste. Cook, stirring, for 1 minute.
3. Add the pomegranate molasses and water and bring to a boil. Reduce heat to low. Cover and simmer until the lentils and rice are tender, about 40 minutes.
4. Stir in the chickpeas and cilantro. Simmer, uncovered, for 15 minutes, to heat through and allow the flavors to blend. Serve immediately.

Rice And Pea Soup
PREP: 5 MINUTES • COOK TIME: 45 MINUTES • TOTAL: 50 MINUTES • SERVES: 4 servings

Ingredients

2 tablespoons olive oil
1 medium onion, minced
2 garlic cloves minced
1 cup Arborio rice
1/4 cup chopped fresh flat-leaf parsley

6 cups vegetable broth or water
Salt and freshly ground black pepper
1 (16-ounce) bag frozen petite green peas

Directions

1. In a large soup pot, heat the oil over medium heat. Add the onion and garlic, cover, and cook until softened about 5 minutes.
2. Uncover and add the rice, broth, and salt and pepper to taste. Bring to a boil, then reduce heat to low. Cover and simmer until the rice begins to soften, about 30 minutes.
3. Stir in the peas and cook, uncovered, for 15 to 20 minutes longer. Stir in the parsley and serve.

Ethiopian Cabbage, Carrot, and Potato Stew
PREP: 10 MINUTES • COOK TIME: 20 MINUTES • TOTAL: 30 MINUTES • SERVES: 6

Ingredients
3 russet potatoes, peeled and cut into ½-inch cubes
2 tablespoons olive oil
6 carrots, peeled, halved lengthwise, and cut into ½-inch slices
1 onion, chopped
4 garlic cloves, minced

1 tablespoon ground turmeric
1 teaspoon ground cumin
1 teaspoon ground ginger
1½ teaspoons sea salt
1½ cups low-sodium vegetable broth, divided
4 cups shredded or thinly sliced green cabbage

Directions
Preparing the Ingredients.
1. Bring a large pot of water to a boil over medium-high heat.
2. Add the potatoes and cook for 10 minutes, or until fork-tender. Drain and set aside. While the potatoes are cooking, heat the oil in a large skillet over medium-high heat. Add the carrots and onion and sauté for 5 minutes. Add the garlic, turmeric, cumin, ginger, and salt and sauté for 1 additional minute, until fragrant. Add the cooked potatoes and 1 cup of broth to the skillet, bring to a boil, and reduce to a simmer. Scatter the cabbage on top of the potatoes. Cover and simmer for 3 minutes.
3. Mix the cabbage into the potatoes, add the remaining ½ cup of broth, cover, and simmer for 5 more minutes, or until the cabbage is wilted and tender. Stir the cabbage from time to time while cooking to incorporate it with the other ingredients as it continues to wilt.

Thai-Inspired Coconut Soup
PREP: 5 MINUTES • COOK TIME: 25 MINUTES • TOTAL: 30 MINUTES • SERVES: 4 servings

Ingredients
1 tablespoon canola or grapeseed oil
1 medium onion, chopped
2 tablespoons minced fresh ginger
2 tablespoons soy sauce
1 tablespoon light brown sugar (optional)
1 teaspoon Asian chili paste

21/2 cups light vegetable broth or water
8 ounces extra-firm tofu, drained and cut into 1/2-inch dice
2 (13.5-ounce) cans unsweetened coconut milk
1 tablespoon fresh lime juice
3 tablespoons chopped fresh cilantro, for garnish

Directions
1. In a large soup pot, heat the oil over medium heat. Add the onion and ginger and cook until softened, about 5 minutes. Stir in the soy sauce, sugar, and chile paste. Add the broth and bring to a boil. Reduce heat to medium and simmer for 15 minutes.
2. Strain the broth and discard solids. Return the broth to the pot over medium heat. Add the tofu and stir in the coconut milk and lime juice. Simmer 5 minutes longer to allow flavors to blend.
3. Ladle into bowls, sprinkle with cilantro, and serve.

Curried Butternut And Red Lentil Soup With Chard
PREP: 5 MINUTES • COOK TIME: 55 MINUTES • TOTAL: 60 MINUTES • SERVES: 4 servings

Ingredients

1 tablespoon olive oil
1 medium onion, chopped
1 medium butternut squash, peeled and diced
1 garlic clove, minced
1 tablespoon minced fresh ginger
1 tablespoon hot or mild curry powder

1 (14.5-ounce) can crushed tomatoes
1 cup red lentils, picked over, rinsed, and drained
5 cups vegetable broth, homemade (see Light Vegetable Broth) or store-bought, or water
Salt and freshly ground black pepper
3 cups chopped stemmed Swiss chard

Directions

1. In a large soup pot, heat the oil over medium heat. Add the onion, squash, and garlic. Cover and cook until softened, about 10 minutes.
2. Stir in the ginger and curry powder, then add the tomatoes, lentils, broth, and salt and pepper to taste. Bring to boil, then reduce heat to low and simmer, uncovered, until the lentils and vegetables are tender, stirring occasionally, about 45 minutes.
3. About 15 minutes before serving, stir in the chard. Taste, adjusting seasonings if necessary, and serve.

Spinach, Walnut, And Apple Soup
PREP: 10 MINUTES • COOK TIME: 20 MINUTES • TOTAL: 30 MINUTES • SERVES: 4 servings

Ingredients

1 tablespoon olive oil
1 small onion, chopped
3 cups vegetable broth, homemade (see Light Vegetable Broth) or store-bought, or water
2 Fuji or other flavorful apples
1 cup apple juice
4 cups fresh spinach

¾ cup ground walnuts
1 teaspoon minced fresh sage or 1/2 teaspoon dried
1/4 teaspoon ground allspice
Salt and freshly ground black pepper
1 cup soy milk
1/4 cup toasted walnut pieces

Directions

1. In a large soup pot, heat the oil over medium heat. Add the onion, cover, and cook until softened, 5 minutes. Add about 1 cup of the vegetable broth, cover, and cook until the onion is very soft, about 5 minutes longer.
2. Peel, core, and chop one of the apples and add it to the pot with the onion and broth. Add the apple juice, spinach, ground walnuts, sage, allspice, the remaining 2 cups broth, and salt and pepper to taste. Bring to a boil, then reduce heat to low and simmer for 10 minutes.
3. Puree the soup in the pot with an immersion blender or in a blender or food processor, in batches if necessary, and return to the pot. Stir in the soy milk and reheat over medium heat until hot.
4. Chop the remaining apple. Ladle the soup into bowls, garnish each bowl with some of the chopped apple, sprinkle with the walnut pieces, and serve.

Squash Soup With Pecans And Ginger
PREP: 10 MINUTES • COOK TIME: 30 MINUTES • TOTAL: 40 MINUTES • SERVES: 4 servings

Ingredients

1/3 cup toasted pecans
2 tablespoons chopped crystallized ginger
1 tablespoon canola or grapeseed oil
1 medium onion, chopped

1 celery rib, chopped
1 teaspoon grated fresh ginger
5 cups vegetable broth, homemade (see Light Vegetable Broth) or store-bought, or water

1 kabocha squash, peeled, seeded, and cut into 1/2-inch dice
1/4 cup pure maple syrup
2 tablespoons soy sauce

1/4 teaspoon ground allspice
Salt and freshly ground black pepper
1 cup plain unsweetened soy milk

Directions

1. In a food processor, combine the pecans and crystallized ginger and pulse until coarsely chopped. Set aside.
2. In a large soup pot, heat the oil over medium heat. Add the onion, celery, and fresh ginger. Cover and cook until softened, about 5 minutes. Stir in the broth and squash, cover, and bring to a boil. Reduce the heat to low and simmer, covered, stirring occasionally, until the squash is tender, about 30 minutes.
3. Stir in the maple syrup, soy sauce, allspice, and salt and pepper to taste. Puree in the pot with an immersion blender or in a blender or food processor, in batches if necessary, and return to the pot.
4. Stir in the soy milk and heat over low heat until hot. Ladle the soup into bowls and sprinkle with the pecan and ginger mixture, and serve.

Root Vegetable Bisque
PREP: 5 MINUTES • COOK TIME: 35 MINUTES • TOTAL: 40 MINUTES • SERVES: 4 to 6 servings

Ingredients

1 tablespoon olive oil
3 large shallots, chopped
2 large carrots, shredded
2 medium parsnips, shredded
1 medium potato, peeled and chopped
2 garlic cloves, minced
1/2 teaspoon dried thyme

1/4 teaspoon dried marjoram
4 cups vegetable broth, homemade (see Light Vegetable Broth) or store-bought, or water
1 cup plain unsweetened soy milk
Salt and freshly ground black pepper
1 tablespoon minced fresh parsley, garnish

Directions

1. In a large soup pot, heat the oil over medium heat. Add the shallots, carrots, parsnips, potato, and garlic. Cover and cook until softened, about 5 minutes. Add the thyme, marjoram, and broth and bring to a boil. Reduce heat to low and simmer, uncovered, until the vegetables are tender, about 30 minutes.
2. Puree the soup in the pot with an immersion blender or in a blender or food processor in batches if necessary, then return to the pot. Stir in the soy milk and taste, adjusting seasonings if necessary. Heat the soup over low heat until hot. Ladle into bowls, sprinkle with parsley, and serve.

Curried Pumpkin Soup
PREP: 5 MINUTES • COOK TIME: 22 MINUTES • TOTAL: 27 MINUTES • SERVES: 4 to 6 servings

Ingredients

1 tablespoon olive oil
1 medium onion, chopped
1 garlic clove, minced
1 teaspoon grated fresh ginger
1 tablespoon hot or mild curry powder
1 (16-ounce) can pumpkin puree or 2 cups cooked fresh pumpkin

3 cups vegetable broth, homemade or water
Salt
1 (13.5-ounce) can unsweetened coconut milk
1 tablespoon minced fresh parsley, for garnish
Mango chutney, for garnish (optional)
Chopped roasted cashews, for garnish (optional)

Directions

1. In a large soup pot, heat the oil over medium heat. Add the onion and garlic and cover and cook until softened, about 7 minutes. Stir in the ginger, curry powder,and cook for 30 seconds over low heat,

stirring constantly. Stir in the pumpkin, broth, and salt to taste and bring to a boil. Reduce heat to low, cover, and simmer, uncovered, until the flavors are blended, about 15 minutes.

2. Use an immersion blender to puree the soup in the pot or transfer in batches to a blender or food processor, puree, then return to the pot, and season with salt and pepper to taste. Add coconut milk and heat until hot.

3. Ladle into soup bowls, sprinkle with parsley and a spoonful of chutney sprinkled with chopped cashews, if using, and serve.

Lemony Lentil And Rice Soup
PREP: 15 MINUTES • COOK TIME: 1 HOUR 10 MINUTES • • SERVES: 6 servings

Ingredients
2 tablespoons olive oil
1 medium onion, chopped
1 medium carrot, cut into 1/4-inch dice
1 celery rib, cut into 1/4-inch dice
11/4 cups brown lentils, picked over, rinsed, and drained
¾ cup long-grain brown rice
1 (14.5-ounce) can crushed tomatoes

2 cups tomato juice
2 bay leaves
1/2 teaspoon ground cumin
6 cups water
1 teaspoon salt
1/4 teaspoon freshly ground black pepper
1 tablespoon fresh lemon juice
2 tablespoons minced fresh parsley

Directions

1. In a large soup pot, heat the oil over medium heat. Add the onion, carrot, and celery. Cover and cook until tender, about 10 minutes.

2. Add the lentils, rice, tomatoes, tomato juice, bay leaves, cumin, water, salt, and pepper. Bring to a boil, then reduce heat to medium low, and simmer, uncovered, until lentils and rice are tender, about 1 hour.

3. Just before serving, remove and discard the bay leaves, and stir in the lemon juice and parsley. Taste, adjusting seasonings if necessary, and serve.

Balsamic Lentil Stew
PREP: 10 MINUTES • COOK TIME: 30 MINUTES • TOTAL: 40 MINUTES • SERVES: 5

Ingredients
1 teaspoon olive oil
4 carrots, peeled and chopped
1 onion, chopped
3 garlic cloves, minced
2 tablespoons balsamic vinegar
4 cups Vegetable Broth or water

1 (28-ounce) can crushed tomatoes
1 tablespoon sugar
2 cups dried lentils or 2 (15-ounce) cans lentils, drained and rinsed
1 teaspoon salt
Freshly ground black pepper

Directions
Preparing the Ingredients
1. Heat the olive oil in a large soup pot over medium heat.
2. Add the carrots, onion, and garlic and sauté for about 5 minutes, until the vegetables are softened. Pour in the vinegar, and let it sizzle to deglaze the bottom of the pot. Add the vegetable broth, tomatoes, sugar, and lentils.
3. Bring to a boil, then reduce the heat to low. Simmer for about 25 minutes, until the lentils are soft. Add the salt and season to taste with pepper. Leftovers will keep in an airtight container for up to 1 week in the refrigerator or up to 1 month in the freezer.

Per Serving (2 cups) Calories: 353; Protein: 22g; Total fat: 2g; Saturated fat: 0g; Carbohydrates: 67g; Fiber: 27g

Tomato Orzo Soup

PREP: 5 MINUTES • COOK TIME: 30 MINUTES • TOTAL: 35 MINUTES • SERVES: 4 servings

Ingredients

1 tablespoon olive oil
1 medium onion, chopped
1 celery rib, minced
3 garlic cloves, minced
1 (28-ounce) can crushed tomatoes
3 cups chopped fresh ripe tomatoes
2 tablespoons chopped fresh basil, for garnish

2 tablespoons tomato paste
3 cups vegetable broth, homemade or water
2 bay leaves
Salt and freshly ground black pepper
1 cup plain unsweetened soy milk
11/2 cups cooked orzo

Directions

1. In large soup pot, heat the oil over medium heat. Add the onion, celery, and garlic. Cover and cook until softened, about 5 minutes. Stir in the canned and fresh tomatoes, tomato paste, broth, sugar, and bay leaves. Season with salt and pepper to taste and bring to a boil. Reduce the heat to low, cover, and simmer, uncovered, until the vegetables are tender, about 20 minutes.
2. Remove and discard bay leaves. Puree the soup in the pot with an immersion blender or in a blender or food processor, in batches if necessary, and return to the pot. Stir in the soy milk, taste, adjusting seasonings if necessary, and heat through.
3. Spoon about 1/3 cup of the orzo into the bottom of each bowl, ladle the hot soup on top, and serve sprinkled with the basil.

Golden Potato Soup

PREP: 5 MINUTES • COOK TIME: 30 MINUTES • TOTAL: 35 MINUTES • SERVES: 4 to 6 servings

Ingredients

1 tablespoon olive oil3 medium shallots, chopped4 cups vegetable broth, homemade (see Light Vegetable Broth) or store-bought, or water
3 medium russet potatoes, peeled and diced

2 medium sweet potatoes, peeled and diced
1 cup plain unsweetened soy milk
Salt and freshly ground black pepper
1 tablespoon minced chives, for garnish

Directions

1. In large saucepan, heat the oil over medium heat. Add the shallots, cover, and cook until softened, about 5 minutes. Add the broth and potatoes and bring to a boil. Reduce heat to low and simmer, uncovered, until the potatoes are soft, about 20 minutes.
2. Puree the potato mixture in the pot with an immersion blender or in a blender or food processor, in batches if necessary, and return to the pot. Stir in the soy milk and season with salt and pepper to taste. Simmer for 5 minutes to heat through and blend flavors.
3. Ladle the soup into bowls, sprinkle with chives, and serve.

Pad Thai Bowl

PREP: 10 MINUTES • COOK TIME: 10 MINUTES • TOTAL: 20 MINUTES • SERVES: 2

Ingredients

7 ounces brown rice noodles

1 teaspoon olive oil, or 1 tablespoon vegetable broth or water

2 carrots, peeled or scrubbed, and julienned

1 cup thinly sliced napa cabbage, or red cabbage

1 red bell pepper, seeded and thinly sliced

2 scallions, finely chopped

2 to 3 tablespoons fresh mint, finely chopped

1 cup bean sprouts

¼ cup Peanut Sauce

¼ cup fresh cilantro, finely chopped

2 tablespoons roasted peanuts, chopped

Fresh lime wedges

Directions

Preparing the Ingredients.

1. Put the rice noodles in a large bowl or pot, and cover with boiling water. Let sit until they soften, about 10 minutes. Rinse, drain, and set aside to cool. Heat the oil in a large skillet to medium-high, and sauté the carrots, cabbage, and bell pepper until softened, 7 to 8 minutes. Toss in the scallions, mint, and bean sprouts and cook for just a minute or two, then remove from the heat.
2. Toss the noodles with the vegetables, and mix in the Peanut Sauce. Transfer to bowls, and sprinkle with cilantro and peanuts. Serve with a lime wedge to squeeze onto the dish for a flavor boost.

Per Serving. Calories: 660; Total fat: 19g; Carbs: 110g; Fiber: 10g; Protein: 15g

Green Pea Risotto

PREP: 5 MINUTES • COOK TIME: 35 MINUTES • TOTAL: 40 MINUTES • SERVES: 4

Ingredients

1 teaspoon vegan butter

4 teaspoons minced garlic (about 4 cloves)

1 cup Arborio rice

2 cups vegetable broth (try a no-chicken broth for a richer flavor)

¼ teaspoon salt

2 tablespoons nutritional yeast

3 tablespoons lemon juice (about 1½ small lemons)

2 cups fresh, canned, or frozen (thawed) green peas

¼ to ½ teaspoon freshly ground black pepper, to taste

Directions

Preparing the Ingredients.

1. In a large skillet over medium-high heat, heat the vegan butter.

   Add the garlic and sauté for about 3 minutes.

   Add the rice, broth, and salt, and stir to combine well.

   Bring to boil. Reduce the heat to low and simmer for about 30 minutes, until the broth is absorbed and the rice is tender. Stir in the nutritional yeast and lemon juice.

   Gently fold in the peas. Taste before seasoning with the pepper.

   Divide the risotto evenly among 4 single-serving containers. Let cool before sealing the lids.
2. Place the airtight containers in the refrigerator for up to 5 days or freeze for up to 2 months. To thaw, refrigerate overnight. Reheat in the microwave for 1½ to 3 minutes.

Per Serving: Calories: 144; Fat: 2g; Protein: 10g; Carbohydrates: 24g; Fiber: 7g; Sugar: 5g; Sodium: 273mg

Three-Bean Chili

PREP: 5 MINUTES • COOK TIME: 55 MINUTES • TOTAL: 60 MINUTES • SERVES: 4 servings

Ingredients

1 tablespoon olive oil

1 medium yellow onion, chopped

3 garlic cloves, minced

1 (28-ounce) can crushed tomatoes

1 (4-ounce) can chopped mild green chiles, drained

1 cup water

3 tablespoons chili powder

1 canned chipotle chile in adobo, minced

1 teaspoon ground cumin

1/2 teaspoon dried marjoram

11/2 cups cooked or 1 (15.5-ounce) can black beans, drained and rinsed

11/2 cups cooked or 1 (15.5-ounce) can Great Northern or other white beans, drained and rinsed

11/2 cups cooked or 1 (15.5-ounce) can dark red kidney beans, drained and rinsed

Salt and freshly ground black pepper

Directions

1. In a large saucepan, heat the oil over medium heat. Add the onion and garlic, cover, and cook until softened, about 7 minutes.
2. Add the tomatoes, green chiles, water, chili powder, chipotle, cumin, marjoram, and sugar. Stir in the black beans, Great Northern beans, and kidney beans and season with salt and pepper to taste. Bring to a boil, then reduce the heat to low and simmer, uncovered, stirring occasionally, for 45 minutes.
3. Uncover, and cook an additional 10 minutes to allow flavors to develop and the chili to thicken. Serve immediately.

Chinese Black Bean Chili

PREP: 15 MINUTES • COOK TIME: 0 MINUTES • TOTAL: 15 MINUTES • SERVES: 4 servings

Ingredients

1 tablespoon olive oil

1 medium yellow onion, finely chopped

2 medium carrots, finely chopped

1 teaspoon grated fresh ginger

2 tablespoons chili powder

1 teaspoon brown sugar

1 (28-ounce) can diced tomatoes, undrained

1/2 cup Chinese black bean sauce

¾ cup water

41/2 cups cooked or 3 (15.5-ounce) cans black beans, drained and rinsed

Salt and freshly ground black pepper

2 tablespoons minced green onion, for garnish

Directions

1. In a large pot, heat the oil over medium heat. Add the onion and carrot. Cover and cook, until softened, about 10 minutes.
2. Stir in the ginger, chili powder, and sugar. Add the tomatoes, black bean sauce, and water. Stir in the black beans and season with salt and pepper to taste.
3. Bring to a boil, then reduce the heat to medium and simmer, covered, until the vegetables are tender, about 30 minutes. Simmer, uncovered, 10 to 15 minutes longer. Serve immediately, garnished with the green onion.

New World Chili

PREP: 5 MINUTES • COOK TIME: 55 MINUTES • TOTAL: 60 MINUTES • SERVES: 4 servings

Ingredients

1 small butternut squash, peeled, halved, and seeded
1 tablespoon olive oil
1 medium onion, chopped
3 cups mild tomato salsa, homemade (see Fresh Tomato Salsa) or store-bought
3 cups cooked or 2 (15.5-ounce) cans pinto beans, drained and rinsed

1 cup frozen lima beans
1 cup fresh or frozen corn kernels
1 canned chipotle chile in adobo, minced
1 cup water
3 tablespoons chili powder
1/2 teaspoon ground allspice
1/2 teaspoon sugar
Salt and freshly ground black pepper

Directions

1. Cut the squash into 1/4-inch dice and set aside. In a large saucepan, heat the oil over medium heat. Add the onion and squash, cover, and cook, until softened, about 10 minutes.
2. Add the salsa, pinto beans, lima beans, corn, and chipotle chile. Stir in the water, chili powder, allspice, sugar, and salt and black pepper to taste. Bring to a boil, then reduce the heat to medium and simmer, covered, until the vegetables are tender, about 45 minutes.
3. Uncover and simmer about 10 minutes longer. Serve immediately.

Lentil Salad With Chiles
PREP: 5 MINUTES • COOK TIME: 40 MINUTES • TOTAL: 45 MINUTES • SERVES: 4 servings

Ingredients

1 cup brown lentils, picked over, rinsed, and drained
4 ripe plum tomatoes, chopped
2 celery ribs, cut into 1/4-inch slices
1 or 2 hot or mild chiles, seeded and minced

1/3 cup chopped green onions
2 tablespoons chopped fresh parsley
4 tablespoons olive oil
2 tablespoons sherry or balsamic vinegar
Salt and freshly ground black pepper

Directions

1. Bring a medium saucepan of salted water to boil over high heat. Add the lentils, return to a boil, then reduce to low. Cover and cook until the lentils are tender, about 40 minutes.
2. Drain the lentils well and transfer to a large bowl. Add the tomatoes, celery, chiles, green onions, parsley, oil, and vinegar. Season with salt and pepper to taste, toss well to combine, and serve.

Jerk-Spiced Red Bean Chili
PREP: 5 MINUTES • COOK TIME: 50 MINUTES • TOTAL: 55 MINUTES • SERVES: 4 servings

Ingredients

1 tablespoon olive oil
1 medium onion, chopped
8 ounces seitan, chopped
3 cups cooked or 2 (15.5-ounce) cans dark red kidney beans, drained and rinsed
1 (14.5-ounce) can crushed tomatoes
1 (14.5-ounce) can diced tomatoes, drained
1 (4-ounce) can chopped mild or hot green chiles, drained
1/2 cup barbecue sauce

1 cup water
1 tablespoon soy sauce
1 tablespoon chili powder
1 teaspoon ground cumin
1 teaspoon ground allspice
1/2 teaspoon ground oregano
1/4 teaspoon ground cayenne
1/2 teaspoon salt
1/4 teaspoon freshly ground black pepper

Directions

1. In a large pot, heat the oil over medium heat. Add the onion and seitan. Cover and cook, until the onion is softened, about 10 minutes.
2. Stir in the kidney beans, crushed tomatoes, diced tomatoes, and chiles. Stir in the barbecue sauce, water, soy sauce, chili powder, cumin, allspice, sugar, oregano, cayenne, salt, and black pepper.
3. Bring to a boil, then reduce the heat to medium and simmer, covered, until the vegetables are tender, about 45 minutes. Uncover and simmer about 10 minutes longer. Serve immediately.

Warm Lentil Salad With Walnuts
PREP: 5 MINUTES • COOK TIME: 45 MINUTES • TOTAL: 50 MINUTES • SERVES: 4 servings

Ingredients

1 cup green lentils, picked over, rinsed, and drained
1 medium shallot, halved
1 garlic clove, crushed
2 tablespoons white wine vinegar
1 tablespoon Dijon mustard
1/4 cup olive oil

1/2 teaspoon dried oregano
1/2 teaspoon salt
1/4 teaspoon freshly ground black pepper
1/2 cup finely chopped red bell pepper
1/3 cup chopped toasted walnuts
1/4 cup finely chopped red onion
2 tablespoons minced fresh parsley

Directions

1. Bring a medium saucepan of salted water to a boil. Add the lentils and return to a boil, then reduce the heat to low. Cover and cook until lentils are tender, about 45 minutes.
2. In a blender or food processor, mince the shallot and garlic. Add the vinegar, mustard, oil, oregano, salt, and black pepper and process until well blended. Set aside.
3. When the lentils are tender, drain well and transfer to a serving bowl. Add the bell pepper, walnuts, onion, and parsley

Falafel Wrap
PREP: 30 MINUTES • COOK TIME: 30 MINUTES • TOTAL: 60 MINUTES • SERVES: 6

Ingredients

FOR THE FALAFEL PATTIES
1 (14-ounce) can chickpeas, drained and rinsed, or 1½ cups cooked
1 zucchini, grated
2 scallions, minced
¼ cup fresh parsley, chopped
2 tablespoons black olives, pitted and chopped (optional)
1 tablespoon tahini, or almond, cashew, or sunflower seed butter
1 tablespoon lemon juice, or apple cider vinegar
½ teaspoon ground cumin
¼ teaspoon paprika

¼ teaspoon sea salt
1 teaspoon olive oil (optional, if frying)
FOR THE WRAP
1 whole-grain wrap or pita
¼ cup Classic *Hummus*
½ cup fresh greens
1 baked falafel patty
¼ cup cherry tomatoes, halved
¼ cup diced cucumber
¼ cup chopped avocado, or *Guacamole*
¼ cup cooked quinoa, or *Tabbouleh Salad* (optional)

Directions

TO MAKE THE FALAFEL

1. Use a food processor to pulse the chickpeas, zucchini, scallions, parsley, and olives (if using) until roughly chopped. Just pulse—don't purée. Or use a potato masher to mash the chickpeas in a large bowl and stir in the grated and chopped veggies.

2. In a small bowl, whisk together the tahini and lemon juice, and stir in the cumin, paprika, and salt. Pour this into the chickpea mixture, and stir well (or pulse the food processor) to combine. Taste and add more salt, if needed. Using your hands, form the mix into 6 patties.

3. You can either panfry or bake the patties. To panfry, heat a large skillet to medium, add 1 teaspoon of olive oil, and cook the patties about 10 minutes on the first side. Flip, and cook another 5 to 7 minutes. To bake them, put them on a baking sheet lined with parchment paper and bake at 350°F for 30 to 40 minutes.

TO MAKE THE WRAP

1. Lay the wrap on a plate and spread the hummus down the center. Then lay on the greens and crumble the falafel patty on top. Add the tomatoes, cucumber, avocado, and quinoa.

2. Fold in both ends, and wrap up as tightly as you can. If you have a sandwich press, you can press the wraps for about 5 minutes. This will travel best in a reusable lunch box, or reusable plastic lunch wrap.

Per Serving (1 wrap) Calories: 546; Total fat: 19g; Carbs: 81g; Fiber: 14g; Protein: 18g

Red Bean Jambalaya
PREP: 5 MINUTES • COOK TIME: 45 MINUTES • TOTAL: 50 MINUTES • SERVES: 4 servings

Ingredients

1 tablespoon olive oil
1 medium yellow onion, chopped
2 celery ribs, chopped
1 medium green bell pepper, chopped
3 garlic cloves, minced
1 cup long-grain rice
3 cups cooked or 2 (15.5-ounce) cans dark red kidney beans, drained and rinsed
1 (14.5-ounce) can diced tomatoes, drained

1 (14.5-ounce) can crushed tomatoes
1 (4-ounce) can mild green chiles, drained
1 teaspoon dried thyme
1/2 teaspoon dried marjoram
1 teaspoon salt
Freshly ground black pepper
21/2 cups vegetable broth, or water
1 tablespoon chopped fresh parsley, for garnish
Tabasco sauce (optional)

Directions

1. In a large saucepan, heat the oil over medium heat. Add the onion, celery, bell pepper, and garlic. Cover and cook until softened, about 7 minutes.

2. Stir in the rice, beans, diced tomatoes, crushed tomatoes, chiles, thyme, marjoram, salt, and black pepper to taste. Add the broth, cover, and simmer until the vegetables are soft and the rice is tender, about 45 minutes.

3. Sprinkle with parsley and a splash of Tabasco, if using, and serve.

Black Bean And Corn Salad With Cilantro Dressing
PREP: 15 MINUTES • COOK TIME: 0 MINUTES • TOTAL: 15 MINUTES • SERVES: 4 servings

Ingredients

2 cups frozen corn, thawed
3 cups cooked or 2 (15.5-ounce) cans black beans, rinsed and drained
1/2 cup chopped red bell pepper
1/4 cup minced red onion
1 (4-ounce) can chopped mild green chiles, drained
2 garlic cloves, crushed

1/4 cup chopped fresh cilantro
1 teaspoon ground cumin
1/2 teaspoon salt (optional)
1/4 teaspoon freshly ground black pepper
2 tablespoons fresh lime juice
2 tablespoons water
1/4 cup olive oil

Directions

1. In a large bowl, combine the corn, beans, bell pepper, onion, and chiles. Set aside.
2. In a blender or food processor, mince the garlic. Add the cilantro, cumin, salt, and black pepper and pulse to blend. Add the lime juice, water, and oil and process until well blended. Pour the dressing over the salad and toss to combine. Taste, adjusting seasonings if necessary, and serve.

Coconut-Peanut Chickpeas And Vegetables
PREP: 5 MINUTES • COOK TIME: 13 MINUTES • TOTAL: 18 MINUTES • SERVES: 4 servings

Ingredients

1 tablespoon olive oil
1 medium onion, chopped
1 medium red bell pepper, chopped
3 garlic cloves, minced
1 tablespoon hot or mild curry powder
2 tablespoons creamy peanut butter
1 (13.5-ounce) can unsweetened coconut milk

3 cups cooked or 2 (15.5-ounce) cans chickpeas, drained and rinsed
1 (14.5-ounce) can diced tomatoes, drained
3 cups fresh baby spinach
Salt and freshly ground black pepper
Crushed unsalted roasted peanuts, for garnish

Directions

1. In a large saucepan, heat the oil over medium heat. Add the onion and bell pepper, cover, and cook until soft, about 10 minutes. Add the garlic and curry powder, stirring until fragrant, about 30 seconds. Add the peanut butter and gradually stir in the coconut milk until well blended. Add the chickpeas, tomatoes, and spinach, stirring to wilt the spinach, about 5 minutes. Season with salt and pepper to taste.
2. Simmer until hot and the flavors are well blended, about 7 minutes. Serve immediately, sprinkled with the peanuts.

Black Beans And Wild Rice
PREP: 5 MINUTES • COOK TIME: 50 MINUTES • TOTAL: 55 MINUTES • SERVES: 4 servings

Ingredients

¾ cup wild rice
3 cups cooked or 2 (15.5-ounce) cans black beans, drained and rinsed
1 (14.5-ounce) can diced tomatoes, undrained
3 cups fresh baby spinach

1 teaspoon dried marjoram
1/2 teaspoon salt
1/4 teaspoon freshly ground black pepper

Directions

1. Combine the wild rice in a large saucepan with 3 cups of salted water. Bring to a boil, then reduce heat to low, cover, and simmer for 40 minutes or until tender. Add the beans, tomatoes, marjoram, salt, and pepper.
2. Cover and cook over low heat, stirring occasionally, until the flavors are well combined, about 15 minutes, adding a splash of water if too dry.
3. Stir in the spinach and cook until the spinach is wilted and the flavors have blended, about 5 minutes. Taste, adjusting seasonings if necessary. Serve immediately.

Moroccan-Spiced Chickpea and Sweet Potato Stew
PREP: 5 MINUTES • COOK TIME: 50 MINUTES • TOTAL: 55 MINUTES • SERVES: 4 to 6 servings

Ingredients

1 tablespoon olive oil
1 large yellow onion, chopped
2 medium carrots, cut into 1/4-inch dice
1 celery rib, cut into 1/4-inch dice
2 garlic cloves, minced
1 teaspoon grated fresh ginger
1 teaspoon ground coriander
1 teaspoon ground cumin
1/2 teaspoon turmeric
1/4 teaspoon ground cinnamon
1/4 teaspoon ground nutmeg
1/2 teaspoon sugar

2 medium sweet potatoes, peeled and cut into 1/2-inch dice
8 ounces green beans, trimmed and cut into 1-inch lengths
11/2 cups cooked or 1 (15.5-ounce) can chickpeas, drained and rinsed
1 (14.5-ounce) can diced tomatoes, undrained
11/2 cups vegetable broth
Salt and freshly ground black pepper
2 tablespoons minced fresh parsley or cilantro
1 teaspoon fresh lemon juice

Directions

1. In a large saucepan, heat the oil over medium heat. Add the onion, carrots, celery, garlic, and ginger. Cover and cook until softened, about 10 minutes.
2. Stir in the coriander, cumin, turmeric, cinnamon, nutmeg, and sugar.
3. Add the sweet potatoes, green beans, chickpeas, and tomatoes with their juice. Stir in the broth and bring to a boil. Reduce heat to low and season with salt and pepper to taste.
4. Cover and simmer until the vegetables are tender, about 40 minutes. Stir in the parsley and lemon juice and cook 10 minutes longer. Taste, adjusting seasonings if necessary, and serve immediately.

White Bean And Broccoli Salad With Parsley-Walnut Pesto
PREP: 10 MINUTES • COOK TIME: 15 MINUTES • TOTAL: 25 MINUTES • SERVES: 4 to 6 servings

Ingredients

1 pound Yukon Gold potatoes, peeled and cut into 1-inch chunks
3 cups broccoli florets
11/2 cups cooked or 1 (15.5-ounce) can cannellini or other white beans, drained and rinsed
1/2 cup kalamata olives, pitted and halved
1/2 cup walnut pieces

2 garlic cloves, finely minced
1/2 cup chopped fresh parsley
1/4 cup walnut oil
1/4 cup olive oil
1/4 cup white wine vinegar
1/2 teaspoon salt (optional)
1/4 teaspoon crushed red pepper

Directions

1. Steam the potatoes until almost tender, about 10 minutes. Steam the broccoli until just tender, about 5 minutes. Drain the potatoes and broccoli and place them in a large bowl. Add the beans, olives, and 1/4 cup of the walnuts and set aside.
2. In a blender or food processor, combine the remaining 1/4 cup walnuts with the garlic and process until well minced. Add the parsley, walnut oil, olive oil, vinegar, salt, sugar, and crushed red pepper and process until blended. Pour the dressing over the salad, toss gently to combine, and serve.

Three-Bean Cassoulet
PREP: 5 MINUTES • COOK TIME: 60 MINUTES • TOTAL: 65 MINUTES • SERVES: 4 to 6 servings

Ingredients

1 tablespoon olive oil
1 medium onion, chopped

2 medium carrots, chopped
1 celery rib, chopped

3 garlic cloves, minced

11/2 cups cooked or 1 (15.5-ounce) cans Navy beans, drained and rinsed

11/2 cups cooked or 1 (15.5-ounce) cans Great Northern beans, drained and rinsed

11/2 cups cooked or 1 (15.5-ounce) cans cannellini beans, drained and rinsed

1 (14.5-ounce) can crushed tomatoes

1 cup vegetable broth

1 tablespoon minced fresh parsley

1 teaspoon dried savory

1 teaspoon dried thyme

1 teaspoon salt

1/4 teaspoon freshly ground black pepper

1/2 cup dry unseasoned bread crumbs

Directions

1. Preheat the oven to 375°F. Lightly oil a 3-quart casserole and set aside.
2. In a large skillet, heat the oil over medium heat. Add the onion, carrots, celery, and garlic. Cover and cook until softened, about 10 minutes.
3. Transfer the vegetable mixture to the prepared casserole. Stir in the beans, tomatoes, broth, parsley, savory, thyme, salt, and pepper. Cover tightly and bake until the vegetables are tender and the flavors are blended, about 45 minutes.
4. Remove the cassoulet from the oven, uncover, and top with the bread crumbs. Return to the oven and bake, uncovered, 10 minutes longer to lightly brown the crumbs. Serve immediately.

Three Lentil Dal
PREP: 5 MINUTES • COOK TIME: 65 MINUTES • TOTAL: 70 MINUTES • SERVES: 6 servings

Ingredients

1/2 cup green lentils, picked over, rinsed, and drained

1/2 cup brown lentils, picked over, rinsed, and drained

3 cups water

Salt

1/2 cup red lentils, picked over, rinsed, and drained

2 tablespoons canola or grapeseed oil

1 medium yellow onion, minced

2 garlic cloves, minced

2 teaspoons grated fresh ginger

1 tablespoon hot or mild curry powder

1/2 teaspoon ground cumin

1/2 teaspoon ground coriander

1/4 teaspoon ground cayenne

1 (14.5-ounce) can crushed tomatoes

Directions

1. Soak the green lentils and brown lentils in separate medium bowls of hot water for 45 minutes. Drain the green lentils and place them in a large saucepan with the water. Bring to a boil. Reduce heat to low and simmer for 10 minutes.
2. Drain the brown lentils and add to the green lentils with salt to taste. Simmer, partially covered, for 20 minutes, stirring occasionally. Add the red lentils and simmer, uncovered, until the sauce thickens and the beans are very soft, 20 to 25 minutes longer.
3. In a large skillet, heat the oil over medium heat. Add the onion, cover, and cook until softened about 10 minutes. Add the garlic and ginger and cook until fragrant, about 30 seconds.
4. Add the curry powder, cumin, coriander, cayenne, and tomatoes, stirring constantly for about 1 minute. Add the tomato mixture to the cooked lentils and stir to mix well. Cook another 10 minutes until the flavors are blended. Taste, adjusting seasonings if necessary. Serve immediately.

Curried Mango Chickpea Wrap
PREP: 15 MINUTES • COOK TIME: 0 MINUTES • TOTAL: 15 MINUTES • SERVES: 3

Ingredients

3 tablespoons tahini

Zest and juice of 1 lime

1 tablespoon curry powder
¼ teaspoon sea salt
3 to 4 tablespoons water
1 (14-ounce) can chickpeas, rinsed and drained, or 1½ cups cooked

1 cup diced mango
1 red bell pepper, seeded and diced small
½ cup fresh cilantro, chopped
3 large whole-grain wraps
1 to 2 cups shredded green leaf lettuce

Directions
Preparing the Ingredients.
1. In a medium bowl, whisk together the tahini, lime zest and juice, curry powder, and salt until the mixture is creamy and thick.

   Add 3 to 4 tablespoons water to thin it out a bit. Or you can process this all in a blender. The taste should be strong and salty, to flavor the whole salad.

   Toss the chickpeas, mango, bell pepper, and cilantro with the tahini dressing. Spoon the salad down the center of the wraps, top with shredded lettuce, and then roll up and enjoy.

Per Serving (1 wrap) Calories: 437; Total fat: 8g; Carbs: 79g; Fiber: 12g; Protein: 15g

Peppered Pinto Beans
PREP: 5 MINUTES • COOK TIME: 20 MINUTES • TOTAL: 25 MINUTES • SERVES: 6

Ingredients
1 teaspoon extra-virgin olive oil or ¼ cup vegetable broth
1 red bell pepper, seeded and diced
1 jalapeño seeded and minced
2 (14.5-ounce) cans pinto beans, rinsed and drained

½ cup vegetable broth
1 teaspoon ground cumin
1 teaspoon chili powder
½ teaspoon salt (optional)
¼ teaspoon freshly ground black pepper

Directions
Preparing the Ingredients.
1. In a large pot over medium-high heat, heat the olive oil.

   Sauté the bell pepper and jalapeño for 3 to 5 minutes.

   Add the beans, broth, cumin, chili powder, salt, and black pepper.

   Bring to a boil. Reduce the heat to low and simmer, uncovered, for 10 minutes.

   Transfer to a large storage container, or scoop about ⅓ cup of beans into each of 6 storage containers. Let cool before sealing the lids.

   Place the airtight containers in the refrigerator for up to 5 days or freeze for up to 3 months. To thaw, refrigerate overnight. Reheat in the microwave for 1½ to 3 minutes.

Per Serving: Calories: 183; Fat: 2g; Protein: 11g; Carbohydrates: 32g; Fiber: 11g; Sugar: 2g; Sodium: 340mg

Maple Baked Beans
PREP: 5 MINUTES • COOK TIME: 45 MINUTES • TOTAL: 50 MINUTES • SERVES: 4 servings

Ingredients
1 tablespoon olive oil
1 medium yellow onion, minced
3 garlic cloves, minced
1 (14.5-ounce) can crushed tomatoes
1/2 cup pure maple syrup

2 tablespoons blackstrap molasses
1 tablespoon soy sauce
11/2 teaspoons dry mustard
1/4 teaspoon ground cayenne
Salt and freshly ground black pepper

3 cups cooked or 2 (15.5-ounce) cans Great Northern beans, drained and rinsed

Directions
1. Preheat the oven to 350°F. Lightly oil a 2-quart casserole and set aside.
2. In a large saucepan, heat the oil over medium heat. Add the onion and garlic. Cover and cook until softened, about 5 minutes.
3. Stir in the tomatoes, maple syrup, molasses, soy sauce, mustard, and cayenne and bring to a boil. Reduce heat to low and simmer, uncovered, until slightly reduced, about 10 minutes. Season with salt and pepper to taste.
4. Place the beans in the prepared casserole. Add the sauce, stirring to combine and coat the beans. Cover and bake until hot and bubbly, about 30 minutes. Serve immediately.

Loaded Black Bean Pizza
PREP: 10 MINUTES • COOK TIME: 20 MINUTES • TOTAL: 30 MINUTES • SERVES: 2 SMALL PIZZAS

Ingredients
2 prebaked pizza crusts
½ cup Spicy Black Bean Dip
1 tomato, thinly sliced
Pinch freshly ground black pepper
1 carrot, grated

Pinch sea salt
1 red onion, thinly sliced
1 avocado, sliced
1.Preheat the oven to 400°F.

Directions
Preparing the Ingredients.
1. Lay the two crusts out on a large baking sheet. Spread half the Spicy Black Bean Dip on each pizza crust. Then layer on the tomato slices with a pinch pepper if you like. Sprinkle the grated carrot with the sea salt and lightly massage it in with your hands. Spread the carrot on top of the tomato, then add the onion.
2. Pop the pizzas in the oven for 10 to 20 minutes, or until they're done to your taste. Top the cooked pizzas with sliced avocado and another sprinkle of pepper.

Per Serving (1 pizza) Calories: 379; Total fat: 13g; Carbs: 59g; Fiber: 15g; Protein: 13g

Black Bean And Bulgur Loaf
PREP: 5 MINUTES • COOK TIME: 60 MINUTES • TOTAL: 65 MINUTES • SERVES: 4 to 6 servings

Ingredients
1 tablespoon olive oil
1 medium yellow onion, minced
1 cup medium-grind bulgur
2 cups water
Salt
3 cups cooked or 2 (15.5-ounce) cans black beans, drained, rinsed, and mashed

1/2 cup quick-cooking oats
1/3 cup wheat gluten flour (vital wheat gluten)
2 tablespoons nutritional yeast
11/2 teaspoons dried thyme
11/2 teaspoons dried savory
1/2 teaspoon dried oregano
1/4 teaspoon freshly ground black pepper

Directions
1. In a large saucepan, heat the oil over medium heat. Add the onion, cover, and cook until softened, 5 minutes. Add the bulgur and water and bring to a boil. Salt the water, reduce heat to low, cover, and

simmer until bulgur is tender and water is absorbed, 15 to 20 minutes. If any water remains, drain well in a fine-mesh sieve, pressing any excess liquid from the bulgur.

2. Preheat the oven to 350°F. Lightly oil a 9-inch loaf pan and set aside. Transfer the bulgur mixture to a large bowl. Add the mashed beans to the bulgur. Stir in the oats, flour, yeast, thyme, savory, oregano, and salt and pepper to taste. Mix well until thoroughly combined.

3. Spoon the mixture into the prepared loaf pan, pressing with your hands to make a smooth loaf. Bake until firm, about 40 minutes. Remove from the oven and set aside to cool for 10 minutes before slicing.

Grilled AHLT
PREP: 5 MINUTES • COOK TIME: 10 MINUTES • TOTAL: 15 MINUTES • SERVES: 1 SANDWHICH

Ingredients
¼ cup Classic *Hummus*
2 slices whole-grain bread
¼ avocado, sliced
½ cup lettuce, chopped

½ tomato, sliced
Pinch sea salt
Pinch freshly ground black pepper
1 teaspoon olive oil, divided

Directions
Preparing the Ingredients.

1. Spread some hummus on each slice of bread. Then layer the avocado, lettuce, and tomato on one slice, sprinkle with salt and pepper, and top with the other slice.

   Heat a skillet to medium heat, and drizzle ½ teaspoon of the olive oil just before putting the sandwich in the skillet.

   Cook for 3 to 5 minutes, then lift the sandwich with a spatula, drizzle the remaining ½ teaspoon olive oil into the skillet, and flip the sandwich to grill the other side for 3 to 5 minutes.

   Press it down with the spatula to seal the vegetables inside. Once done, remove from the skillet and slice in half to serve.

   You can also toast the bread and assemble as a simple sandwich, or brush the bread with olive oil, assemble the sandwich, and put in the toaster oven for 10 to 15 minutes at 350°F.

Per Serving Calories: 322; Total fat: 14g; Carbs: 40g; Fiber: 11g; Protein: 12g

Chickpea and Vegetable Loaf
PREP: 15 MINUTES • COOK TIME: 10 MINUTES • TOTAL: 25 MINUTES • SERVES: 4 servings

Ingredients
1 small white potato, peeled and shredded
1 medium carrot, shredded
1 small yellow onion, chopped
2 garlic cloves, minced
11/2 cups cooked or 1 (15.5-ounce) can chickpeas, drained and rinsed
¾ cup wheat gluten flour or chickpea flour, or more if needed

¾ cup quick-cooking oats
1/2 cup dry unseasoned bread crumbs
1/4 cup minced fresh parsley
1 tablespoon soy sauce
1 teaspoon dried savory
1/2 teaspoon dried sage
1 teaspoon salt
1/4 teaspoon freshly ground black pepper

Directions

1. Preheat the oven to 350°F. Lightly oil a 9-inch loaf pan and set aside. Squeeze the excess liquid from the shredded potato and place it in a food processor, along with the carrot, onion, and garlic. Add the chickpeas and pulse to blend the Ingredients while retaining some texture. Add the flour, oats, bread crumbs, parsley, soy sauce, savory, sage, salt, and black pepper. Pulse just until blended.

2. Scrape the mixture onto a lightly floured work surface. Use your hands to form the mixture into a loaf, adding more flour or oats if the mixture is too loose. Place the loaf in the prepared pan, smoothing the

top. Bake until firm and golden, about 1 hour. Remove from oven and let stand for 10 minutes before slicing.

Red Lentil Patties In Pita
PREP: 15 MINUTES • COOK TIME: 20 MINUTES • TOTAL: 35 MINUTES • SERVES: 4 pitas

Ingredients
1/2 cup red lentils, picked over, rinsed, and drained
2 tablespoons olive oil
1/2 cup minced onion
1 small potato, peeled and shredded
1/2 cup roasted cashews
1/4 cup chickpea flour or wheat gluten flour
1 tablespoon minced fresh parsley

2 teaspoons hot or mild curry powder
1/2 teaspoon salt
1/8 teaspoon ground cayenne
4 (7-inch) whole-grain pita breads, warmed and halved
Shredded romaine lettuce
Fresh Mint and Coconut Chutney or your favorite chutney

Directions
1. Bring a small saucepan of salted water to boil over high heat. Add the lentils, return to a boil, then reduce heat to low. Cover and cook until tender, about 15 minutes. Drain well, then return to the saucepan and cook over low heat for 1 to 2 minutes, stirring, to evaporate any remaining moisture. Set aside.
2. In a large skillet, heat 1 tablespoon of the oil over medium heat. Add the onion and potato, cover, and cook until soft, about 5 minutes. Set aside.
3. In a food processor, process the cashews until finely ground. Add the cooked lentils and the onion-potato mixture and pulse to combine. Add the flour, parsley, curry powder, salt, and cayenne. Process until just mixed, leaving some texture. Shape the mixture into 8 small patties.
4. In a large skillet, heat the remaining 1 tablespoon of oil over medium heat. Add the patties and cook until browned on both sides, about 5 minutes per side.
Stuff a patty inside each pita half, along with some shredded lettuce and a spoonful of chutney. Serve immediately.

Black Bean Burgers
PREP: 15 MINUTES • COOK TIME: 0 MINUTES • TOTAL: 15 MINUTES • SERVES: 4 burgers

Ingredients
3 tablespoons olive oil
1/2 cup minced onion
1 garlic clove, minced
11/2 cups cooked or 1 (15.5-ounce) can black beans, drained and rinsed
1 tablespoon minced fresh parsley
1/2 cup dry unseasoned bread crumbs

1/4 cup wheat gluten flour (vital wheat gluten)
1 teaspoon smoked paprika
1/2 teaspoon dried thyme
Salt and freshly ground black pepper
4 burger rolls
4 lettuce leaves
1 ripe tomato, cut into 1/4-inch slices

Directions
1. In a small skillet, heat 1 tablespoon of the oil over medium heat. Add the onion and garlic and cook until softened, about 5 minutes.
2. Transfer the onion mixture to a food processor. Add the beans, parsley, bread crumbs, flour, paprika, thyme, and salt and pepper to taste. Process until well combined, leaving some texture. Shape the mixture into 4 equal patties and refrigerate for 20 minutes.
3. In a large skillet, heat the remaining 2 tablespoons oil over medium heat. Add the burgers and cook until browned on both sides, turning once, about 5 minutes per side.

Serve the burgers on the rolls with lettuce and tomato slices.

White Bean And Walnut Patties
PREP: 10 MINUTES • COOK TIME: 7 MINUTES • TOTAL: 17 MINUTES • SERVES: 4 patties

Ingredients
1/4 cup diced onion
1 garlic clove, crushed
¾ cup walnut pieces
¾ cup canned or cooked white beans, drained and rinsed
¾ cup wheat gluten flour (vital wheat gluten)
2 tablespoons minced fresh parsley
1 tablespoon soy sauce
1 teaspoon Dijon mustard, plus more to serve

1/2 teaspoon salt
1/2 teaspoon ground sage
1/2 teaspoon sweet paprika
1/4 teaspoon turmeric
1/4 teaspoon freshly ground black pepper
2 tablespoons olive oil
Bread or rolls of choice
Lettuce leaves and sliced tomatoes

Directions
1. In a food processor, combine the onion, garlic, and walnuts and process until finely ground.
2. Cook the beans in a small skillet over medium heat, stirring, for 1 to 2 minutes to evaporate any moisture. Add the beans to the food processor along with the flour, parsley, soy sauce, mustard, salt, sage, paprika, turmeric, and pepper. Process until well blended. Shape the mixture into 4 equal patties.
3. In a large skillet, heat the oil over medium heat. Add the patties and cook until browned on both sides, about 5 minutes per side.
4. Serve on your favorite sandwich bread with mustard, lettuce, and sliced tomatoes.

Italian Lentils
PREP: 5 MINUTES • COOK TIME: 40 MINUTES • TOTAL: 45 MINUTES • SERVES: 6

Ingredients
5 cups water
2¼ cups dry French or brown lentils, rinsed and drained
3 teaspoons minced garlic (about 3 cloves)
1 bay leaf

½ teaspoon dried basil
½ teaspoon dried oregano
½ teaspoon dried rosemary
½ teaspoon dried thyme

Directions
Preparing the Ingredients.
1. In a large pot, combine the water, lentils, garlic, bay leaf, basil, oregano, rosemary, and thyme. Bring to a boil. Reduce the heat to low, cover, and simmer for 25 to 40 minutes, until tender, stirring occasionally. Drain any excess cooking liquid.
   Transfer to a large storage container, or scoop 1 cup of lentils into each of 6 storage containers. Let cool before sealing the lids.
2. Place the airtight containers in the refrigerator for up to 5 days or freeze for up to 3 months. To thaw, refrigerate overnight. Reheat in the microwave for 1½ to 3 minutes.

Per Serving (1 cup): Calories: 257; Fat: 1g; Protein: 19g; Carbohydrates: 44g; Fiber: 22g; Sugar: 2g; Sodium: 5mg

Curry Spiced Lentil Burgers
PREP: 40 MINUTES • COOK TIME: 30 MINUTES • TOTAL: 70 MINUTES • SERVES: 12 BURGUERS

Ingredients

1 cup lentils
2½ to 3 cups water
3 carrots, grated
1 small onion, diced

¾ cup whole-grain flour (see Options for gluten-free below)
1½ to 2 teaspoons curry powder
½ teaspoon sea salt
Pinch freshly ground black pepper

Directions

Preparing the Ingredients.

1. Put the lentils in a medium pot with the water. Bring to a boil and then simmer for about 30 minutes, until soft. While the lentils are cooking, put the carrots and onion in a large bowl. Toss them with the flour, curry powder, salt, and pepper.
2. When the lentils are cooked, drain off any excess water, then add them to the bowl with the veggies. Use a potato masher or a large spoon to mash them slightly, and add more flour if you need to get the mixture to stick together. The amount of flour depends on how much water the lentils absorbed, and on the texture of the flour, so use more or less until the mixture sticks when you form it into a ball. Scoop up ¼-cup portions and form into 12 patties. You can either panfry or bake the burgers.
3. To panfry, heat a large skillet to medium, add a tiny bit of oil, and cook the burgers about 10 minutes on the first side. Flip, and cook another 5 to 7 minutes. To bake them, put them on a baking sheet lined with parchment paper and bake at 350°F for 30 to 40 minutes.
4. For the whole-grain flour, use whatever flour you like. Sorghum, rice, oat, buckwheat, and even almond meal would work and make these gluten-free. The flour in this recipe is just a binding agent, so it can be any type.

Per Serving (1 burger) Calories: 114; Total fat: 1g; Carbs: 22g; Fiber: 7g; Protein: 6g

Vegetable Fried Rice
PREP: 5 MINUTES • COOK TIME: 15 MINUTES • TOTAL: 20 MINUTES • SERVES: 4 servings

Ingredients

2 tablespoons canola or grapeseed oil
1 medium yellow onion, finely chopped
1 large carrot, finely chopped
1 medium zucchini, finely chopped
2 garlic cloves, minced
2 teaspoons grated fresh ginger
3 green onions, minced

1/2 teaspoon turmeric (optional)
31/2 cups cold cooked long-grain rice
1 cup frozen peas, thawed
3 tablespoons soy sauce
2 teaspoons mirin or dry white wine
1 tablespoon toasted sesame oil

Directions

1. In a large skillet, heat the canola oil over medium-high heat. Add the onion, carrot, and zucchini and stir-fry until softened, about 5 minutes. Add the garlic, ginger, and green onions and stir-fry until softened, about 3 minutes.
2. Stir in the turmeric, if using. Add the rice, peas, soy sauce, and mirin and stir-fry until hot, about 5 minutes. Drizzle with the sesame oil, toss to combine, and taste, adjusting seasonings and adding more soy sauce if necessary. Serve immediately.

Red Pepper Lentils
PREP: 5 MINUTES • COOK TIME: 20 MINUTES • TOTAL: 25 MINUTES • SERVES: 4

Ingredients

1 teaspoon extra-virgin olive oil or canola oil or 2 teaspoons water or vegetable broth
2 teaspoons minced garlic (about 2 cloves)
2 teaspoons grated fresh ginger
½ teaspoon ground cumin
½ teaspoon fennel seeds

1 large red bell pepper, seeded and chopped
1 large tomato, chopped
1 cup dried red lentils
2¼ cups water
2 tablespoons lemon juice (about 1 small lemon)

Directions
Preparing the Ingredients.
1. In a large pot over medium-high heat, heat the olive oil.
   Add the garlic and ginger and sauté for 3 minutes, stirring frequently to keep the garlic from sticking. Add the cumin, fennel, red bell pepper, tomato, lentils, and water. Bring to a boil, cover, and reduce the heat to medium-low or low to simmer until the lentils are tender, about 15 minutes. Remove from the heat, and stir in the lemon juice. Transfer to a large storage container, or scoop ½ cup of lentils into each of 4 storage containers. Let cool before sealing the lids.
2. Place the airtight containers in the refrigerator for up to 5 days or freeze for up to 3 months. To thaw, refrigerate overnight. Reheat in the microwave for 1½ to 3 minutes.

   Per Serving: Calories: 206; Fat: 2g; Protein: 13g; Carbohydrates: 34g; Fiber: 16g; Sugar: 4g; Sodium: 9mg

Lemon and Thyme Couscous
PREP: 5 MINUTES • COOK TIME: 10 MINUTES • TOTAL: 15 MINUTES • SERVES: 6

Ingredients
2¾ cups vegetable stock
juice and zest of 1 lemon
2 tablespoons chopped fresh thyme
1½ cups couscous

¼ cup chopped fresh parsley
sea salt
freshly ground black pepper

Directions
Preparing the Ingredients.
1. In a medium pot, bring the vegetable stock, lemon juice, and thyme to a boil. Stir in the couscous, cover, and remove from the heat.
2. Allow to sit, covered, until the -couscous absorbs the liquid and softens, about 5 minutes. Fluff with a fork. Stir in the lemon zest and parsley. Season with salt and pepper. Serve hot.

Wild Rice And Millet Croquettes
PREP: 5 MINUTES • COOK TIME: 20 MINUTES • TOTAL: 25 MINUTES • SERVES: 4 to 6 servings

Ingredients
¾ cup cooked millet
1/2 cup cooked wild rice
3 tablespoons olive oil
1/4 cup minced onion
1 celery rib, finely minced

1/4 cup finely shredded carrot
1/3 cup all-purpose flour
1/4 cup chopped fresh parsley
2 teaspoons dried dillweed
Salt and freshly ground black pepper

Directions
1. Place the cooked millet and wild rice in a large bowl and set aside.

2. In a medium skillet, heat 1 tablespoon of the oil over medium heat. Add the onion, celery, and carrot. Cover and cook until softened, 5 minutes. Add the vegetables to the cooked grains. Stir in the flour, parsley, dillweed, and salt and pepper to taste. Mix until well combined. Refrigerate until chilled, about 20 minutes.

3. Use your hands to shape the mixture into small patties and set aside. In a large skillet, heat the remaining 2 tablespoons oil over medium heat. Add the croquettes and cook until golden brown, turning once, about 8 minutes total. Serve immediately.

Caribbean Rice, Squash, And Peas
PREP: 5 MINUTES • COOK TIME: 40 MINUTES • TOTAL: 45 MINUTES • SERVES: 4 servings

Ingredients

2 tablespoons olive oil
1 small yellow onion, chopped
2 cups peeled, seeded, and diced butternut or other winter squash
3 garlic cloves, minced
1 teaspoon dried thyme

1/2 teaspoon ground cumin
11/2 cups cooked or 1 (15.5-ounce) can black-eyed peas, drained and rinsed
1 cup long-grain rice
21/2 cups hot water
2 tablespoons chopped fresh cilantro

Directions

1. In a large saucepan, heat the oil over medium heat. Add the onion, cover, and cook until softened, about 5 minutes. Add the squash, garlic, thyme, and cumin. Cover and cook until the squash is softened, about 10 minutes. Stir in the peas, rice, and water.

2. Bring to a boil, then reduce heat to low. Cover and simmer until the rice is cooked, about 30 minutes. Fluff with a fork and sprinkle with cilantro. Serve immediately.

Green Tea Rice With Lemon Snow Peas And Tofu
PREP: 7 MINUTES • COOK TIME: 30 MINUTES • TOTAL: 37 MINUTES • SERVES: 4 servings

Ingredients

3 cups water
4 green tea bags
11/2 cups white sushi rice
2 tablespoons canola or grapeseed oil
8 ounces extra-firm tofu, drained and cut into 1/4-inch dice

3 green onions, minced
2 cups snow peas, trimmed and cut diagonally into 1-inch pieces
1 tablespoon fresh lemon juice
1 teaspoon grated lemon zest
Salt and freshly ground black pepper

Directions

1. In a large saucepan, bring the water to a boil. Add the tea bags and remove from the heat. Let stand for 7 minutes and remove and discard the tea bags. Rinse the rice under running water until the water runs clear, then add to the brewed tea. Cover and cook over medium heat until tender, about 25 minutes. Remove from heat and set aside.

2. In a large skillet, heat the oil over medium heat. Add the tofu and cook until golden brown, 5 minutes. Add the green onions and snow peas and cook until softened, 3 minutes. Stir in the lemon juice and zest.

3. In a large bowl, combine the cooked rice with the tofu and snow pea mixture. Season with salt and pepper to taste, and serve immediately.

Brown Rice And Lentil Pilaf
PREP: 15 MINUTES • COOK TIME: 50 MINUTES • TOTAL: 65 MINUTES • SERVES: 4 to 6 servings

Ingredients

1 tablespoon olive oil
1 large yellow onion, minced
1 medium carrot, chopped
2 garlic cloves, minced
1 cup long-grain brown rice
11/2 teaspoons ground coriander

1/2 teaspoon ground cumin
3 cups water
Salt
3 tablespoons minced fresh cilantro
Freshly ground black pepper

Directions

1. Bring a saucepan of salted water to a boil over high heat. Add the lentils, return to a boil, then reduce heat to medium and cook for 15 minutes. Drain and set aside. In a large saucepan, heat the oil over medium heat. Add the onion, carrot, and garlic, cover, and cook until tender, 10 minutes.
2. Add the lentils to the vegetable mixture. Add the rice, coriander, and cumin. Stir in the water and bring to a boil. Reduce heat to low, salt the water, and cook, covered, until the lentils and rice are tender, about 30 minutes. Remove from heat and set aside for 10 minutes.
3. Transfer to a large bowl, fluff with a fork, and sprinkle with the cilantro and freshly ground black pepper. Serve immediately.

Savory Beans And Rice
PREP: 5 MINUTES • COOK TIME: 40 MINUTES • TOTAL: 55 MINUTES • SERVES: 4 servings

Ingredients

1 tablespoon olive oil
3 green onions, chopped
1 teaspoon grated fresh ginger
1 cup brown basmati rice
2 cups water
1 tablespoon soy sauce

Salt
11/2 cups cooked or 1 (15.5-ounce) can Great Northern white beans, drained and rinsed
1 tablespoon nutritional yeast
1 tablespoon minced fresh savory or 11/2 teaspoons dried

Directions

1. In a large saucepan, heat the oil over medium heat. Add the green onions and ginger and cook until fragrant, about 1 minute. Add the rice, water, soy sauce, and salt to taste. Cover and bring to a boil.
2. Reduce heat to low and simmer, covered, until the rice is tender, about 30 minutes. Stir in the beans, nutritional yeast, and savory. Cook, uncovered, stirring, until heated through and the liquid is absorbed, about 10 minutes. Serve immediately.

Mexican Green Rice And Beans
PREP: 10 MINUTES • COOK TIME: 40 MINUTES • TOTAL: 50 MINUTES • SERVES: 4 servings

Ingredients

1 large green bell pepper
2 or 3 small fresh jalapeño or other hot green chiles
21/2 cups vegetable broth
1/2 cup coarsely chopped fresh parsley
1 small yellow onion, chopped
2 garlic cloves, chopped
1/4 teaspoon freshly ground black pepper
1 teaspoon sugar

1/2 teaspoon dried oregano
1/4 teaspoon ground cumin
3 tablespoons canola or grapeseed oil
1 cup long-grain white rice
Salt
11/2 cups cooked or 1 (15.5-ounce) can dark red kidney beans, drained and rinsed
2 tablespoons minced fresh cilantro, garnish

Directions

1. Roast the bell pepper and chiles over a gas flame or under a broiler until the skin blisters, turning on all sides. Place in a paper bag for 5 minutes. Use a damp towel to rub off scorched bits of skin. Stem, seed, and chop the bell pepper and chiles and place them in a food processor. Add 1 cup of the broth, parsley, onion, garlic, pepper, sugar, oregano, and cumin and process until smooth. Set aside.
2. In a large skillet, heat the oil over medium heat. Add the rice and stir constantly for a few minutes to coat the rice with the oil. Add the pureed vegetables and simmer, stirring occasionally, for 5 minutes. Add the remaining 11/2 cups broth and bring to a boil. Reduce the heat to medium, add salt to taste, cover, and cook until the liquid is absorbed, about 30 minutes. About 10 minutes before ready to serve, stir in the kidney beans. Garnish with cilantro and serve immediately.

Balsamic Black Beans
PREP: 5 MINUTES • COOK TIME: 20 MINUTES • TOTAL: 25 MINUTES • SERVES: 5

Ingredients
1 teaspoon extra-virgin olive oil or vegetable broth
½ cup diced sweet onion
1 teaspoon ground cumin
1 teaspoon ground cardamom (optional)

2 (14.5-ounce) cans black beans, rinsed and drained
¼ to ½ cup vegetable broth
2 tablespoons balsamic vinegar

Directions
Preparing the Ingredients.
1. In a large pot over medium-high heat, heat the olive oil.
   Add the onion, cumin, and cardamom (if using) and sauté for 3 to 5 minutes, until the onion is translucent. Add the beans and ¼ cup broth, and bring to a boil. Add up to ½ cup more of broth for "soupier" beans.
   Cover, reduce the heat, and simmer for 10 minutes. Add the balsamic vinegar, increase the heat to medium-high, and cook for 3 more minutes uncovered. Transfer to a large storage container, or divide the beans evenly among 5 single-serving storage containers. Let cool before sealing the lids.
2. Place the airtight containers in the refrigerator for up to 5 days or freeze for up to 2 months. To thaw, refrigerate overnight. Reheat in the microwave for 1½ to 3 minutes.

Per Serving: Calories: 200; Fat: 2g; Protein: 13g; Carbohydrates: 34g; Fiber: 12g; Sugar: 1g; Sodium: 41mg

Pesto & White Bean Pasta
PREP: 15 MINUTES • COOK TIME: 10 MINUTES • TOTAL: 25 MINUTES • SERVES: 4

Ingredients
8 ounces rotini pasta, cooked according to the package directions, drained, and rinsed with cold water to cool
1½ cups canned cannellini beans or navy beans, drained and rinsed

½ cup Spinach Pesto
1 cup chopped tomato or red bell pepper
¼ red onion, finely diced
½ cup chopped pitted black olives

Directions
Preparing the Ingredients.
1. In a large bowl, combine the pasta, beans, and pesto. Toss to combine.

2. Add the tomato, red onion, and olives, tossing thoroughly. Store leftovers in an airtight container in the refrigerator for up to 1 week.

Per Serving Calories: 544; Protein: 23g; Total fat: 17g; Saturated fat: 3g; Carbohydrates: 83g; Fiber: 13g

Dilly White Beans
PREP: 5 MINUTES • COOK TIME: 20 MINUTES • TOTAL: 5 MINUTES • SERVES: 6

Ingredients
1 teaspoon extra-virgin olive oil or ¼ cup vegetable broth
1 small sweet onion, cut into half-moon slices
2 (14.5-ounce) cans great northern beans, rinsed and drained
½ cup vegetable broth
2 teaspoons dried dill
½ teaspoon salt (optional)
¼ teaspoon freshly ground black pepper

Directions
Preparing the Ingredients.
1. In a large skillet or wok over medium-high heat, heat the olive oil. Sauté the onion slices for 3 to 5 minutes, until the onion is translucent.
2. Add the beans, broth, dill, salt (if using), and pepper. Bring to a boil. Reduce the heat to low and simmer, uncovered, for 10 minutes.
   Transfer to a large storage container, or scoop ½ cup of beans into each of 6 storage containers. Let cool before sealing the lids.

Per Serving: Calories: 155; Fat: 1g; Protein: 10g; Carbohydrates: 26g; Fiber: 9g; Sugar: 1g; Sodium: 67mg

Quinoa Pilaf
PREP: 10 MINUTES • COOK TIME: 15 MINUTES • TOTAL: 25 MINUTES • SERVES: 4

Ingredients
1 cup quinoa
2 cups vegetable stock
¼ cup pine nuts
2 tablespoons olive oil

½ onion, chopped
⅓ cup chopped fresh parsley
sea salt
freshly ground black pepper

Directions
Preparing the Ingredients.
1. In a medium pot, bring the quinoa and vegetable stock to a boil over medium-high heat, stirring occasionally. Reduce to a simmer.
2. Cover and cook until the quinoa is soft, about 15 minutes. Meanwhile, heat a large sauté pan over medium-high heat. Add the pine nuts to the dry hot pan and toast, stirring frequently, until the nuts are fragrant, 2 to 3 minutes. Remove the pine nuts from the pan and set aside. Add the olive oil to the same pan and heat until it shimmers. Add the onion and cook until soft, about 5 minutes. When the quinoa is soft and all the liquid is absorbed, remove it from the heat and fluff it with a fork. Stir in the pine nuts, onion, and parsley. Season with salt and pepper. Serve hot.

Five-Spice Farro
PREP: 3 MINUTES • COOK TIME: 35 MINUTES • TOTAL: 38 MINUTES • SERVES: 4

Ingredients

1 cup dried farro, rinsed and drained | 1 teaspoon five-spice powder

Directions

Preparing the Ingredients.

1. In a medium pot, combine the farro, five-spice powder, and enough water to cover.
   Bring to a boil; reduce the heat to medium-low, and simmer for 30 minutes. Drain off any excess water.
   Transfer to a large storage container, or scoop 1 cup farro into each of 4 storage containers. Let cool before sealing the lids.
   Place the airtight containers in the refrigerator for 1 week or freeze for up to 3 months. To thaw, refrigerate overnight. Reheat in the microwave for 1½ to 3 minutes.

Per Serving: Calories: 73; Fat: 0g; Protein: 3g; Carbohydrates: 15g; Fiber: 1g; Sugar: 0g; Sodium: 0mg

Italian Rice With Seitan And Mushrooms
PREP: 15 MINUTES • COOK TIME: 0 MINUTES • TOTAL: 15 MINUTES • SERVES: 4 servings

Ingredients

2 cups water
1 cup long-grain brown or white rice
2 tablespoons olive oil
1 medium yellow onion, chopped
2 garlic cloves, minced
8 ounces seitan, homemade or store-bought, chopped

8 ounces white mushrooms, chopped
1 teaspoon dried basil
1/2 teaspoon ground fennel seed
1/4 teaspoon crushed red pepper
Salt and freshly ground black pepper

Directions

1. In a large saucepan, bring the water to boil over high heat. Add the rice, reduce the heat to low, cover, and cook until tender, about 30 minutes.
2. In a large skillet, heat the oil over medium heat. Add the onion, cover, and cook until softened, about 5 minutes. Add the seitan and cook uncovered until browned. Stir in the mushrooms and cook until tender, about 5 minutes longer. Stir in the basil, fennel, crushed red pepper, and salt and black pepper to taste.
3. Transfer the cooked rice to large serving bowl. Stir in the seitan mixture and mix thoroughly. Add a generous amount of black pepper and serve immediately.

Spanish Rice And Beans
PREP: 10 MINUTES • COOK TIME: 40 MINUTES • TOTAL: 50 MINUTES • SERVES: 4 servings

Ingredients

1 tablespoon olive oil
1 medium yellow onion, chopped
1 medium green bell pepper, chopped
2 garlic cloves, minced
1 (14.5-ounce) can diced tomatoes, undrained
1 tablespoon capers, chopped if large
1/4 teaspoon crushed red pepper

11/2 cups long-grain brown rice
3 cups vegetable broth
Salt
11/2 cups cooked or 1 (15.5-ounce) can dark red kidney beans, drained and rinsed
1/4 cup sliced pitted kalamata olives
2 tablespoons minced fresh parsley

Directions

1. In a large saucepan, heat the oil over medium heat. Add the onion, bell pepper, and garlic. Cover and cook until softened, about 5 minutes. Add the tomatoes and their juice, the capers, and the crushed red pepper. Stir to combine and simmer for 5 minutes to blend the flavors.
2. Add the rice and broth and bring to a boil, then reduce heat to low. Add salt to taste. Cover and cook until the rice is tender and the liquid is evaporated, 30 to 40 minutes. Remove from heat and stir in the beans, olives, and parsley. Cover and set aside for 10 minutes before serving. Serve immediately.

GGB Bowl
PREP: 10 MINUTES • COOK TIME: 5 MINUTES • TOTAL: 15 MINUTES • SERVES: 2

Ingredients
2 teaspoons olive oil
1 cup cooked brown rice, quinoa, or your grain of choice
1 (15-ounce) can chickpeas or your beans of choice, rinsed and drained

1 bunch spinach or kale, stemmed and roughly chopped
1 tablespoon soy sauce or gluten-free tamari
Sea salt
Black pepper

Directions
Preparing the Ingredients.
1. In a large skillet, heat the oil over medium heat.
2. Add the rice, beans, and greens and stir continuously until the greens have wilted and everything is heated through, 3 to 5 minutes. Drizzle in the soy sauce, mix to combine, and season with salt and pepper.

Brown Rice With Artichokes, Chickpeas, And Tomatoes
PREP: 5 MINUTES • COOK TIME: 30 MINUTES • TOTAL: 35 MINUTES • SERVES: 4 servings

Ingredients
2 tablespoons olive oil
3 garlic cloves, minced
1 cup frozen artichokes hearts, thawed and chopped
1 teaspoon dried basil
1/2 teaspoon dried marjoram

11/2 cups cooked or 1 (15.5-ounce) can chickpeas, drained and rinsed
11/2 cups long-grain brown rice
3 cups vegetable broth
Salt and freshly ground black pepper
1 cup ripe grape tomatoes, quartered
2 tablespoons minced fresh parsley

Directions
1. In a large saucepan, heat the oil over medium heat. Add the garlic and cook until softened, about 1 minute. Add the artichokes, basil, marjoram, and chickpeas. Stir in the rice and broth. Season with salt and pepper to taste.
2. Cover tightly and reduce heat to low. Simmer until the rice is cooked, about 30 minutes. Transfer to a serving bowl, add the tomatoes and parsley, taste, adjusting seasonings if necessary, and fluff with a fork. Serve immediately.

Fried Rice
PREP: 10 MINUTES • COOK TIME: 15 MINUTES • TOTAL: 25 MINUTES • SERVES: 6

Ingredients
2 tablespoons sesame oil
1 onion, diced

1 carrot, diced
1 cup sugar snap peas

1 cup sliced shiitake mushrooms
2 garlic cloves, minced
1 tablespoon grated fresh ginger

¼ cup soy sauce
2 cups prepared rice (brown or white)
3 green onions (white and green parts), chopped

Directions
Preparing the Ingredients.
1. In a large sauté pan or wok, heat the sesame oil until it shimmers. Add the onion and carrot. Cook until the vegetables soften, about 3 minutes. Add the peas and mushrooms and cook, stirring frequently, until they soften, 5 to 7 minutes. Add the garlic and ginger and cook until they are fragrant, about 30 seconds.
2. Add the soy sauce and rice. Cook, stirring, until heated through. Stir in the green onions and serve immediately.

Baked Wild Rice
PREP: 5 MINUTES • COOK TIME: 1 HOUR 10 MINUTES • TOTAL: 1 HOUR 15MINUTES• SERVES: 4

Ingredients
1 tablespoon vegan butter or extra-virgin olive oil or 2 tablespoons water
1 cup chopped white or yellow onion
½ cup chopped carrot
½ cup chopped celery

1 cup chopped mushrooms
1½ cups wild rice
4 cups vegetable broth
1 cup chopped dried cranberries or cherries
½ cup chopped pistachios

Directions
Preparing the Ingredients.
1. Preheat the oven to 375ºF.
2. In a Dutch oven with a lid or in a large, oven-safe skillet over medium-high heat, heat the vegan butter. Add the onion, carrot, and celery and sauté for 5 minutes. Add the mushrooms and sauté for 3 more minutes. Stir in the rice and broth, mixing well.
3. Cover with a lid or aluminum foil and bake for 30 minutes Remove the pan from the oven, uncover, and stir in the dried cranberries. Return to the oven uncovered and bake for 20 to 30 minutes longer, until the liquid is absorbed and the rice is tender. Remove from the oven and stir in the pistachios. Divide the rice evenly among 4 storage containers. Let cool before sealing the lids.

Per Serving: Calories: 355; Fat: 8g; Protein: 11g; Carbohydrates: 63g; Fiber: 7g; Sugar: 14g; Sodium: 496mg

Stovetop   Thanksgiving Rice Stuffing
PREP: 10 MINUTES • COOK TIME: 15 MINUTES • TOTAL: 25 MINUTES • SERVES: 8

Ingredients
¼ cup vegan butter
1 onion, chopped
2 celery stalks, thinly sliced
1 (8-ounce) package baby bella or white button mushrooms, stemmed and sliced
3 garlic cloves, minced
½ cup low-sodium vegetable broth

½ cup dried cranberries or cherries
½ cup chopped walnuts, toasted
2 cups cooked wild-rice blend or brown rice
1 teaspoon poultry seasoning
1 teaspoon sea salt
Chopped fresh parsley, for garnish

Directions
Preparing the Ingredients.

1. Melt the butter in a large skillet over medium heat.
2. Add the onion, celery, and mushrooms and sauté for 5 minutes, or until soft. Add the garlic and sauté for 1 additional minute, or until fragrant. Add the broth, cranberries, and walnuts. Bring to a boil, cover, reduce the heat, and simmer for 5 minutes, or until fragrant. Add the rice, poultry seasoning, and salt and mix well to combine. Continue to cook, uncovered, for 4 minutes, stirring occasionally, or until heated through and all the liquid evaporates. Transfer to a serving dish and garnish with parsley.

Easy Kitchari
PREP: 20 MINUTES • COOK TIME: 20 MINUTES • TOTAL: 40 MINUTES • SERVES: 5

Ingredients

½ cup yellow mung beans or split peas
½ cup basmati rice
1 small red onion, diced
1 (14.5-ounce) can diced tomatoes
5 teaspoons minced garlic (about 5 cloves)
1 jalapeño, seeded
½ teaspoon ground ginger or 2 tablespoons minced fresh ginger
1 teaspoon ground turmeric
2 tablespoons to ¼ cup water
1 teaspoon extra-virgin olive oil or 1 to 2 tablespoons vegetable broth

1¼ teaspoons ground cumin
1¼ teaspoons ground coriander
1 teaspoon fennel seeds
4 cups chopped vegetables (mix of carrot, cauliflower, summer or winter squash, broccoli, and/or potatoes)
3 cups water
Juice of 1 large lemon
1 to 2 teaspoons salt, to taste
½ teaspoon freshly ground black pepper

Directions
Preparing the Ingredients.
1. Rinse and drain the beans and rice. Transfer to a small bowl and soak in water for 15 minutes.
2. In a food processor or blender, purée the onion, tomatoes with their juices, garlic, jalapeño, ginger, turmeric, and 2 tablespoons of water, adding water as necessary, until you reach a sauce consistency that pours easily and is not chunky.
3. In a large pot over medium-high heat, heat the olive oil. Add the cumin, coriander, and fennel seeds and sauté, stirring constantly, just until fragrant.
Transfer the purée to the pot. Drain and rinse the soaked rice and beans, and add them to the pot. Add the chopped vegetables and water and combine well.
Bring to a boil. Cover, reduce the heat to low, and simmer for 15 to 20 minutes, until the beans and rice are soft but not mushy. Add the lemon juice, and taste before adding the salt and pepper. Into each of 5 single-serving storage containers, spoon 2 cups.
Let cool before sealing.

Per Serving: Calories: 234; Fat: 3g; Protein: 7g; Carbohydrates: 47g; Fiber: 13g; Sugar: 5g; Sodium: 862mg

Chickpea And Artichoke Curry
PREP: 10 MINUTES • COOK TIME: 15 MINUTES • TOTAL: 25 MINUTES • SERVES: 4

Ingredients

1 teaspoon extra-virgin olive oil or 2 teaspoons vegetable broth
1 small onion, diced
2 teaspoons minced garlic (2 cloves)

1 (14.5-ounce) can chickpeas, rinsed and drained
1 (14.5-ounce) can artichoke hearts, drained and quartered
2 teaspoons curry powder

½ teaspoon ground coriander
½ teaspoon ground cumin

1 (5.4-ounce) can unsweetened coconut milk

Directions
Preparing the Ingredients.
1. In a large skillet or pot over medium-high heat, heat the olive oil. Add the onion and garlic and sauté for about 5 minutes. Add the chickpeas, artichoke hearts, curry powder, coriander, and cumin. Stir to combine well.
2. Pour the coconut milk into the pot, mix well, and bring to a boil. Cover, reduce the heat to low, and simmer for 10 minutes.
   Divide the curry evenly among 4 wide-mouth glass jars or single-compartment containers. Let cool before sealing the lids.

   Per Serving: Calories: 267; Fat: 12g; Protein: 9g; Carbohydrates: 36g; Fiber: 11g; Sugar: 3g; Sodium: 373mg

Curried Lentils (Pressure cooker)
PREP: 6 MINUTES • PRESSURE: 20 MINUTES • TOTAL: 60 MINUTES • PRESSURE LEVEL: HIGH • RELEASE: NATURAL • SERVES 6-8

Ingredients
1 tablespoon coconut oil
2 tablespoons mild curry powder
1 teaspoon ground ginger
½ teaspoon ground turmeric (optional)
1 cup dried green lentils or brown lentils

3 cups water
1 teaspoon freshly squeezed lime juice (optional)
½ teaspoon salt
Freshly ground black pepper (optional)

Directions
1. **Preparing the Ingredients.** On your electric pressure cooker, select Sauté. Add the coconut oil, curry powder, ginger, and turmeric (if using) and toss to toast for 1 minute. Add the lentils and toss with the spices. Add the water. Cancel Sauté.
2. **High pressure for 20 minutes.** Close and lock the lid and ensure the pressure valve is sealed, then select High Pressure and set the time for 20 minutes.
3. **Pressure Release.** Once the cook time is complete, let the pressure release naturally, about 30 minutes.
4. Once all the pressure has released, carefully unlock and remove the lid. Stir in the lime juice (if using). Season with the salt and pepper, if you like.
   PER SERVING Calories: 212; Total fat: 5g; Protein: 13g; Sodium: 2mg; Fiber: 16g

Pest Pearled Barley
PREP: 1 MINUTE • COOK TIME: 50 MINUTES • TOTAL: 51 MINUTES • SERVES: 4

Ingredients
1 cup dried barley
2½ cups vegetable broth

½ cup Parm-y Kale Pesto

Directions
Preparing the Ingredients.
1. In a medium saucepan, combine the barley and broth and bring to a boil.
2. Cover, reduce the heat to low, and simmer for about 45 minutes, until tender.
   Remove from the stove and let stand for 5 minutes. Fluff the barley, then gently fold in the pesto. Scoop about ¾ cup into each of 4 single-compartment storage containers. Let cool before sealing the lids.

Per Serving: Calories: 237; Fat: 6g; Protein: 9g; Carbohydrates: 40g; Fiber: 11g; Sugar: 2g; Sodium: 365mg

Spicy Picnic Beans
PREP: 15 MINUTES • COOK TIME: 15 MINUTES • TOTAL: 30 MINUTES • SERVES: 6

Ingredients
1 jalapeño, cut into strips
1 red bell pepper, cut into strips
1 green bell pepper, cut into strips
1 onion, chopped
5 garlic cloves, minced
two 15-ounce cans pinto beans, drained and rinsed

one 15-ounce can kidney beans, drained and rinsed
one 15-ounce can chickpeas, drained and rinsed
one 18-ounce bottle barbecue sauce
½ teaspoon chipotle powder
sea salt
freshly ground black pepper

Directions
Preparing the Ingredients.
1. In the bowl of a food processor, combine the jalapeño, bell peppers, onion, and garlic and blend for ten 1-second pulses, stopping halfway through to scrape down the sides of the bowl. In a large pot, combine the processed mixture with the beans, barbecue sauce, and chipotle powder.
2. Simmer over medium-high heat, stirring frequently to blend the flavors, about 15 minutes. Season with salt and pepper. Serve hot. You can make this ahead of time and store it in a tightly sealed container for up to 3 days in the refrigerator. The flavors will blend and deepen as the beans rest.

Chipotle Chickpeas (Pressure Cooker)
PREP: 8 MINUTES • PRESSURE: 20 MINUTES • TOTAL: 45 MINUTES • PRESSURE LEVEL: HIGH • RELEASE: NATURAL• SERVES 4-6

Ingredients
1 cup dried chickpeas, soaked in water overnight
2 cups water
¼ cup sun-dried tomatoes, chopped
1 to 2 tablespoons olive oil
2 teaspoons ground chipotle pepper
1½ teaspoons ground cumin

1½ teaspoons onion powder
1 teaspoon dried oregano
¾ teaspoon garlic powder
½ teaspoon smoked paprika
¼ to ½ teaspoon salt

Directions
1. **Preparing the Ingredients.** Drain and rinse the chickpeas, drain again, and put them in your electric pressure cooker's cooking pot. Add the water, sun-dried tomatoes, olive oil, chipotle pepper, cumin, onion powder, oregano, garlic powder, and paprika.
2. **High pressure for 20 minutes**. Lock the lid and ensure the pressure valve is sealed, then select High Pressure and set the time for 20 minutes.
3. **Pressure Release.** Once the cook time is complete, let the pressure release naturally, about 15 minutes. Once all the pressure has released, unlock and remove the lid. Taste and season with salt and more oil or seasonings if you like.

PER SERVING Calories: 280; Total fat: 7g; Protein: 13g; Sodium: 168mg; Fiber: 12g

Cinnamon Chickpeas (Pressure Cooker)
PREP: 12 MINUTES • PRESSURE: 30 MINUTES • TOTAL: 50 MINUTES • PRESSURE LEVEL: HIGH • RELEASE: NATURAL• SERVES 4-6

Ingredients
1 cup dried chickpeas, soaked in water overnight

2 cups water

2 teaspoons ground cinnamon, plus more as needed
½ teaspoon ground nutmeg (optional)

1 tablespoon coconut oil
2 to 4 tablespoons unrefined sugar or brown sugar, plus more as needed

Directions

1. **Preparing the Ingredients.** Drain and rinse the chickpeas, then put them in your electric pressure cooker's cooking pot. Add the water, cinnamon, and nutmeg (if using).
2. **High pressure for 30 minutes.** Lock the lid and ensure the pressure valve is sealed, then select High Pressure and set the time for 30 minutes.
3. **Pressure Release.** Once the cook time is complete, let the pressure release naturally, about 15 minutes. Once all the pressure has released, unlock and remove the lid. Drain any excess water from the chickpeas and add them back to the pot. Stir in the coconut oil and sugar. Taste and add more cinnamon, if desired.

   Select Sauté and cook for about 5 minutes, stirring the chickpeas occasionally, until there's no liquid left and the sugar has melted onto the chickpeas. Transfer to a bowl and toss with additional sugar if you want to add a crunchy texture.

PER SERVING Calories: 253; Total fat: 7g; Protein: 11g; Sodium: 9mg; Fiber: 10g

Lentil Spinach Curry
PREP: 5 MINUTES • COOK TIME: 30 MINUTES • TOTAL: 35 MINUTES • SERVES: 4

Ingredients

1 teaspoon olive oil
1 onion, chopped
½-inch piece fresh ginger, peeled and minced
1 to 2 tablespoons mild curry powder
1½ cups dried green or brown lentils
2½ cups water or Vegetable Broth
1 cup canned diced tomatoes

2 to 4 cups finely chopped raw spinach
½ cup nondairy milk
2 tablespoons soy sauce (optional)
1 tablespoon apple cider vinegar or rice vinegar
1 teaspoon salt (or 2 teaspoons if omitting soy sauce)

Directions

Preparing the Ingredients.

1. Heat the olive oil in a large pot over medium heat. Add the onion, and sauté for about 3 minutes, until soft.
2. Add the ginger, and cook for 1 minute more. Stir in the curry powder, lentils, and water. Bring to a boil, turn the heat to low, and cover the pot. Simmer for 15 to 20 minutes, until the lentils are soft. Stir in the tomatoes, spinach, milk, soy sauce (if using), vinegar, and salt. Simmer for about 3 minutes, until heated through. If you prefer, use an immersion blender to half-blend this in the pot for a creamier texture and to hide the spinach. Store in an airtight container for 4 to 5 days in the refrigerator or up to 1 month in the freezer.

Per Serving Calories: 313; Protein: 21g; Total fat: 3g; Saturated fat: 0g; Carbohydrates: 52g; Fiber: 24g

Peas and Pesto Rice
PREP: 5 MINUTES • COOK TIME: 5 MINUTES • TOTAL: 10 MINUTES • SERVES: 3

Ingredients

1 cup Pistachio Pesto or store bought vegan pesto
1 cup frozen peas, thawed
2 cups cooked brown rice

Directions

Preparing the Ingredients.

1. In a large skillet, warm the pesto sauce and peas over low heat for 3 to 5 minutes, until heated through. Add the rice and mix until everything is coated.

White Bean Burgers

PREP: 10 MINUTES • COOK TIME: 10 MINUTES • TOTAL: 20 MINUTES • SERVES: 4

Ingredients

1 tablespoon olive oil, plus more for coating the baking sheet
¼ cup couscous
¼ cup boiling water
1 (15-ounce) can white beans, drained and rinsed
2 tablespoons balsamic vinegar
2 tablespoons chopped sun-dried tomatoes or olives
½ teaspoon garlic powder or 1 garlic clove, finely minced
½ teaspoon salt
4 burger buns
Lettuce leaves, for serving
Tomato slices, for serving
Condiments of choice, such as ketchup, olive tapenade, *Creamy Tahini Dressing*, and/or *Spinach Pesto*

Directions

Preparing the Ingredients.

If baking, preheat the oven to 350°F.

1. Coat a rimmed baking sheet with olive oil or line it with parchment paper or a silicone mat. In a medium heat-proof bowl, combine the couscous and boiling water.
2. Cover and set aside for about 5 minutes. Once the couscous is soft and the water is absorbed, fluff it with a fork. Add the beans, and mash them to a chunky texture. Add the vinegar, olive oil, sun-dried tomatoes, garlic powder, and salt; stir until combined but still a bit chunky. Divide the mixture into 4 portions, and shape each into a patty. Put the patties on the prepared baking sheet, and bake for 25 to 30 minutes, until slightly crispy on the edges. Alternatively, heat some olive oil in a large skillet over medium heat, then add the patties, making sure each has oil under it.
3. Fry for about 5 minutes, until the bottoms are browned. Flip, adding more oil as needed, and fry for about 5 minutes more. Serve the burgers on buns with lettuce, tomato, and your choice of condiments.

Chickpeas with Lemon and Spinach

PREP: 10 MINUTES • COOK TIME: 10 MINUTES • TOTAL: 20 MINUTES • SERVES: 4

Ingredients

3 tablespoons olive oil
one 15-ounce can chickpeas, drained and rinsed
10 ounces baby spinach
½ teaspoon sea salt
juice and zest of 1 lemon
freshly ground black pepper

Directions

Preparing the Ingredients.

1. In a large sauté pan, heat the olive oil over medium-high heat until it shimmers. Add the chickpeas and cook until they are heated through, about 5 minutes.
2. Add the spinach and stir just until it wilts, about 5 minutes. Add the salt, lemon juice, lemon zest, and pepper and stir to combine. Serve immediately.

Brown Rice and Lentils
PREP: 10 MINUTES • COOK TIME: 15 MINUTES • TOTAL: 25 MINUTES • SERVES: 4

Ingredients
2 tablespoons olive oil
1 onion, diced
1 carrot, diced
1 celery stalk, diced
two 15-ounce cans lentils, drained and rinsed
one 15-ounce can diced tomatoes with juice
1 tablespoon dried rosemary
1 tablespoon garlic powder
2 cups prepared brown rice
sea salt
freshly ground black pepper

Directions
Preparing the Ingredients.
1. In a large pot, heat the olive oil over medium-high heat until it shimmers.
2. Add the onion, carrot, and celery and cook until the vegetables soften, about 5 minutes. Add the lentils, tomatoes, rosemary, and garlic powder. Lower the heat to -medium-low and simmer to blend the flavors, 5 to 7 minutes. Stir the rice into lentils and heat through, 2 to 3 minutes. Season with salt and -pepper and serve immediately.

Grilled Portobello with Mashed Potatoes and Green Beans

PREP: 20 MINUTES • COOK TIME: 40 MINUTES • TOTAL: 60 MINUTES • SERVES: 4

Ingredients

FOR THE GRILLED PORTOBELLOS

4 large portobello mushrooms

1 teaspoon olive oil

Pinch sea salt

FOR THE MASHED POTATOES

6 large potatoes, scrubbed or peeled, and chopped

3 to 4 garlic cloves, minced

½ teaspoon olive oil

½ cup non-dairy milk

2 tablespoons coconut oil (optional)

2 tablespoons nutritional yeast (optional)

Pinch sea salt

FOR THE GREEN BEANS

2 cups green beans, cut into 1-inch pieces

2 to 3 teaspoons coconut oil

Pinch sea salt

1 to 2 tablespoons nutritional yeast (optional)

Directions

1. **TO MAKE THE GRILLED PORTOBELLOS**

   Preheat the grill to medium, or the oven to 350°F.

   Take the stems out of the mushrooms.

   Wipe the caps clean with a damp paper towel, then dry them. Spray the caps with a bit of olive oil, or put some oil in your hand and rub it over the mushrooms.

   Rub the oil onto the top and bottom of each mushroom, then sprinkle them with a bit of salt on top and bottom.

   Put them bottom side facing up on a baking sheet in the oven, or straight on the grill. They'll take about 30 minutes in the oven, or 20 minutes on the grill. Wait until they're soft and wrinkling around the edges. If you keep them bottom up, all the delicious mushroom juice will pool in the cap. Then at the very end, you can flip them over to drain the juice. If you like it, you can drizzle it over the mashed potatoes.

2. **TO MAKE THE MASHED POTATOES**

   Boil the chopped potatoes in lightly salted water for about 20 minutes, until soft. While they're cooking, sauté the garlic in the olive oil, or bake them whole in a 350°F oven for 10 minutes, then squeeze out the flesh. Drain the potatoes, reserving about ½ cup water to mash them. In a large bowl, mash the potatoes with a little bit of the reserved water, the cooked garlic, milk, coconut oil (if using), nutritional yeast (if using), and salt to taste. Add more water, a little at a time, if needed, to get the texture you want. If you use an immersion blender or beater to purée them, you'll have some extra-creamy potatoes.

3. **TO MAKE THE GREEN BEAN**

   Heat a medium pot with a small amount of water to boil, then steam the green beans by either putting them directly in the pot or in a steaming basket.

Once they're slightly soft and vibrantly green, 7 to 8 minutes, take them off the heat and toss them with the oil, salt, and nutritional yeast (if using).

Per Serving: Calories: 263; Total fat: 7g; Carbs: 43g; Fiber: 7g; Protein: 10g

Tahini Broccoli Slaw
PREP: 15 MINUTES • COOK TIME: 0 MINUTES • TOTAL: 15 MINUTES • SERVES: 4 to 6 servings

Ingredients

1/4 cup tahini (sesame paste)
2 tablespoons white miso
1 tablespoon rice vinegar
1 tablespoon toasted sesame oil
2 teaspoons soy sauce
1 (12-ounce) bag broccoli slaw
2 green onions, minced
1/4 cup toasted sesame seeds

Directions

1. In a large bowl, whisk together the tahini, miso, vinegar, oil, and soy sauce. Add the broccoli slaw, green onions, and sesame seeds and toss to coat.
2. Set aside for 20 minutes before serving.

Steamed Cauliflower
PREP: 5 MINUTES • COOK TIME: 10 MINUTES • TOTAL: 15 MINUTES • SERVES: 6

Ingredients

1 large head cauliflower
1 cup water
½ teaspoon salt
1 teaspoon red pepper flakes (optional)

Directions

Preparing the Ingredients.

1. Remove any leaves from the cauliflower, and cut it into florets.
   In a large saucepan, bring the water to a boil. Place a steamer basket over the water, and add the florets and salt. Cover and steam for 5 to 7 minutes, until tender. In a large bowl, toss the cauliflower with the red pepper flakes (if using). Transfer the florets to a large airtight container or 6 single-serving containers. Let cool before sealing the lids.

Per Serving: Calories: 35; Fat: 0g; Protein: 3g; Carbohydrates: 7g; Fiber: 4g; Sugar: 4g; Sodium: 236mg

Roasted Cauliflower Tacos

PREP: 10 MINUTES • COOK TIME: 30 MINUTES • TOTAL: 40 MINUTES

• SERVES: 8 TACOS

Ingredients

FOR THE ROASTED CAULIFLOWER

1 head cauliflower, cut into bite-size pieces
1 tablespoon olive oil (optional)
2 tablespoons whole-wheat flour
2 tablespoons nutritional yeast
1 to 2 teaspoons smoked paprika
½ to 1 teaspoon chili powder
Pinch sea salt

FOR THE TACOS

2 cups shredded lettuce
2 cups cherry tomatoes, quartered
2 carrots, scrubbed or peeled, and grated
½ cup Fresh Mango Salsa
½ cup *Guacamole*
8 small whole-grain or corn tortillas
1 lime, cut into 8 wedges

Directions

1. **TO MAKE THE ROASTED CAULIFLOWER**
   Preheat the oven to 350°F. Lightly grease a large rectangular baking sheet with olive oil, or line it with parchment paper. In a large bowl, toss the cauliflower pieces with oil (if using), or just rinse them so they're wet. The idea is to get the seasonings to stick. In a smaller bowl, mix together the flour, nutritional yeast, paprika, chili powder, and salt.
   Add the seasonings to the cauliflower, and mix it around with your hands to thoroughly coat. Spread the cauliflower on the baking sheet, and roast for 20 to 30 minutes, or until softened.

2. **TO MAKE THE TACOS.** Prep the veggies, salsa, and guacamole while the cauliflower is roasting. Once the cauliflower is cooked, heat the tortillas for just a few minutes in the oven or in a small skillet. Set everything out on the table, and assemble your tacos as you go. Give a squeeze of fresh lime just before eating.

Per Serving (1 taco): Calories: 198; Total fat: 6g; Carbs: 32g; Fiber: 6g; Protein: 7g

Cajun Sweet Potatoes

PREP: 5 MINUTES • COOK TIME: 30 MINUTES • TOTAL: 35 MINUTES • SERVES: 4

Ingredients

2 pounds sweet potatoes
2 teaspoons extra-virgin olive oil
½ teaspoon ground cayenne pepper
½ teaspoon smoked paprika
½ teaspoon dried oregano
½ teaspoon dried thyme
½ teaspoon garlic powder

½ teaspoon salt (optional)
Directions

Preparing the Ingredients.

1. Preheat the oven to 400ºF. Line a baking sheet with parchment paper.
    Wash the potatoes, pat dry, and cut into ¾-inch cubes. Transfer to a large bowl, and pour the olive oil over the potatoes.
    In a small bowl, combine the cayenne, paprika, oregano, thyme, and garlic powder. Sprinkle the spices over the potatoes and combine until the potatoes are well coated. Spread the potatoes on the prepared baking sheet in a single layer. Season with the salt (if using). Roast for 30 minutes, stirring the potatoes after 15 minutes.
    Divide the potatoes evenly among 4 single-serving containers. Let cool completely before sealing.

Per Serving: Calories: 219; Fat: 3g; Protein: 4g; Carbohydrates: 46g; Fiber: 7g; Sugar: 9g; Sodium: 125mg

Creamy Mint-Lime Spaghetti Squash
PREP: 10 MINUTES • COOK TIME: 30 MINUTES • TOTAL: 40 MINUTES • SERVES: 3

Ingredients
FOR THE DRESSING
3 tablespoons tahini
Zest and juice of 1 small lime
2 tablespoons fresh mint, minced
1 small garlic clove, pressed
1 tablespoon nutritional yeast
Pinch sea salt
FOR THE SPAGHETTI SQUASH
1 spaghetti squash
Pinch sea salt
1 cup cherry tomatoes, chopped
1 cup chopped bell pepper, any color
Freshly ground black pepper

Directions

1. TO MAKE THE DRESSING
    Make the dressing by whisking together the tahini and lime juice until thick, stirring in water if you need it, until smooth, then add the rest of the ingredients. Or you can purée all the ingredients in a blender.

2. TO MAKE THE SPAGHETTI SQUASH. Put a large pot of water on high and bring to a boil. Cut the squash in half and scoop out the seeds. Put the squash halves in the pot with the salt, and boil for about 30 minutes. Carefully remove the squash from the pot and let it cool until you can safely handle it. Set half the squash aside for another meal. Scoop out the squash from the skin, which stays hard like a shell, and break the strands apart. The flesh absorbs water while boiling, so set the "noodles" in a strainer for 10 minutes, tossing occasionally to drain. Transfer the cooked spaghetti squash to a large bowl and toss with the mint-lime dressing. Then top with the cherry tomatoes and bell pepper. Add an extra sprinkle of nutritional yeast and black pepper, if you wish.

Per Serving: Calories: 199; Total fat: 10g; Carbs: 27g; Fiber: 5g; Protein: 7g

Smoky Coleslaw
PREP: 10 MINUTES • COOK TIME: 0 MINUTES • TOTAL: 10 MINUTES • SERVES: 6

Ingredients
1 pound shredded cabbage
⅓ cup vegan mayonnaise
¼ cup unseasoned rice vinegar
3 tablespoons plain vegan yogurt or plain soymilk
1 tablespoon vegan sugar
½ teaspoon salt
¼ teaspoon freshly ground black pepper
¼ teaspoon smoked paprika
¼ teaspoon chipotle powder

Directions
Preparing the Ingredients.
1. Put the shredded cabbage in a large bowl. In a medium bowl, whisk the mayonnaise, vinegar, yogurt, sugar, salt, pepper, paprika, and chipotle powder.
    Pour over the cabbage, and mix with a spoon or spatula and until the cabbage shreds are coated. Divide the coleslaw evenly among 6 single-serving containers. Seal the lids.

Per Serving: Calories: 73; Fat: 4g; Protein: 1g; Carbohydrates: 8g; Fiber: 2g; Sugar: 5g; Sodium: 283mg

Simple Sesame Stir-Fry
PREP: 10 MINUTES • COOK TIME: 20 MINUTES • TOTAL: 30 MINUTES • SERVES: 4

Ingredients
1 cup quinoa
2 cups water
Pinch sea salt
1 head broccoli
1 to 2 teaspoons untoasted sesame oil, or olive oil
1 cup snow peas, or snap peas, ends trimmed and cut in half
1 cup frozen shelled edamame beans, or peas
2 cups chopped Swiss chard, or other large-leafed green
2 scallions, chopped
2 tablespoons water
1 teaspoon toasted sesame oil
1 tablespoon tamari, or soy sauce
2 tablespoons sesame seeds

Directions
Preparing the Ingredients.

1. Put the quinoa, water, and sea salt in a medium pot, bring it to a boil for a minute, then turn to low and simmer, covered, for 20 minutes. The quinoa is fully cooked when you see the swirl of the grains with a translucent center, and it is fluffy. Do not stir the quinoa while it is cooking.
2. Meanwhile, cut the broccoli into bite-size florets, cutting and pulling apart from the stem. Also chop the stem into bite-size pieces. Heat a large skillet to high, and sauté the broccoli in the untoasted sesame oil, with a pinch of salt to help it soften. Keep this moving continuously, so that it doesn't burn, and add an extra drizzle of oil if needed as you add the rest of the vegetables. Add the snow peas next, continuing to stir. Add the edamame until they thaw. Add the Swiss chard and scallions at the same time, tossing for only a minute to wilt. Then add 2 tablespoons of water to the hot skillet so that it sizzles and finishes the vegetables with a quick steam.
3. Dress with the toasted sesame oil and tamari, and toss one last time. Remove from the heat immediately. Serve a scoop of cooked quinoa, topped with stir-fry and sprinkled with some sesame seeds, and an extra drizzle of tamari and/or toasted sesame oil if you like.

Per Serving: Calories: 334; Total fat: 13g; Carbs: 42g; Fiber: 9g; Protein: 17g

Mediterranean Hummus Pizza
PREP: 10 MINUTES • COOK TIME: 30 MINUTES • TOTAL: 25 MINUTES • SERVES: 2 PIZZAS

Ingredients
½ zucchini, thinly sliced
½ red onion, thinly sliced
1 cup cherry tomatoes, halved
2 to 4 tablespoons pitted and chopped black olives
Pinch sea salt
Drizzle olive oil (optional)
2 prebaked pizza crusts
½ cup Classic Hummus, or Roasted Red Pepper Hummus
2 to 4 tablespoons *Cheesy Sprinkle*

Directions
Preparing the Ingredients.
1. Preheat the oven to 400°F. Place the zucchini, onion, cherry tomatoes, and olives in a large bowl, sprinkle them with the sea salt, and toss them a bit. Drizzle with a bit of olive oil (if using), to seal in the flavor and keep them from drying out in the oven.
2. Lay the two crusts out on a large baking sheet. Spread half the hummus on each crust, and top with the veggie mixture and some Cheesy Sprinkle. Pop the pizzas in the oven for 20 to 30 minutes, or until the veggies are soft.

Per Serving (1 pizza) Calories: 500; Total fat: 25g; Carbs: 58g; Fiber: 12g; Protein: 19g

Baked Brussels Sprouts
PREP: 10 MINUTES • COOK TIME: 40 MINUTES • TOTAL: 50 MINUTES • SERVES: 4

Ingredients
1 pound Brussels sprouts

2 teaspoons extra-virgin olive or canola oil
4 teaspoons minced garlic (about 4 cloves)
1 teaspoon dried oregano
½ teaspoon dried rosemary
½ teaspoon salt
¼ teaspoon freshly ground black pepper
1 tablespoon balsamic vinegar

Directions
Preparing the Ingredients.
1. Preheat the oven to 400ºF. Line a rimmed baking sheet with parchment paper. Trim and halve the Brussels sprouts. Transfer to a large bowl. Toss with the olive oil, garlic, oregano, rosemary, salt, and pepper to coat well.
2. Transfer to the prepared baking sheet. Bake for 35 to 40 minutes, shaking the pan occasionally to help with even browning, until crisp on the outside and tender on the inside. Remove from the oven and transfer to a large bowl. Stir in the balsamic vinegar, coating well.
   Divide the Brussels sprouts evenly among 4 single-serving containers. Let cool before sealing the lids.

Per Serving: Calories: 77; Fat: 3g; Protein: 4g; Carbohydrates: 12g; Fiber: 5g; Sugar: 3g; Sodium: 320mg

Minted Peas
PREP: 5 MINUTES • COOK TIME: 5 MINUTES • TOTAL: 10 MINUTES • SERVES: 4

Ingredients
1 tablespoon olive oil
4 cups peas, fresh or frozen (not canned)
½ teaspoon sea salt

freshly ground black pepper
3 tablespoons chopped fresh mint

Directions
Preparing the Ingredients.
1. In a large sauté pan, heat the olive oil over medium-high heat until hot. Add the peas and cook, about 5 minutes.
   Remove the pan from heat. Stir in the salt, season with pepper, and stir in the mint.
   Serve hot.

Edamame Donburi
PREP: 5 MINUTES • COOK TIME: 20 MINUTES • TOTAL: 25 MINUTES • SERVES: 4 servings

Ingredients
1 cup fresh or frozen shelled edamame
1 tablespoon canola or grapeseed oil
1 medium yellow onion, minced
5 shiitake mushroom caps, lightly rinsed, patted dry, and cut into 1/4-inch strips
1 teaspoon grated fresh ginger

3 green onions, minced
8 ounces firm tofu, drained and crumbled
2 tablespoons soy sauce
3 cups hot cooked white or brown rice
1 tablespoon toasted sesame oil
1 tablespoon toasted sesame seeds, for garnish

Directions
1. In a small saucepan of boiling salted water, cook the edamame until tender, about 10 minutes. Drain and set aside.

2. In a large skillet, heat the canola oil over medium heat. Add the onion, cover, and cook until softened, about 5 minutes. Add the mushrooms and cook, uncovered, 5 minutes longer. Stir in the ginger and green onions. Add the tofu and soy sauce and cook until heated through, stirring to combine well, about 5 minutes. Stir in the cooked edamame and cook until heated through, about 5 minutes.
3. Divide the hot rice among 4 bowls, top each with the edamame and tofu mixture, and drizzle on the sesame oil. Sprinkle with sesame seeds and serve immediately.

Sicilian Stuffed Tomatoes
PREP: 10 MINUTES • COOK TIME: 30 MINUTES • TOTAL: 40 MINUTES • SERVES: 4 servings

Ingredients
2 cups water
1 cup couscous
Salt
3 green onions, minced
1/3 cup golden raisins
1 teaspoon finely grated orange zest

4 large ripe tomatoes
1/3 cup toasted pine nuts
1/4 cup minced fresh parsley
Freshly ground black pepper
2 teaspoons olive oil

Directions
1. Preheat the oven to 375°F. Lightly oil a 9 x 13-inch baking pan and set aside. In a large saucepan, bring the water to a boil over high heat. Stir in the couscous and salt to taste and remove from the heat. Stir in the green onions, raisins, and orange zest. Cover and set aside for 5 minutes.
2. Cut a 1/2-inch-thick slice off the top of each of the tomatoes. Scoop out the pulp, keeping the tomato shells intact. Chop the pulp and place it in a large bowl. Add the couscous mixture along with the pine nuts, parsley, and salt and pepper to taste. Mix well.
3. Fill the tomatoes with the mixture and place them in the prepared pan. Drizzle the tomatoes with the oil, cover with foil, and bake until hot, about 20 minutes. Serve immediately.

Basic Baked Potatoes
PREP: 5 MINUTES • COOK TIME: 60 MINUTES • TOTAL: 65 MINUTES • SERVES: 5

Ingredients
5 medium Russet potatoes or a variety of potatoes, washed and patted dry
1 to 2 tablespoons extra-virgin olive oil

¼ teaspoon salt
¼ teaspoon freshly ground black pepper

Directions
Preparing the Ingredients.
1. Preheat the oven to 400ºF. Pierce each potato several times with a fork or a knife. Brush the olive oil over the potatoes, then rub each with a pinch of the salt and a pinch of the pepper.
2. Place the potatoes on a baking sheet and bake for 50 to 60 minutes, until tender. Place the potatoes on a baking rack and cool completely. Transfer to an airtight container or 5 single-serving containers. Let cool before sealing the lids.

Per Serving: Calories: 171; Fat: 3g; Protein: 4g; Carbohydrates: 34g; Fiber: 5g; Sugar: 3g; Sodium: 129mg

Orange-Dressed Asparagus
PREP: 5 MINUTES • COOK TIME: 10 MINUTES • TOTAL: 15 MINUTES • SERVES: 4 servings

Ingredients

1 medium shallot, minced
2 teaspoons orange zest
1/3 cup fresh orange juice
1 tablespoon fresh lemon juice

Pinch sugar
2 tablespoons olive oil
Salt and freshly ground black pepper
1 pound asparagus, tough ends trimmed

Directions

1. In a small bowl, combine the shallot, orange zest, orange juice, lemon juice, sugar, and oil. Add salt and pepper to taste and mix well. Set aside to allow flavors to blend, for 5 to 10 minutes.
2. Steam the asparagus until just tender, 4 to 5 minutes. If serving hot, arrange on a serving platter and drizzle the dressing over the asparagus. Serve at once.
3. If serving chilled, run the asparagus under cold water to stop the cooking process and retain the color. Drain on paper towels, then cover and refrigerate until chilled, about 1 hour. To serve, arrange the asparagus on a serving platter and drizzle with the dressing.

Broccoli With Almonds
PREP: 5 MINUTES • COOK TIME: 15 MINUTES • TOTAL: 20 MINUTES • SERVES: 4 servings

Ingredients

1 pound broccoli, cut into small florets
2 tablespoons olive oil
3 garlic cloves, minced
1 cup thinly sliced white mushrooms

1/4 cup dry white wine
2 tablespoons minced fresh parsley
Salt and freshly ground black pepper
1/2 cup slivered toasted almonds

Directions

1. Steam the broccoli until just tender, about 5 minutes. Run under cold water and set aside.
2. In a large skillet, heat 1 tablespoon of the oil over medium heat. Add the garlic and mushrooms and cook until soft, about 5 minutes. Add the wine and cook 1 minute longer. Add the steamed broccoli and parsley and season with salt and pepper to taste. Cook until the liquid is evaporated and the broccoli is hot, about 3 minutes.
3. Transfer to a serving bowl, drizzle with the remaining 1 tablespoon oil and the almonds, and toss to coat. Serve immediately.

Glazed Curried Carrots
PREP: 5 MINUTES • COOK TIME: 15 MINUTES • TOTAL: 20 MINUTES • SERVES: 6

Ingredients

1 pound carrots, peeled and thinly sliced
2 tablespoons olive oil
2 tablespoons curry powder
2 tablespoons pure maple syrup

juice of ½ lemon
sea salt
freshly ground black pepper

Directions
Preparing the Ingredients.

1. Place the carrots in a large pot and cover with water. Cook on medium-high heat until tender, about 10 minutes. Drain the carrots and return them to the pan over medium-low heat.
2. Stir in the olive oil, curry powder, maple syrup, and lemon juice. Cook, stirring constantly, until the liquid reduces, about 5 minutes. Season with salt and pepper and serve immediately.

Miso Spaghetti Squash

Ingredients

1 (3-pound) spaghetti squash
1 tablespoon hot water

1 tablespoon unseasoned rice vinegar
1 tablespoon white miso

Directions

Preparing the Ingredients.

1. Preheat the oven to 400ºF. Line a rimmed baking sheet with parchment paper. Halve the squash lengthwise and place, cut-side down, on the prepared baking sheet.
2. Bake for 35 to 40 minutes, until tender. Cool until the squash is easy to handle. With a fork, scrape out the flesh, which will be stringy, like spaghetti. Transfer to a large bowl. In a small bowl, combine the hot water, vinegar, and miso with a whisk or fork. Pour over the squash. Gently toss with tongs to coat the squash. Divide the squash evenly among 4 single-serving containers. Let cool before sealing the lids.

Per Serving: Calories: 117; Fat: 2g; Protein: 3g; Carbohydrates: 25g; Fiber: 0g; Sugar: 0g; Sodium: 218mg

Braised Cabbage And Apples

PREP: 5 MINUTES • COOK TIME: 25 MINUTES • TOTAL: 30 MINUTES • SERVES: 6 servings

Ingredients

2 tablespoons olive oil
1 small head red cabbage, shredded
1 small head savoy cabbage, shredded
1 Granny Smith apple
1 red cooking apple, such as Rome or Gala

2 tablespoons sugar
1 cup water
1/4 cup cider vinegar
Salt and freshly ground black pepper

Directions

1. In a large saucepan, heat the oil over medium heat. Add the shredded red and savoy cabbage, cover, and cook until slightly wilted, 5 minutes.
2. Core the apples and cut them into 1/4-inch dice. Add the apples to the cabbage, along with the sugar, water, vinegar, and salt and pepper to taste. Reduce heat to low, cover, and simmer until the cabbage and apples are tender, stirring frequently, about 20 minutes. Serve immediately.

Marsala Carrots

PREP: 5 MINUTES • COOK TIME: 20 MINUTES • TOTAL: 25 MINUTES • SERVES: 4 servings

Ingredients

2 tablespoons vegan margarine
1 pound carrots, cut diagonally into 1/4-inch slices
Salt and freshly ground black pepper

1/2 cup Marsala
1/4 cup water
1/4 cup chopped fresh parsley, for garnish

Directions

1. In a large skillet, melt the margarine over medium heat. Add the carrots and toss well to coat evenly with the margarine. Cover and cook, stirring occasionally, for 5 minutes.
2. Season with salt and pepper to taste, tossing to coat. Add the Marsala and water. Reduce heat to low, cover, and simmer until the carrots are tender, about 15 minutes.

3. Uncover and cook over medium-high heat until the liquid is reduced into a syrupy sauce, stirring to prevent burning.
Transfer to a serving bowl and sprinkle with parsley. Serve immediately.

Garlic And Herb Zoodles
PREP: 10 MINUTES • COOK TIME: 2 MINUTES • TOTAL: 12 MINUTES • SERVES: 4

Ingredients
1 teaspoon extra-virgin olive oil or 2 tablespoons vegetable broth
1 teaspoon minced garlic (about 1 clove)
4 medium zucchini, spiralized
½ teaspoon dried basil

½ teaspoon dried oregano
¼ to ½ teaspoon red pepper flakes, to taste
¼ teaspoon salt (optional)
¼ teaspoon freshly ground black pepper

Directions
Preparing the Ingredients.
1. In a large skillet over medium-high heat, heat the olive oil.
2. Add the garlic, zucchini, basil, oregano, red pepper flakes, salt (if using), and black pepper. Sauté for 1 to 2 minutes, until barely tender. Divide the zoodles evenly among 4 storage containers. Let cool before sealing the lids.

Per Serving: Calories: 44; Fat: 2g; Protein: 3g; Carbohydrates: 7g; Fiber: 2g; Sugar: 3g; Sodium: 20mg

Ratatouille (Pressure cooker)
PREP: 15 MINUTES • PRESSURE: 6 MINUTES • TOTAL: 45 MINUTES • PRESSURE LEVEL: HIGH • RELEASE: NATURAL• SERVES 4-6

Ingredients
1 onion, diced
4 garlic cloves, minced
1 to 2 teaspoons olive oil
1 cup water
3 or 4 tomatoes, diced
1 eggplant, cubed

1 or 2 bell peppers, any color, seeded and chopped
1½ tablespoons dried herbes de Provence (or any mixture of dried basil, oregano, thyme, marjoram, and rosemary)
½ teaspoon salt
Freshly ground black pepper

Directions
1. **Preparing the Ingredients.** On your electric pressure cooker, select Sauté. Add the onion, garlic, and olive oil. Cook for 4 to 5 minutes, stirring occasionally, until the onion is softened. Add the water, tomatoes, eggplant, bell peppers, and herbes de Provence. Cancel Sauté.
2. **High pressure for 6 minutes.** Close and lock the lid and ensure the pressure valve is sealed, then select High Pressure and set the time for 6 minutes.
3. **Pressure Release.** Once the cook time is complete, let the pressure release naturally, about 20 minutes. Once all the pressure has released, carefully unlock and remove the lid. Let cool for a few minutes, then season with salt and pepper.

PER SERVING Calories: 101; Total fat: 2g; Protein: 4g; Sodium: 304mg; Fiber: 7g

Cardamom Carrots With Orange

Ingredients

1 pound carrots, cut into 1/4-inch slices
2 tablespoons vegan margarine
1 tablespoon finely grated orange zest

1/2 teaspoon ground cardamom
Salt
Ground cayenne

Directions

1. Steam the carrots until tender, about 7 minutes. Set aside.
2. In a large skillet, melt the margarine over medium heat. Add the carrots, orange zest, and cardamom and season with salt and cayenne to taste. Cook, stirring occasionally, until flavors are blended, about 2 minutes. Serve immediately

Ginger-Tamari Braised Eggplant
PREP: 5 MINUTES • COOK TIME: 15 MINUTES • TOTAL: 20 MINUTES • SERVES: 4 servings

Ingredients

2 garlic cloves, minced
2 teaspoons grated fresh ginger
2 tablespoons tamari soy sauce
1 tablespoon dry sherry
1 teaspoon toasted sesame oil
1/2 teaspoon sugar

1 tablespoon canola or grapeseed oil
2 medium Asian eggplants, unpeeled and cut into
1-inch thick slices
1/4 cup water
2 green onions, minced

Directions

1. In a small bowl, combine the garlic, ginger, tamari, sherry, sesame oil, and sugar. Mix well and set aside. In a large skillet, heat the canola oil over medium heat. Add the eggplant slices and cook until slightly softened, turning once, about 8 minutes.
2. Pour the ginger-tamari sauce over the eggplant. Add the water, cover, and simmer until the eggplant is tender, about 10 minutes. Remove the lid and cook until liquid is reduced by half, about 5 minutes.
3. Transfer the eggplant to a serving platter and garnish with the green onions. Serve immediately.

Roasted   Sweet-and-Sour Cauliflower
PREP: 5 MINUTES • COOK TIME: 25 MINUTES • TOTAL: 30 MINUTES • SERVES: 4

Ingredients

1 head cauliflower, cut into bite-size florets
2 tablespoons olive oil
¾ cup organic cane sugar
⅔ cup water
⅓ cup apple cider vinegar or white vinegar
1 tablespoon ketchup

¼ cup soy sauce or gluten-free tamari
2 tablespoons cornstarch
4 cups cooked brown rice
2 scallions, chopped, for garnish (optional)
White sesame seeds, for garnish (optional)

Directions
Preparing the Ingredients.
1. Preheat the oven to 450°F. Line a baking sheet with parchment paper.
2. In a large bowl, toss the cauliflower florets with the oil and spread out on the prepared baking sheet. Roast for 15 minutes, toss with a spatula, and roast for an additional 10 minutes, or until fork-tender. While the cauliflower is roasting, mix together the sugar, water, vinegar, and ketchup in a large skillet. Bring the mixture to a boil over medium-high heat, then reduce to a simmer.

In a small bowl, whisk together the soy sauce and cornstarch to create a slurry. Slowly stir the slurry into the sauce until well combined and the sauce thickens, 2 to 4 minutes. When the cauliflower is finished, transfer to the skillet and toss well to coat with the sauce.

3. Divide the rice among 4 bowls, top with the cauliflower, and garnish with scallions and sesame seeds, if desired.

Spicy Fruit And Veggie Gazpacho
PREP: 10 MINUTES • COOK TIME: 0 MINUTES • TOTAL: 10 MINUTES • SERVES: 8

Ingredients
2 large tomatoes

1 serrano chile, seeded

4 cups cubed fresh watermelon, divided

2 teaspoons unseasoned rice vinegar or white wine vinegar

¼ cup extra-virgin olive oil or 2 to 3 tablespoons vegetable broth

1 large cucumber, peeled, seeded, and diced

1 small red onion, diced

1 small red bell pepper, seeded and diced

¼ cup minced fresh dill

Salt

Freshly ground black pepper

Directions
Preparing the Ingredients.
1. In a blender, purée the tomatoes, chile, and 2 cups of watermelon. Pour in the vinegar and olive oil and pulse. Add the cucumber, onion, bell pepper, and dill and purée until smooth. Taste before seasoning with salt and black pepper.
2. In a large bowl, pour the gazpacho over the remaining 2 cups of watermelon. Scoop 1½ cups of gazpacho into each of 8 single-serving containers. Seal the lids.

Per Serving: Calories: 106; Fat: 7g; Protein: 2g; Carbohydrates: 12g; Fiber: 2g; Sugar: 8g; Sodium: 28mg

Maple Dijon Burgers
PREP: 20 MINUTES • COOK TIME: 30 MINUTES • TOTAL: 50 MINUTES • SERVES: 12 BURGERS

Ingredients
1 red bell pepper

1 (19-ounce) can chickpeas, rinsed and drained, or 2 cups cooked

1 cup ground almonds

2 teaspoons Dijon mustard

2 teaspoons maple syrup

1 garlic clove, pressed

Juice of ½ lemon

1 teaspoon dried oregano

½ teaspoon dried sage

1 cup spinach

1 to 1½ cups rolled oats

Directions
Preparing the Ingredients.
1. Preheat the oven to 350°F. Line a large baking sheet with parchment paper.
2. Cut the red pepper in half, remove the stem and seeds, and put on the baking sheet cut side up in the oven. Roast in the oven while you prep the other ingredients.
3. Put the chickpeas in the food processor, along with the almonds, mustard, maple syrup, garlic, lemon juice, oregano, sage, and spinach. Pulse until things are thoroughly combined but not puréed. When the red pepper is softened a bit, about 10 minutes, add it to the processor along with the oats and pulse until they are chopped just enough to form patties. If you don't have a food processor, mash the

chickpeas with a potato masher or fork, and make sure everything else is chopped up as finely as possible, then stir together.

4. Scoop up ¼-cup portions and form into 12 patties, and lay them out on the baking sheet. Put the burgers in the oven and bake until the outside is lightly browned, about 30 minutes.

Per Serving (1 burger): Calories: 200; Total fat: 11g; Carbs: 21g; Fiber: 6g; Protein: 8g

Caramelized Root Vegetables
PREP: 5 MINUTES • COOK TIME: 25 MINUTES • TOTAL: 30 MINUTES • SERVES: 4 servings

Ingredients

2 tablespoons olive oil
2 garlic cloves, minced
4 medium shallots, halved or quartered
3 large carrots, cut into 1-inch chunks
3 large parsnips, cut into 1-inch chunks

2 small turnips, cut into 1-inch dice
1/2 cup light brown sugar
1/4 cup water
1/4 cup sherry vinegar
Salt and freshly ground black pepper

Directions

1. In a large skillet, heat the oil over medium heat. Add the garlic and shallots and cook for 1 minute to soften. Add the carrots, parsnips, and turnips and cook, stirring, until lightly brown and softened, about 5 minutes.
2. Stir in the sugar and 2 tablespoons of the water and cook, stirring until the sugar dissolves, about 5 minutes.
3. Stir in the remaining 2 tablespoons water and the vinegar and simmer for 2 to 3 minutes to blend the flavors. Season with salt and pepper to taste. Cover and cook on low until the vegetables are soft, about 25 minutes, stirring occasionally.
   Serve immediately.

Sushi-Style Quinoa
PREP: 2 MINUTES • COOK TIME: 25 MINUTES • TOTAL: 27 MINUTES • SERVES: 4

Ingredients

2 cups water
1 cup dry quinoa, rinsed

¼ cup unseasoned rice vinegar
¼ cup mirin or white wine vinegar

Directions

Preparing the Ingredients.
1. In a large saucepan, bring the water to a boil. Add the quinoa to the boiling water, stir, cover, and reduce the heat to low. Simmer for 15 to 20 minutes, until the liquid is absorbed. Remove from the heat and let stand for 5 minutes.
2. Fluff with a fork. Add the vinegar and mirin, and stir to combine well.
   Divide the quinoa evenly among 4 mason jars or single-serving containers. Let cool before sealing the lids.

Per Serving: Calories: 192; Fat: 3g; Protein: 6g; Carbohydrates: 34g; Fiber: 3g; Sugar: 4g; Sodium: 132mg

Pepper Medley
PREP: 10 MINUTES • COOK TIME: 15 MINUTES • TOTAL: 25 MINUTES • SERVES: 4

Ingredients

3 tablespoons olive oil
1 red bell pepper, sliced
1 orange bell pepper, sliced
1 yellow bell pepper, sliced
1 green bell pepper, sliced

2 garlic cloves, minced
3 tablespoons red wine vinegar
sea salt
freshly ground black pepper
2 tablespoons chopped fresh basil

Directions

Preparing the Ingredients.

1. In a large sauté pan, heat the olive oil over medium-high heat until it shimmers. Add the bell peppers and cook, stirring frequently, until softened, 7 to 10 minutes. Add the garlic and cook until it is fragrant, about 30 seconds. Add the vinegar, using a spoon to scrape any browned bits off the bottom of the pan. Simmer until the vinegar reduces, 2 to 3 minutes. Season with salt and pepper. Stir in the basil and serve immediately.

Sautéed Citrus Spinach
PREP: 10 MINUTES • COOK TIME: 10 MINUTES • TOTAL: 20 MINUTES • SERVES: 4

Ingredients

2 tablespoons olive oil
1 shallot, chopped
2 garlic cloves, minced
10 ounces baby spinach

zest and juice of 1 orange
sea salt
freshly ground black pepper

Directions

Preparing the Ingredients.

1. In a large sauté pan, heat the olive oil over medium-high heat until it shimmers. Add the shallot and cook until soft, about 3 minutes. Add the garlic and cook until it is fragrant, about 30 seconds. Add the spinach, orange juice, and orange zest.
2. Cook, stirring, until the spinach wilts, 2 to 3 minutes. Season with salt and pepper.
Serve warm.

Vegetable Paella
PREP: 10 MINUTES • COOK TIME: 45 MINUTES • TOTAL: 55 MINUTES • SERVES: 4 servings

Ingredients

2 tablespoons olive oil
2 medium carrots, cut into 1/4-inch slices
1 celery rib, cut into 1/4-inch slices
1 medium yellow onion, chopped
1 medium red bell pepper, cut into 1/2-inch dice
3 garlic cloves, chopped
8 ounces green beans, trimmed and cut into 1-inch pieces
11/2 cups cooked or 1 (15.5-ounce) can dark red kidney beans, drained and rinsed
1 (14.5-ounce) can diced tomatoes, drained

21/2 cups vegetable broth
Salt
1/2 teaspoon dried marjoram
1/2 teaspoon crushed red pepper
1/2 teaspoon ground fennel seed
1/4 teaspoon saffron or turmeric
¾ cup long-grain rice
2 cups oyster mushrooms, lightly rinsed and patted dry
1 (14-ounce) can artichoke hearts, drained and quartered

Directions

1. In a large saucepan, heat the oil over medium heat. Add the carrots, celery, onion, bell pepper, and garlic. Cover and cook for 10 minutes.
2. Add the green beans, kidney beans, tomatoes, broth, salt, oregano, crushed red pepper, fennel seed, saffron, and rice. Cover and simmer for 30 minutes.
3. Stir in the mushrooms and artichoke hearts. Taste, adjusting seasonings, adding more salt if necessary. Cover and simmer 15 minutes longer. Serve immediately.

Quinoa And Chickpea Pilaf With Orange And Pistachios
PREP: 10 MINUTES • COOK TIME: 30 MINUTES • TOTAL: 40 MINUTES • SERVES: 4 servings

Ingredients

1 tablespoon olive oil
1 medium red onion, minced
11/2 cups quinoa, well rinsed
3 cups vegetable broth or water
Salt

3 cups or 2 (15.5-ounce) cans chickpeas, drained and rinsed
1/4 teaspoon ground cayenne
1 tablespoon minced fresh chives
1 orange, peeled, segmented, and chopped
1/2 cup shelled pistachios

Directions

1. In a large saucepan, heat the oil over medium heat. Add the onion, cover, and cook until tender, 10 minutes. Stir in the quinoa, add the broth, and bring to a boil.
2. Reduce heat to low, add salt to taste, cover, and simmer until the quinoa has absorbed all the liquid, 20 to 30 minutes. Remove from heat and set aside for 5 minutes, then stir in the chickpeas, cayenne, chives, orange, and pistachios. Taste, adjusting seasonings if necessary. Serve immediately.

Potato And Artichoke Gratin With Spinach And Pine Nuts
PREP: 5 MINUTES • COOK TIME: 50 MINUTES • TOTAL: 55 MINUTES • SERVES: 4 servings

Ingredients

1 (10-ounce) package frozen artichoke hearts
2 tablespoons olive oil
2 garlic cloves, minced
5 cups fresh baby spinach
Salt and freshly ground black pepper
1 teaspoon dried basil

1/2 teaspoon dried thyme
2 large russet potatoes, peeled and cut into 1/4-inch slices
1/2 cup vegetable broth
2 tablespoons nutritional yeast
1/2 cup coarsely ground pine nuts

Directions

1. Preheat the oven to 375°F. Lightly oil a 2-quart gratin dish or casserole. If using frozen artichoke hearts, cook them in a small saucepan of boiling salted water until tender, about 12 minutes. Drain well. Cut the artichoke hearts into thin slices and set aside.
2. In a large skillet, heat 1 tablespoon of the oil over medium heat. Add the garlic, spinach, and salt and pepper to taste. Cover and cook until the spinach is wilted, stirring occasionally, about 2 minutes. Stir in the basil, thyme, and salt and pepper to taste. Set aside.
3. Layer half of the potato slices in the prepared gratin dish. Season with salt and pepper to taste. Top with the sliced artichokes, followed by the spinach mixture. Top with a layer of the remaining potatoes.
4. In a small bowl, combine the broth and nutritional yeast and stir until blended. Pour over the gratin. Sprinkle ground pine nuts on top of the gratin and drizzle with the 1 tablespoon remaining oil. Cover

with foil and bake until the potatoes are tender, about 40 minutes. Uncover and bake until the top is golden brown, about 10 minutes longer. Serve immediately.

Chard And New Potato Gratin With Herbes De Provence
PREP: 5 MINUTES • COOK TIME:1 HOUR 10 MINUTES • TOTAL: 15 MINUTES • SERVES: 4 servings

Ingredients
3 tablespoons olive oil
1 medium yellow onion, minced
3 garlic cloves, minced
1 medium bunch Swiss chard, tough stems removed and coarsely chopped

Salt and freshly ground black pepper
2 pounds new potatoes, unpeeled and cut into 1/4-inch slices
1 teaspoon herbes de Provence
2 tablespoons vegan Parmesan

Directions
1. Preheat the oven to 350°F. Lightly oil a 9- or 10-inch square baking pan or large gratin dish. Heat 1 tablespoon of the oil in a large skillet over medium heat. Add the onion and garlic, cover, and cook to soften, about 5 minutes. Add the Swiss chard and cook, uncovered, turning it until it is wilted. Season with salt and pepper and set aside.
2. Layer half of the potatoes in the bottom of the prepared pan, overlapping as necessary. Season with some of the herbes de Provence and salt and pepper to taste. Drizzle with 1 tablespoon of the olive oil. Add the chard and onion mixture in a layer across the potatoes. Season with salt and herbes de Provence and top with the remaining potatoes. Drizzle with the remaining tablespoon of the oil and season with salt and pepper.
3. Cover tightly with aluminum foil and bake until the vegetables are tender, about 1 hour. Sprinkle with vegan Parmesan and bake 10 minutes longer. Serve hot directly from the gratin dish.

Quinoa And Mixed Vegetable Sauté
PREP: 5 MINUTES • COOK TIME: 45 MINUTES • TOTAL: 50 MINUTES • SERVES: 4 servings

Ingredients
3 cups water
Salt
11/2 cups quinoa, well rinsed
1 tablespoon olive oil
1 small red onion, chopped
1 medium red bell pepper, chopped

1 medium zucchini, chopped
2 cups cooked shelled edamame
2 cups frozen corn kernels, thawed
2 ripe Roma tomatoes, chopped
Freshly ground black pepper
3 tablespoons chopped fresh parsley

Directions
1. In a large saucepan, bring the water to a boil over high heat. Salt the water and add the quinoa. Reduce the heat to medium and cook 20 to 30 minutes. Remove from the heat and set aside.
2. In a large skillet, heat the oil over medium heat. Add the onion and bell pepper, cover, and cook until softened, 5 minutes. Add the zucchini and cook, uncovered, until softened, about 7 minutes, stirring occasionally. Stir in the edamame, corn, tomatoes, and salt and black pepper to taste. Cook 5 minutes, stirring occasionally, until heated through.
3. Add the cooked quinoa and parsley and stir gently to combine. Serve immediately.

Stuffed Eggplant Rolls
PREP: 5 MINUTES • COOK TIME: 45 MINUTES • TOTAL: 50 MINUTES • SERVES: 4 servings

Ingredients

1 large or 2 medium eggplants
Salt and freshly ground black pepper
1 tablespoon olive oil
2 garlic cloves, minced
2 green onions, chopped
1/4 cup ground pine nuts

2 tablespoons finely chopped oil-packed sun-dried tomatoes
3 tablespoons golden raisins
3 tablespoons vegan Parmesan
1 tablespoon minced fresh parsley
2 cups marinara sauce

Directions

1. Preheat the oven to 375°F. Lightly oil a large baking sheet and a 9 x 13-inch baking pan and set side. Cut the eggplants lengthwise into 1/4-inch-thick slices and arrange them on the prepared baking sheet. Bake until partially softened, about 15 minutes. Remove from the oven, sprinkle with salt and pepper to taste, and set aside to cool.
2. In a large skillet, heat the oil over medium heat. Add the garlic, green onions, and pine nuts and cook, stirring for 1 minute. Stir in the tomatoes, raisins, Parmesan, parsley, and salt and pepper to taste. Mix well. Taste, adjusting seasonings if necessary.
3. Spread about 2 tablespoons of the stuffing mixture onto each of the softened eggplant slices and roll up the eggplant. Arrange the eggplant bundles, seam side down, in the prepared baking pan. Top with the marinara sauce, cover tightly with foil, and bake until tender and hot, about 30 minutes. Serve immediately.

Artichoke-Walnut Tart
PREP: 5 MINUTES • COOK TIME: 50 MINUTES • TOTAL: 55 MINUTES • SERVES: 4 servings

Ingredients

1 (10-ounce) package frozen artichoke hearts
1 frozen puff pastry sheet, thawed
1/2 cup toasted walnut pieces
8 ounces extra-firm tofu, drained and crumbled
3 green onions, minced
2 teaspoons fresh lemon juice

2 tablespoons minced fresh parsley
1 tablespoon minced fresh marjoram, or 1 teaspoon dried
Salt and freshly ground black pepper
2 ripe plum tomatoes, sliced paper thin

Directions

1. Preheat the oven to 400°F. Cook the artichoke hearts in a small saucepan of boiling salted water until tender, about 12 minutes. Drain and set aside.
2. On a lightly floured work surface, roll out the pastry, then press it into the bottom and up the sides of a 9-inch tart pan or pie plate. Trim and crimp the edges. Partially bake the crust for 10 minutes. Remove from the oven and set aside.
4. Coarsely chop 2 of the artichoke hearts and set aside. In a food processor, combine the remaining artichoke hearts, ¾ cup of the walnuts, tofu, and green onions and process until finely chopped. Add the lemon juice, parsley, marjoram, and salt and pepper to taste and process until well blended. Spoon the mixture into a bowl and add the remaining 1/4 cup walnuts and reserved artichokes. Stir to blend.
5. Spread the artichoke-walnut mixture evenly over the partially baked pastry. Arrange the tomato slices on top, overlapping slightly. Season with salt and pepper to taste. Bake until the crust is golden brown and the filling is hot, about 25 minutes. Cool 10 to 15

Broccoli And White Beans With Potatoes And Walnuts
PREP: 5 MINUTES • COOK TIME: 35 MINUTES • TOTAL: 40 MINUTES • SERVES: 4 servings

Ingredients

11/2 pounds fingerling potatoes
4 cups broccoli florets
3 tablespoons olive oil
3 garlic cloves, minced
¾ cup chopped walnut pieces
1/4 teaspoon crushed red pepper

11/2 cups or 1 (15.5-ounce) can white beans, drained and rinsed
1 teaspoon dried savory
Salt and freshly ground black pepper
1 tablespoon fresh lemon juice

Directions

1. Steam the potatoes until tender, about 20 minutes. Set aside. Steam the broccoli until crisp-tender, about 7 minutes. Set aside.
2. In a large skillet, heat 2 tablespoons of the oil over medium heat. Add the garlic, walnuts, and crushed red pepper. Cook until the garlic is softened, about 1 minute.
3. Stir in the steamed potatoes and broccoli. Add the beans and savory and season with salt and black pepper to taste. Cook until heated through, about 5 minutes. Sprinkle with lemon juice and drizzle with the remaining 1 tablespoon olive oil.
   Serve immediately.

Bell Peppers Stuffed With White Beans And Mushrooms
PREP: 5 MINUTES • COOK TIME: 40 MINUTES • TOTAL: 45 MINUTES • SERVES: 4 servings

Ingredients

2 large or 4 small red or yellow bell peppers
2 tablespoons olive oil
1 small yellow onion, minced
2 garlic cloves, minced
12 ounces white mushrooms, lightly rinsed, patted dry, and chopped

3 cups cooked or 2 (15.5-ounce) cans white beans, drained, rinsed, and mashed
1 cup finely chopped walnuts
2 tablespoons minced fresh parsley or dillweed
1/2 cup dry unseasoned bread crumbs
Salt and freshly ground black pepper

Directions

1. Cut the bell peppers in half lengthwise and remove the seeds and membranes. Cook the peppers in a pot of boiling water to soften slightly, 3 to 4 minutes. Drain and set aside. Preheat the oven to 375°F. Lightly oil a 9 x 13-inch baking pan and set aside.
2. In a large skillet, heat the oil over medium heat. Add the onion, cover, and cook until softened, about 5 minutes. Add the garlic and mushrooms and cook, uncovered, 5 minutes longer. Add the beans, walnuts, parsley, and 1/4 cup of the bread crumbs to the mushroom mixture. Season with salt and black pepper to taste and mix well.
3. Stuff the softened pepper halves with the enough of the stuffing mixture to fill the peppers (1/2 to 1 cup, depending on the size of the pepper) and arrange stuffing side up in the prepared baking pan. Cover with foil and bake for 20 minutes. Uncover, sprinkle with the remaining bread crumbs, and continue baking until the peppers are hot and the crumbs are golden brown, about 10 minutes longer. Serve immediately.

Roasted Rosemary Potatoes
PREP: 5 MINUTES • COOK TIME: 30 MINUTES • TOTAL: 35 MINUTES • SERVES: 4

Ingredients

1½ pounds baby red potatoes, halved
2 tablespoons olive oil

3 garlic cloves, minced
1 tablespoon minced fresh rosemary

¾ teaspoon sea salt

Directions
Preparing the Ingredients.
1. Preheat the oven to 425°F. Line a baking sheet with parchment paper.
2. In a large bowl, toss the potatoes with the oil, garlic, rosemary, and salt until well combined. Spread the potatoes evenly on the prepared baking sheet and bake for 15 minutes. Toss with a spatula and bake for an additional 15 minutes, or until golden brown.

Roasted Asparagus with Balsamic Reduction
PREP: 10 MINUTES • COOK TIME: 25 MINUTES • TOTAL: 35 MINUTES • SERVES: 4

Ingredients
1½ pounds asparagus, trimmed
2 tablespoons olive oil
½ teaspoon sea salt

¼ teaspoon freshly ground black pepper
⅓ cup balsamic vinegar
juice and zest of 1 meyer lemon

Directions
Preparing the Ingredients.
1. Preheat the oven to 375°F. On a large rimmed baking sheet, toss the asparagus with the olive oil, salt, and pepper and then spread the asparagus out into a single layer. Roast for 20 to 25 minutes, stirring once, until tender and beginning to brown.
2. While the asparagus is roasting, put the vinegar in a small saucepan and bring it to a boil over medium-high heat. Turn down the heat to low and simmer until reduced to a thick syrup, about 8 minutes. When the asparagus is roasted, remove the baking sheet from the oven. Add the lemon juice and zest and toss to coat.
Transfer to a serving platter and drizzle the balsamic reduction over the top. Serve immediately.

Three-Green Tian
PREP: 15 MINUTES • COOK TIME: 60 MINUTES • TOTAL: 75 MINUTES • SERVES: 4 to 6 servings

Ingredients
2 medium baking potatoes, cut into 1/4-inch slices
3 medium zucchini, cut into 1/4-inch slices on the diagonal
¾ cup olive oil
Salt and freshly ground black pepper
1 medium yellow onion, chopped
3 garlic cloves, minced

3 cups packed fresh spinach leaves, tough stems removed and coarsely chopped
2 cups packed stemmed and chopped kale
2 cups stemmed and chopped Swiss chard
1 cup loosely packed fresh basil leaves
5 to 6 ripe plum tomatoes, cut into 1/4-inch slices
¾ cup fresh bread crumbs
3 tablespoons vegan Parmesan

Directions
1. Preheat the oven to 400°F. Lightly oil a 9 x 13-inch baking pan and set aside. Lightly oil two large baking sheets and arrange the potato slices on one of them, overlapping as needed. Arrange the zucchini slices on the other, overlapping as needed. Drizzle with 1 or 2 tablespoons of the oil and season with salt and pepper to taste. Bake the zucchini slices until softened, about 10 minutes, and the potato slices until softened, about 20 minutes. Remove from the oven and set aside.
2. In a large skillet, heat 1 tablespoon of the oil over medium heat. Add the onion and garlic. Cover and cook until softened, about 5 minutes. Stir in the spinach, kale, and chard and season with salt and pepper to taste. Cover and cook until the greens are wilted, about 7 minutes.

3. Transfer the greens mixture to a blender or food processor and process with the basil and 3 tablespoons of the remaining oil until smooth. Season with salt and pepper to taste.
4. Line the bottom of the prepared pan with a half of the cooked potato slices, overlapping as needed. Spoon a very thin layer of the pureed greens evenly over the potatoes. Arrange a layer of half of the cooked zucchini slices on top, overlapping as needed, followed by more of the pureed greens. Arrange a layer of tomato slices on top, followed by more of the greens. Repeat using the remaining potato, zucchini, and tomato slices and the remaining pureed greens, seasoning each layer with salt and pepper to taste.
5. Cover tightly with foil and bake until the vegetables are tender, about 45 minutes. Remove from the oven and sprinkle the tian with the bread crumbs and Parmesan and drizzle with the remaining olive oil. Return to the oven and bake uncovered for 10 minutes to brown the topping. Serve immediately.

Kasha With Roasted Sweet Potatoes And Peas
PREP: 5 MINUTES • COOK TIME: 50 MINUTES • TOTAL: 55 MINUTES • SERVES: 4 servings

Ingredients
2 large sweet potatoes, peeled and cut into 1/2-inch dice
2 tablespoons olive oil
Salt and freshly ground black pepper

1 large yellow onion, finely chopped
1 cup coarse kasha (buckwheat groats)
2 cups vegetable broth or water
1 cup frozen peas

Directions
1. Preheat the oven to 425°F. Spread the sweet potatoes on a lightly oiled baking pan and drizzle with 1 tablespoon of the oil. Season with salt and pepper to taste and roast until tender, about 25 minutes, stirring once about halfway through. Set aside.
2. In a large skillet, heat the remaining 1 tablespoon oil over medium heat. Add the onion, cover, and cook, stirring occasionally, until browned, about 10 minutes. Stir in the kasha. Add the broth and bring to a boil. Reduce the heat to low, cover, and simmer until the kasha is cooked, about 15 minutes.
3. Add the peas and roasted sweet potatoes and season with salt and pepper to taste. Stir gently to combine. Serve immediately.

Millet, Chard, And White Bean Casserole
PREP: 5 MINUTES • COOK TIME: 45 MINUTES • TOTAL: 50 MINUTES • SERVES: 4 to 6 servings

Ingredients
2¾ cups water
1 cup millet
Salt
1 tablespoon olive oil
1 medium yellow onion, chopped
1 medium red bell pepper, chopped
2 garlic cloves, minced
3 cups chopped stemmed Swiss chard
Salt and freshly ground black pepper

11/2 cups cooked or 1 (15.5-ounce) can Great Northern beans, drained and rinsed
1 cup ripe cherry tomatoes, quartered
2 tablespoons fresh lemon juice
1/4 cup nutritional yeast (optional)
2 tablespoons minced fresh dillweed
2 tablespoons minced fresh parsley
1/3 cup dry unseasoned bread crumbs

Directions
1. In a large saucepan, bring the water to a boil over high heat. Add the millet and 1/2 teaspoon of salt and return to a boil. Reduce the heat to low, cover, and simmer until tender, 30 to 40 minutes. Set aside.

2. Preheat the oven to 350°F. Lightly oil a 2-quart casserole and set aside. In a large skillet, heat the oil over medium heat. Add the onion and bell pepper, cover, and cook until softened, 7 minutes. Add the garlic and chard and season with salt and black pepper to taste. Cover and cook, stirring occasionally, until the chard is wilted, about 5 minutes. Stir the chard mixture into the cooked millet, along with the beans, tomatoes, lemon juice, yeast, dillweed, and parsley.
3. Transfer the mixture to the prepared casserole and sprinkle evenly with the bread crumbs. Bake, uncovered

Mushroom Goulash
PREP: 5 MINUTES • COOK TIME: 45 MINUTES • TOTAL: 50 MINUTES • SERVES: 4 servings

Ingredients

1 tablespoon olive oil
1 large yellow onion, chopped
3 garlic cloves, minced
1 large russet potato, cut into 1/2-inch dice
4 large portobello mushrooms, lightly rinsed, patted dry, and cut into 1-inch chunks
1 tablespoon tomato paste

1/2 cup dry white wine
11/2 tablespoons sweet Hungarian paprika
1 teaspoon caraway seeds
11/2 cups fresh or canned sauerkraut, drained
11/2 cups vegetable broth
Salt and freshly ground black pepper
1/2 cup vegan sour cream

Directions

1. In large saucepan, heat the oil over medium heat. Add the onion, garlic, and potato. Cover and cook until softened, about 10 minutes. Add the mushrooms and cook, uncovered, 3 minutes longer. Stir in the tomato paste, wine, paprika, caraway seeds, and sauerkraut. Add the broth and bring to a boil, then reduce heat to low and season with salt and pepper to taste. Cover and simmer until the vegetables are soft and the flavor is developed, about 30 minutes.
2. Spoon about 1 cup of liquid into a small bowl. Add the sour cream, stirring to blend. Stir the sour cream mixture back into the saucepan and taste, adjusting seasonings if necessary. Serve immediately.

Tamarind Eggplant With Bell Peppers And Mango
PREP: 5 MINUTES • COOK TIME: 35 MINUTES • TOTAL: 40 MINUTES • SERVES: 4 servings

Ingredients

1/2 cup olive oil
1 medium yellow onion, cut into 1/2-inch dice
3 small Asian eggplants, peeled and cut into 1-inch chunks
1 medium red pepper, cut into 1/2-inch dice
1 medium yellow bell pepper, cut into 1/2-inch dice
3 garlic cloves, minced

1 serrano or other small hot chile, seeded and minced
2 tablespoons tamarind paste
1/2 cup fresh orange juice
2 teaspoons light brown sugar
Salt and freshly ground black pepper
1 ripe mango, peeled, pitted, and cut into 1/2-inch dice
1/2 cup finely chopped fresh cilantro

Directions

1. In a large skillet, heat the oil over medium heat. Add the onion, cover, and cook until softened, 5 minutes. Add the eggplants, red and yellow bell peppers, garlic, and chile. Cook, covered, until softened, 10 minutes.
2. Add the tamarind paste, orange juice, sugar, and salt and black pepper to taste. Bring to a boil, then reduce heat to low and simmer, uncovered, until the vegetables are soft and the liquid thickens and reduces by half, about 20 minutes.

3. Stir in the mango and cilantro and serve immediately.

Artichoke And Chickpea Loaf
PREP: 15 MINUTES • COOK TIME: 1 HOUR 15 MINUTES • TOTAL: 15 MINUTES • SERVES: 6 to 8 servings

Ingredients
1 large russet potato, peeled and cut into 1/2-inch dice
1 (10-ounce) package frozen artichoke hearts
1/4 cup olive oil
1 large yellow onion, chopped
11/2 cups or 1 (15.5-ounce) can chickpeas, drained and rinsed
1/4 cup vegetable broth
2 tablespoons tahini
11/2 tablespoons soy sauce
11/2 tablespoons fresh lemon juice
2/3 cup wheat gluten flour (vital wheat gluten)
2/3 cup chickpea flour
1/2 cup nutritional yeast
1 teaspoon dried marjoram
1 teaspoon dried thyme
1 teaspoon salt
1/4 teaspoon freshly ground black pepper
1/2 cup chopped oil-packed sun-dried tomatoes
1/4 cup minced fresh parsley

Directions
1. Preheat the oven to 375°F. Lightly oil a 9-inch loaf pan or square baking pan. Steam the potato and artichoke hearts (if using frozen) until tender, about 15 minutes. Blot off any excess moisture and set aside, reserving 2 of the artichoke hearts. Chop the reserved artichoke hearts and set aside.
2. In a large skillet, heat the oil over medium heat. Add the onion, cover, and cook until tender, about 10 minutes. Stir in the steamed potatoes and artichoke hearts.
    Spoon the potato and artichoke mixture into a food processor. Add the chickpeas, broth, tahini, soy sauce, and lemon juice, and blend until smooth.
3. In a large bowl, combine both kinds of flour, the nutritional yeast, marjoram, thyme, salt, and pepper and stir to combine well.
4. Add the wet Ingredients to the dry Ingredients. Add the sun-dried tomatoes, parsley, and reserved chopped artichoke hearts and mix until well combined. Scrape the mixture into the prepared. Bake until firm and golden brown, about 1 hour. Let sit at room temperature for 15 minutes before slicing.

Lemon Broccoli Rabe
PREP: 10 MINUTES • COOK TIME: 10 MINUTES • TOTAL: 20 MINUTES • SERVES: 4

Ingredients
8 cups water
sea salt
2 bunches broccoli rabe, chopped
3 tablespoons olive oil
3 garlic cloves, minced
pinch of cayenne pepper
zest of 1 lemon
freshly ground black pepper

Directions
Preparing the Ingredients.
1. In a large pot, bring 8 cups of the water to a boil. Add a pinch of salt and the broccoli rabe. Cook until the broccoli rabe is slightly softened, about 2 minutes. Drain.
2. In a large sauté pan, heat the olive oil over medium-high heat until it shimmers. Add the garlic and cook until it is fragrant, about 30 seconds. Stir in the broccoli rabe, cayenne, and lemon zest.
    Season with salt and black pepper. Serve immediately.

Buttered Carrot Noodles with Kale
PREP: 10 MINUTES • COOK TIME: 10 MINUTES • TOTAL: 20 MINUTES • SERVES: 4

Ingredients
¼ cup vegan butter
½ cup chopped onion
1 pound carrots, peeled and sliced with a potato peeler or spiralizer

1 bunch lacinato kale, stemmed and thinly sliced
¼ cup chopped fresh parsley
¼ teaspoon sea salt
½ teaspoon black pepper

Directions
Preparing the Ingredients.
1. In a large skillet, melt the butter over medium heat. Add the onion and sauté for 3 minutes, or until soft. Add the carrots and sauté for 3 minutes more, tossing in the butter until the carrots begin to brown on the edges. Add the kale and sauté for an additional 2 minutes, or until wilted. Mix in the parsley, salt, and pepper.

Tempeh And Vegetable Stir-Fry
PREP: 5 MINUTES • COOK TIME: 45 MINUTES • TOTAL: 50 MINUTES • SERVES: 4 servings

Ingredients
8 ounces tempeh
Salt and freshly ground black pepper
2 teaspoons cornstarch
3 cups small broccoli florets
2 tablespoons canola or grapeseed oil
3 tablespoons soy sauce
2 tablespoons water
1 tablespoon mirin

1/2 teaspoon crushed red pepper
2 teaspoons toasted sesame oil
1 medium red bell pepper, cut into 1/2-inch slices
8 ounces white mushrooms, lightly rinsed, patted dry, and cut into 1/2-inch slices
2 garlic cloves, minced
3 tablespoons minced green onions
1 teaspoon grated fresh ginger

Directions
1. In a medium saucepan of simmering water, cook the tempeh for 30 minutes. Drain, pat dry, and set aside to cool. Cut the tempeh into 1/2-inch cubes and place in a shallow bowl. Season with salt and black pepper to taste, sprinkle with the cornstarch, and toss to coat. Set aside.
2. Lightly steam the broccoli until almost tender, about 5 minutes. Run under cold water to stop the cooking process and retain the bright green color. Set aside.
3. In a large skillet or wok, heat 1 tablespoon of the canola oil over medium-high heat. Add the tempeh and stir-fry until golden brown, about 5 minutes. Remove from the skillet and set aside.
4. In a small bowl, combine the soy sauce, water, mirin, crushed red pepper, and sesame oil. Set aside.
5. Reheat the same skillet over medium-high heat. Add the remaining 1 tablespoon of canola oil. Add the bell pepper and mushrooms and stir-fry until softened, about 3 minutes. Add the garlic, green onions, and ginger and stir-fry 1 minute. Add the steamed broccoli and fried tempeh and stir-fry for 1 minute. Stir in the soy sauce mixture and stir-fry until the tempeh and vegetables are hot and well coated with the sauce. Serve immediately.

Maple-Bourbon Acorn Squash
PREP: 10 MINUTES • COOK TIME: 30 MINUTES • TOTAL: 40 MINUTES • SERVES: 4

Ingredients
1 acorn squash (1 to 2 pounds), seeded and cut into ½-inch slices
½ cup bourbon

⅓ cup maple syrup
¼ cup vegan butter
¼ teaspoon ground cinnamon

2 pinches sea salt

Directions

Preparing the Ingredients.

1. Preheat the oven to 425°F. Line a baking sheet with parchment paper. Spread the squash slices on the prepared baking sheet and bake for 20 minutes.
2. Meanwhile, in a small saucepot, combine the bourbon, maple syrup, and butter. Melt over low heat and stir until well combined.

   Flip the squash, drizzle with the bourbon mixture, and sprinkle with the cinnamon and salt. Bake for 8 to 10 more minutes, until the liquid has started to caramelize and the squash is fork-tender.

Summer Squash Skillet
PREP: 10 MINUTES • COOK TIME: 10 MINUTES • TOTAL: 20 MINUTES • SERVES: 4

Ingredients

2 tablespoons olive oil, divided
1 red onion, sliced
3 garlic cloves, sliced
2 medium green zucchini, halved lengthwise and sliced into ¼-inch half moons

2 medium yellow summer squashes, halved lengthwise and sliced into ¼-inch half moons
1 teaspoon Italian seasoning
½ teaspoon sea salt, plus more if needed
¼ teaspoon black pepper, plus more if needed

Directions

Preparing the Ingredients.

1. Heat 1 tablespoon of olive oil in a large skillet over medium heat. Add the red onion and sauté for 5 minutes, or until soft and stringy.

   Add the garlic and sauté for 1 additional minute, or until fragrant.

   Add the remaining 1 tablespoon of olive oil, the zucchini and squashes, Italian seasoning, salt, and pepper. Mix until well combined. Continue cooking for 4 to 6 minutes, tossing the vegetables every couple of minutes to ensure even cooking. The zucchini and yellow squash will start to brown slightly and be fork-tender when ready. Add more salt and pepper to taste.

Spaghetti Squash Primavera
PREP: 10 MINUTES • COOK TIME: 40 MINUTES • TOTAL: 50 MINUTES • SERVES: 4

Ingredients

1 large spaghetti squash (roughly 4 pounds), halved and seeded
3 tablespoons olive oil, divided
1 onion, chopped
2 cups chopped broccoli florets
½ cup pitted and sliced green olives
1 cup halved cherry tomatoes
3 garlic cloves, minced

1½ teaspoons Italian seasoning
¾ teaspoon sea salt
½ teaspoon black pepper
Pine nuts, for garnish (optional)
Walnut Parmesan or store-bought vegan Parmesan, for garnish (optional)
Red pepper flakes, for garnish (optional)

Directions

Preparing the Ingredients.

1. Preheat the oven to 400°F. Line a baking sheet with parchment paper.
2. Brush the rims and the insides of both squash halves with 1 tablespoon of olive oil. Place on the prepared baking sheet, cut-sides down.

3. Bake for 35 to 45 minutes, until a fork can easily pierce the flesh. Set aside until cool enough to handle, 10 to 15 minutes.

While the squash is cooling, heat 1 tablespoon of olive oil in a large skillet over medium heat.

Add the onion and broccoli and sauté for 3 minutes, or until the onion is soft. Add the olives and tomatoes and cook for an additional 3 to 5 minutes, until the broccoli is fork-tender and the tomatoes have started to wilt. Add the garlic and cook for 1 additional minute, or until fragrant. Remove from the heat. Use a fork to gently pull the squash flesh from the skin and separate the flesh into strands. The strands wrap around the squash horizontally, so rake your fork in the same direction as the strands to make the longest spaghetti squash noodles. Toss the noodles into the skillet with the vegetables. Add the final 1 tablespoon of olive oil, Italian seasoning, salt, and pepper and mix well to combine. Divide among bowls and garnish with pine nuts, Parmesan, and red pepper flakes, if desired.

Sweet and Spicy Brussels Sprout Hash
PREP: 10 MINUTES • COOK TIME: 15 MINUTES • TOTAL: 25 MINUTES • SERVES: 4

Ingredients

3 tablespoons olive oil
2 shallots, thinly sliced
1½ pounds brussels sprouts, trimmed and cut into thin slices
3 tablespoons apple cider vinegar

1 tablespoon pure maple syrup
½ teaspoon sriracha sauce (or to taste)
sea salt
freshly ground black pepper

Directions
Preparing the Ingredients.
1. In a large sauté pan, heat the olive oil over medium-high heat until it shimmers.
2. Add the shallots and Brussels sprouts and cook, stirring frequently, until the vegetables soften and begin to turn golden brown, about 10 minutes. Stir in the vinegar, using a spoon to scrape any browned bits from the bottom of the pan. Stir in the maple syrup and Sriracha. Simmer, stirring frequently, until the liquid reduces, 3 to 5 minutes. Season with salt and pepper and serve immediately.

Mindful Mushroom Stroganoff
PREP: 10 MINUTES • COOK TIME: 15 MINUTES • TOTAL: 25 MINUTES • SERVES: 6

Ingredients

1 tablespoon olive oil
1 onion, chopped
2 (8-ounce) packages baby bella or white button mushrooms, stemmed and sliced
4 garlic cloves, minced
¼ cup low-sodium vegetable broth
1 teaspoon paprika

½ teaspoon sea salt
½ teaspoon black pepper
¼ cup Sour Cream or store-bought vegan sour cream
4 tablespoons chopped fresh parsley, divided
1 pound pasta of your choice, cooked

Directions
Preparing the Ingredients.
1. Heat the oil in a large skillet over medium heat.
2. Add the onion and mushrooms and sauté for 5 to 8 minutes, until the mushrooms are soft and have reduced in size. Add the garlic and sauté for 1 additional minute, or until fragrant. Add the broth, paprika, salt, and pepper and cook for 5 more minutes, or until well incorporated and heated through. Remove from the heat and stir in the sour cream and 2 tablespoons of parsley. Toss with the cooked pasta, divide into 6 portions, and sprinkle with the remaining 2 tablespoons of parsley.

Eggplant & Chickpea Curry with Couscous
PREP: 10 MINUTES • COOK TIME: 10 MINUTES • TOTAL: 20 MINUTES • SERVES: 3

Ingredients

1 tablespoon olive oil
1 onion, chopped
1 eggplant, diced
Salt
1-inch piece fresh ginger, peeled and minced (optional)
1 (15-ounce) can chickpeas, drained and rinsed

1 tomato, chopped, or 1 cup canned diced tomatoes
1½ cups couscous
2¼ cups boiling water
6 tablespoons Coconut Curry Sauce
Chopped fresh cilantro or parsley, for garnish (optional)

Directions
Preparing the Ingredients.
1. Heat the olive oil in a large skillet over medium heat.
2. Add the onion, eggplant, and a pinch of salt, and sauté for about 5 minutes, until the vegetables are softened. Add the ginger (if using), chickpeas, and tomato, and cook for about 5 minutes more, until everything is heated through and the tomato is softened. Meanwhile, in a medium heat-proof bowl, combine the couscous and boiling water. Cover and set aside.
3. Stir the coconut curry sauce into the cooked vegetables. Fluff the couscous with a fork. Divide it among three bowls or lunch containers. Top with the veggies and chopped herbs (if using). Store the cooked ingredients in airtight containers for 4 to 5 days in the refrigerator or up to 1 month in the freezer.

Lemon Broccoli Rabe
PREP: 10 MINUTES • COOK TIME: 10 MINUTES • TOTAL: 20 MINUTES • SERVES: 4

Ingredients

8 cups water
sea salt
2 bunches broccoli rabe, chopped
3 tablespoons olive oil

3 garlic cloves, minced
pinch of cayenne pepper
zest of 1 lemon
freshly ground black pepper

Directions
Preparing the Ingredients.
1. In a large pot, bring 8 cups of the water to a boil.
2. Add a pinch of salt and the broccoli rabe. Cook until the broccoli rabe is slightly softened, about 2 minutes. Drain. In a large sauté pan, heat the olive oil over medium-high heat until it shimmers. Add the garlic and cook until it is fragrant, about 30 seconds. Stir in the broccoli rabe, cayenne, and lemon zest. Season with salt and black pepper.
Serve immediately.

Eggplant Parmesan
PREP: 10 MINUTES • COOK TIME: 15 MINUTES • TOTAL: 25 MINUTES • SERVES: 1

Ingredients

¼ cup nondairy milk
¼ cup bread crumbs or panko
2 tablespoons nutritional yeast (optional)
¼ teaspoon salt

4 (¼-inch-thick) eggplant slices, peeled if desired
1 tablespoon olive oil, plus more as needed
4 tablespoons Simple Homemade Tomato Sauce
4 teaspoons Parm Sprinkle

Directions
Preparing the Ingredients.

1. Put the milk in a shallow bowl. In another shallow bowl, stir together the bread crumbs, nutritional yeast (if using), and salt.
2. Dip one eggplant slice in the milk, making sure both sides get moistened. Dip it into the bread crumbs, flipping to coat both sides. Transfer to a plate and repeat to coat the remaining slices. Heat the olive oil in a large skillet over medium heat and add the breaded eggplant slices, making sure there is oil under each.
3. Cook for 5 to 7 minutes, until browned. Flip, adding more oil as needed. Top each slice with 1 tablespoon tomato sauce and 1 teaspoon Parm Sprinkle. Cook for 5 to 7 minutes more.

Per Serving Calories: 460; Protein: 23g; Total fat: 31g; Saturated fat: 4g; Carbohydrates: 31g; Fiber: 13g

Red Peppers and Kale
PREP: 5 MINUTES • COOK TIME: 15 MINUTES • TOTAL: 20 MINUTES • SERVES: 4

Ingredients
2 bunches kale, stalks removed and cut into small pieces
3 tablespoons olive oil
½ onion, chopped
2 red bell peppers, cut into strips

3 garlic cloves, minced
¼ teaspoon red pepper flakes
sea salt
freshly ground black pepper

Directions
Preparing the Ingredients.

1. In steamer basket in a pan, steam the kale until it softens, 5 to 10 minutes. Remove from the heat and set aside. Meanwhile, in a sauté pan, heat the olive oil over medium-high heat until it -shimmers.
2. Add the onion and bell peppers and cook until soft, about 5 minutes. Add the garlic and cook until it is fragrant, about 30 seconds. Remove from the heat and stir in the kale and red pepper flakes. Season with salt and black pepper and serve immediately.

Cauliflower Alfredo Your Way
PREP: 5 MINUTES • COOK TIME: 15 MINUTES • TOTAL: 20 MINUTES • SERVES: 6

Ingredients
4 cups bite-size cauliflower florets
1½ cups unsweetened soy or almond milk
¼ cup soft or silken tofu
Juice of ½ lemon
2 tablespoons Dijon mustard
1½ teaspoons onion powder
1½ teaspoons sea salt

1 teaspoon garlic powder
¼ teaspoon black pepper, plus more for garnish (optional)
1 pound pasta of your choice, cooked
vegan Parmesan, for garnish (optional)
Chopped fresh parsley, for garnish (optional)

Directions
Preparing the Ingredients.

1. Steam the cauliflower for 10 to 12 minutes until fork-tender, then transfer to a blender.

2. Add the milk, tofu, lemon juice, mustard, onion powder, salt, garlic powder, and pepper and blend for 1 to 2 minutes, until creamy and smooth. Toss the cooked pasta with the sauce and divide among 6 serving bowls. Garnish with Parmesan, parsley, and more pepper, if desired.

Sweet Potato Quesadilla
PREP: 10 MINUTES • COOK TIME: 10 MINUTES • TOTAL: 20 MINUTES • SERVES: 1

Ingredients
1 to 2 teaspoons olive oil, plus more as needed
¼ onion, chopped
Salt
½ cooked sweet potato
½ cup canned black beans, drained and rinsed
½ to 1 teaspoon chili powder

1 teaspoon freshly squeezed lime juice
1 large flour or corn tortilla
¼ cup grated vegan cheese (optional)
Loaded Guacamole, for serving
Salsa, for serving
Sour Cream, for serving

Directions
Preparing the Ingredients.
1. Heat the olive oil in a large skillet over medium heat.
2. Add the onion and a pinch of salt, and sauté for about 5 minutes, until the onion is soft. Meanwhile, in a medium bowl, mash together the sweet potato, black beans, chili powder, lime juice, and a pinch of salt. Stir the onion into the sweet potato mixture, adding another drizzle of olive oil if your sweet potatoes look dry.
3. Spread the mixture onto half of the tortilla, and sprinkle with the cheese (if using). Fold the other side of the tortilla over to close. Return the skillet to medium heat and add another drizzle of olive oil. Gently transfer the filled tortilla to the pan and cook for about 2 minutes. Flip the tortilla, adding another drizzle of olive oil if needed, and cook for about 2 minutes more, until lightly browned. Transfer to a plate, slice in thirds, and enjoy with scoops of guacamole, sour cream, and salsa.

Per Serving Calories: 526; Protein: 17g; Total fat: 11g; Saturated fat: 2g; Carbohydrates: 93g; Fiber: 15g

Steamed Broccoli with Walnut Pesto
PREP: 5 MINUTES • COOK TIME: 10 MINUTES • TOTAL: 15 MINUTES • SERVES: 4

Ingredients
1 pound broccoli florets
2 cups chopped fresh basil
¼ cup olive oil

4 garlic cloves
½ cup walnuts
pinch of cayenne pepper

Directions
Preparing the Ingredients.
1. Put the broccoli in a large pot and cover with water.
2. Bring to a simmer over medium-high heat and cook until the broccoli is tender, about 5 minutes. Meanwhile, in a food processor, combine the basil, olive oil, garlic, walnuts, and cayenne and blend for ten 1-second pulses, scraping down the bowl halfway through processing. Drain the broccoli and return to the pan. Toss with the pesto.
Serve immediately.

Black Bean Taco Salad Bowl

PREP: 15 MINUTES • COOK TIME: 5 MINUTES • TOTAL: 20 MINUTES • SERVES: 3

Ingredients

FOR THE BLACK BEAN SALAD

1 (14-ounce) can black beans, drained and rinsed, or 1½ cups cooked

1 cup corn kernels, fresh and blanched, or frozen and thawed

¼ cup fresh cilantro, or parsley, chopped

Zest and juice of 1 lime

1 to 2 teaspoons chili powder

Pinch sea salt

1½ cups cherry tomatoes, halved

Pinch chili powder

FOR 1 BOWL

1 cup fresh greens (lettuce, spinach, or whatever you like)

1 red bell pepper, seeded and chopped

2 scallions, chopped

FOR 1 SERVING OF TORTILLA CHIPS

1 large whole-grain tortilla or wrap

1 teaspoon olive oil

Pinch sea salt

Pinch freshly ground black pepper

Pinch dried oregano

¾ cup cooked quinoa, or brown rice, millet, or other whole grain

¼ cup chopped avocado, or *Guacamole*

¼ cup Fresh Mango Salsa

Directions

Preparing the Ingredients.

1. **TO MAKE THE BLACK BEAN SALAD**
   Toss all the ingredients together in a large bowl.
2. **TO MAKE THE TORTILLA CHIPS**
   Brush the tortilla with olive oil, then sprinkle with salt, pepper, oregano, chili powder, and any other seasonings you like. Slice it into eighths like a pizza.
   Transfer the tortilla pieces to a small baking sheet lined with parchment paper and put in the oven or toaster oven to toast or broil for 3 to 5 minutes, until browned. Keep an eye on them, as they can go from just barely done to burned very quickly.
3. **TO MAKE THE BOWL**
   Lay the greens in the bowl, top with the cooked quinoa, ⅓ of the black bean salad, the avocado, and salsa.
   Per Serving: Calories: 589; Total fat: 14g; Carbs: 101g; Fiber: 20g; Protein: 21g

Romaine And Grape Tomato Salad With Avocado And Baby Peas

PREP: 15 MINUTES • COOK TIME: 0 MINUTES • TOTAL: 15 MINUTES • SERVES: 4 servings

Ingredients

1 garlic clove, chopped

1 tablespoon chopped shallot

1/2 teaspoon dried basil

1/2 teaspoon salt

1/8 teaspoon freshly ground black pepper

1/4 teaspoon brown sugar (optional)

3 tablespoons white wine vinegar

1/3 cup olive oil

1 medium head romaine lettuce, cut into 1/4-inch strips

12 ripe grape tomatoes, halved

1/2 cup frozen baby peas, thawed

8 kalamata olives, pitted

1 ripe Hass avocado

Directions

1. In a blender or food processor, combine the garlic, shallot, basil, salt, pepper, sugar, and vinegar until smooth. Add the oil and blend until emulsified. Set aside.

2. In a large bowl, combine the lettuce, tomatoes, peas, and olives. Pit and peel the avocado and cut into 1/2-inch dice. Add to the bowl, along with enough dressing to lightly coat. Toss gently to combine and serve.

Warm Vegetable "Salad"
PREP: 10 MINUTES • COOK TIME: 15 MINUTES • TOTAL: 25 MINUTES • SERVES: 4

Ingredients
Salt for salting water, plus ½ teaspoon (optional)
4 red potatoes, quartered
1 pound carrots, sliced into ¼-inch-thick rounds
1 tablespoon extra-virgin olive oil (optional)

2 tablespoons lime juice
2 teaspoons dried dill
¼ teaspoon freshly ground black pepper
1 cup Cashew Cream or Parm-y Kale Pesto

Directions
Preparing the Ingredients.
1. In a large pot, bring salted water to a boil. Add the potatoes and cook for 8 minutes. Add the carrots and continue to boil for another 8 minutes, until both the potatoes and carrots are crisp tender. Drain and return to the pot. Add the olive oil (if using), lime juice, dill, remaining ½ teaspoon of salt (if using), and pepper, and stir to coat well.
2. Divide the vegetables evenly among 4 single-compartment storage containers or wide-mouth pint glass jars, and spoon ¼ cup of cream or pesto over the vegetables in each. Let cool before sealing the lids.

Per Serving: Calories: 393; Fat: 15g; Protein: 10g; Carbohydrates: 52g; Fiber: 9g; Sugar: 8g; Sodium: 343mg

Rice Salad With Cashews And Dried Papaya
PREP: 15 MINUTES • COOK TIME: 0 MINUTES • TOTAL: 15 MINUTES • SERVES: 4 servings

Ingredients
31/2 cups cooked brown rice
1/2 cup chopped roasted cashews
1/2 cup thinly sliced dried papaya
4 green onions, chopped
Salt and freshly ground black pepper

3 tablespoons fresh lime juice
2 teaspoons agave nectar
1 teaspoon grated fresh ginger
1/3 cup grapeseed oil

Directions
1. In a large bowl, combine the rice, cashews, papaya, and green onions. Set aside.
2. In a small bowl, combine the lime juice, agave nectar, and ginger. Whisk in the oil and season with the salt and pepper to taste. Pour the dressing over the rice mixture, mix well, and serve.

Spinach Salad With Orange-Dijon Dressing
PREP: 10 MINUTES • COOK TIME: 0 MINUTES • TOTAL: 10 MINUTES • SERVES: 4 servings

Ingredients
2 tablespoons Dijon mustard
2 tablespoons olive oil
1/4 cup fresh orange juice
1 teaspoon agave nectar
1/2 teaspoon salt
1/4 teaspoon freshly ground black pepper

2 tablespoons minced fresh parsley
1 tablespoon minced green onions
5 cups fresh baby spinach, torn into bite-size pieces
1 navel orange, peeled and segmented
1/2 small red onion, sliced paper thin

Directions

1. In a blender or food processor combine the mustard, oil, orange juice, agave nectar, salt, pepper, parsley, and green onions. Blend well and set aside.
2. In a large bowl, combine the spinach, orange, and onion. Add the dressing, toss gently to combine, and serve.

Caramelized Onion And Beet Salad
PREP: 10 MINUTES • COOK TIME: 40 MINUTES • TOTAL: 50 MINUTES • SERVES: 4

Ingredients

3 medium golden beets
2 cups sliced sweet or Vidalia onions
1 teaspoon extra-virgin olive oil or no-beef broth
Pinch baking soda

¼ to ½ teaspoon salt, to taste
2 tablespoons unseasoned rice vinegar, white wine vinegar, or balsamic vinegar

Directions

Preparing the Ingredients.

1. Cut the greens off the beets, and scrub the beets.
2. In a large pot, place a steamer basket and fill the pot with 2 inches of water.
   Add the beets, bring to a boil, then reduce the heat to medium, cover, and steam for about 35 minutes, until you can easily pierce the middle of the beets with a knife.
   Meanwhile, in a large, dry skillet over medium heat, sauté the onions for 5 minutes, stirring frequently. Add the olive oil and baking soda, and continuing cooking for 5 more minutes, stirring frequently. Stir in the salt to taste before removing from the heat. Transfer to a large bowl and set aside.
3. When the beets have cooked through, drain and cool until easy to handle. Rub the beets in a paper towel to easily remove the skins. Cut into wedges, and transfer to the bowl with the onions. Drizzle the vinegar over everything and toss well.
   Divide the beets evenly among 4 wide-mouth jars or storage containers. Let cool before sealing the lids.

Per Serving: Calories: 104; Fat: 2g; Protein: 3g; Carbohydrates: 20g; Fiber: 4g; Sugar: 14g; Sodium: 303mg

Treasure Barley Salad
PREP: 10 MINUTES • COOK TIME: 30 MINUTES • TOTAL: 40 MINUTES • SERVES: 4 to 6 servings

Ingredients

1 cup pearl barley
11/2 cups cooked or 1 (15.5-ounce) can navy beans, drained and rinsed
1 celery rib, finely chopped
1 medium carrot, shredded
3 green onions, minced
1/2 cup chopped pitted kalamata olives

1/2 cup dried cherries or sweetened dried cranberries
1/2 cup toasted pecans pieces, coarsely chopped
1/2 cup minced fresh parsley
1 garlic clove, pressed
3 tablespoons sherry vinegar
Salt and freshly ground black pepper
1/4 cup grapeseed oil

Directions

1. In a large saucepan, bring 21/2 cups salted water to boil over high heat. Add the barley and return to a boil. Reduce heat to low, cover, and simmer until the barley is tender, about 30 minutes. Transfer to a serving bowl.

2. Add the beans, celery, carrot, green onions, olives, cherries, pecans, and parsley. Set aside.
3. In a small bowl, combine the garlic, vinegar, and salt and pepper to taste. Whisk in the oil until well blended. Pour the dressing over the salad, toss to combine, and serve.

Golden Couscous Salad

PREP: 5 MINUTES • COOK TIME: 12 MINUTES • TOTAL: 17 MINUTES • SERVES: 4 servings

Ingredients

1/4 cup olive oil
1 medium shallot, minced
1/2 teaspoon ground coriander
1/2 teaspoon turmeric
1/4 teaspoon ground cayenne
1 cup couscous
2 cups vegetable broth, homemade or store-bought, or water
Salt

1 medium yellow bell pepper, chopped
1 medium carrot, shredded
1/2 cup chopped dried apricots
1/4 cup golden raisins
1/4 cup chopped unsalted roasted cashews
11/2 cups cooked or 1 (15.5-ounce) can chickpeas, drained and rinsed
2 tablespoons minced fresh cilantro leaves
2 tablespoons fresh lemon juice

Directions

1. In a large saucepan, heat 1 tablespoon of the oil over medium heat. Add the shallot, coriander, turmeric, cayenne, and couscous and stir until fragrant, about 2 minutes, being careful not to burn. Stir in the broth and salt to taste. Bring to a boil, then remove from the heat, cover, and let stand for 10 minutes.
2. Transfer the cooked couscous to a large bowl. Add the bell pepper, carrot, apricots, raisins, cashews, chickpeas, and cilantro. Toss gently to combine and set aside.
3. In a small bowl, combine the remaining 3 tablespoons of oil with the lemon juice, stirring to blend. Pour the dressing over the salad, toss gently to combine, and serve.

Chopped Salad

PREP: 15 MINUTES • COOK TIME: 0 MINUTES • TOTAL: 15 MINUTES • SERVES: 4 servings

Ingredients

¾ cup olive oil
1/4 cup white wine vinegar
2 teaspoons Dijon mustard
1 garlic clove
1 tablespoon minced green onions
1/2 teaspoon salt (optional)
1/4 teaspoon ground black pepper
1/2 small head romaine lettuce, chopped
1/2 small head iceberg lettuce, chopped
11/2 cups cooked or 1 (15.5-ounce) can chickpeas, drained and rinsed

2 ripe tomatoes, cut into 1/2-inch dice
1 medium English cucumber, peeled, halved lengthwise, and chopped
2 celery ribs, chopped celery
1 medium carrot, chopped
1/2 cup halved pitted kalamata olives
3 small red radishes, chopped
2 tablespoons chopped fresh parsley
1 ripe Hass avocado, pitted, peeled, and cut into 1/2-inch dice

Directions

1. In a blender or food processor, combine the oil, vinegar, mustard, garlic, green onions, salt, and pepper. Blend well and set aside.
2. In a large bowl, combine the romaine and iceberg lettuces. Add the chickpeas, tomatoes, cucumber, celery, carrot, olives, radishes, parsley, and avocado. Add enough dressing to lightly coat. Toss gently to combine and serve.

Warm Lentil Salad with Red Wine Vinaigrette
PREP: 10 MINUTES • COOK TIME: 50 MINUTES • TOTAL: 60 MINUTES • SERVES: 4

Ingredients

1 teaspoon olive oil plus ¼ cup, divided, or 1 tablespoon vegetable broth or water
1 small onion, diced
1 garlic clove, minced
1 carrot, diced
1 cup lentils
1 tablespoon dried basil
1 tablespoon dried oregano

1 tablespoon red wine or balsamic vinegar (optional)
2 cups water
¼ cup red wine vinegar or balsamic vinegar
1 teaspoon sea salt
2 cups chopped Swiss chard
2 cups torn red leaf lettuce
4 tablespoons Cheesy Sprinkle

Directions

Preparing the Ingredients.

1. Heat 1 teaspoon of the oil in a large pot on medium heat, then sauté the onion and garlic until they are translucent, about 5 minutes.
Add the carrot and sauté until it is slightly cooked, about 3 minutes. Stir in the lentils, basil, and oregano, then add the wine or balsamic vinegar (if using).
Pour the water into the pot and turn the heat up to high to bring to a boil.

2. Turn the heat down to a simmer and let the lentils cook, uncovered, 20 to 30 minutes, until they are soft but not falling apart.

3. While the lentils are cooking, whisk together the red wine vinegar, olive oil, and salt in a small bowl and set aside. Once the lentils have cooked, drain any excess liquid and stir in most of the red wine vinegar dressing. Set a little bit of dressing aside. Add the Swiss chard to the pot and stir it into the lentils. Leave the heat on low and cook, stirring, for at least 10 minutes. Toss the lettuce with the remaining dressing. Place some lettuce on a plate, and top with the lentil mixture. Finish the plate off with a little Cheesy Sprinkle and enjoy.

Per Serving Calories: 387; Total fat: 17g; Carbs: 42g; Fiber: 19g; Protein: 18g

Carrot And Orange Salad With Cashews And Cilantro
PREP: 15 MINUTES • COOK TIME: 0 MINUTES • TOTAL: 15 MINUTES • SERVES: 4 servings

Ingredients

1 pound carrots, shredded
2 oranges, peeled, segmented, and chopped
1/2 cup unsalted roasted cashews
1/4 cup chopped fresh cilantro
2 tablespoons fresh orange juice

2 tablespoons fresh lime juice
2 teaspoons brown sugar(optional)
Salt (optional) and freshly ground black pepper
1/3 cup olive oil

Directions

1. In a large bowl, combine the carrots, oranges, cashews, and cilantro and set aside.

2. In a small bowl, combine the orange juice, lime juice, sugar, and salt and pepper to taste. Whisk in the oil until blended. Pour the dressing over the carrot mixture, stirring to lightly coat. Taste, adjusting seasonings if necessary. Toss gently to combine and serve.

Not-Tuna Salad
PREP: 5 MINUTES • COOK TIME: 0 MINUTES • TOTAL: 5 MINUTES • SERVES: 4

Ingredients

1 (15.5-ounce) can chickpeas, drained and rinsed
1 (14-ounce) can hearts of palm, drained and chopped
½ cup chopped yellow or white onion

½ cup diced celery
¼ cup vegan mayonnaise, plus more if needed
½ teaspoon salt
¼ teaspoon freshly ground black pepper

Directions
Preparing the Ingredients.
1. In a medium bowl, use a potato masher or fork to roughly mash the chickpeas until chunky and "shredded." Add the hearts of palm, onion, celery, vegan mayonnaise, salt, and pepper.
2. Combine and add more mayonnaise, if necessary, for a creamy texture. Into each of 4 single-serving containers, place ¾ cup of salad. Seal the lids.

Per Serving: Calories: 214; Fat: 6g; Protein: 9g; Carbohydrates: 35g; Fiber: 8g; Sugar: 1g; Sodium: 765mg

Red Bean And Corn Salad
PREP: 15 MINUTES • COOK TIME: 0 MINUTES • TOTAL: 15 MINUTES • SERVES: 4

Ingredients
¼ cup Cashew Cream or other salad dressing
1 teaspoon chili powder
2 (14.5-ounce) cans kidney beans, rinsed and drained

2 cups frozen corn, thawed, or 2 cups canned corn, drained
1 cup cooked farro, barley, or rice (optional)
8 cups chopped romaine lettuce

Directions
Preparing the Ingredients.
1. Line up 4 wide-mouth glass quart jars.
2. In a small bowl, whisk the cream and chili powder. Pour 1 tablespoon of cream into each jar. In each jar, add ¾ cup kidney beans, ½ cup corn, ¼ cup cooked farro (if using), and 2 cups romaine, punching it down to fit it into the jar. Close the lids tightly.

Per Serving: Calories: 303; Fat: 9g; Protein: 14g; Carbohydrates: 45g; Fiber: 15g; Sugar: 6g; Sodium: 654mg

Mango And Snow Pea Salad
PREP: 15 MINUTES • COOK TIME: 0 MINUTES • TOTAL: 15 MINUTES • SERVES: 4 servings

Ingredients
1/2 teaspoon minced garlic
1/2 teaspoon grated fresh ginger
1/4 cup creamy peanut butter
1 tablespoon plus 1 teaspoon light brown sugar
1/4 teaspoon crushed red pepper
3 tablespoons rice vinegar
3 tablespoons water
1 tablespoon soy sauce
2 cups snow peas, trimmed and lightly blanched

2 ripe mangos, peeled, pitted, cut into 1/2-inch dice
1 large carrot, shredded
1 medium cucumber, peeled, halved lengthwise, and seeded
3 cups shredded romaine lettuce
1/2 cup chopped unsalted roasted peanuts, for garnish

Directions
1. In a small bowl, combine the garlic, ginger, peanut butter, sugar, and crushed red pepper. Stir in the vinegar, water, and soy sauce. Taste, adjusting seasonings, if necessary, and set aside.

2. Cut the snow peas diagonally into a thin matchsticks and place in a large bowl. Add the mangos and carrot. Cut the cucumber into 1/4-inch slices and add to the bowl.
3. Pour the dressing onto the salad and toss gently to combine. Spoon the salad onto a bed of shredded lettuce, sprinkle with peanuts, and serve.

Cucumber-Radish Salad With Tarragon Vinaigrette
PREP: 15 MINUTES • COOK TIME: 0 MINUTES • TOTAL: 15 MINUTES • SERVES: 4 servings

Ingredients
2 medium English cucumbers, peeled, halved, seeded, cut into 1/4-inch slices
6 small red radishes, cut into 1/8-inch slices
21/2 tablespoons tarragon vinegar
1/4 cup olive oil

1/2 teaspoon dried tarragon
1/4 teaspoon sugar
Salt and freshly ground black pepper

Directions
1. In a large bowl, combine the cucumbers and the radishes and set aside.
2. In a small bowl, combine the vinegar, tarragon, sugar, and salt and pepper to taste. Whisk in the oil until well blended, then add the dressing to the salad. Toss gently to combine and serve.

Italian-Style Pasta Salad
PREP: 5 MINUTES • COOK TIME: 10 MINUTES • TOTAL: 15 MINUTES • SERVES: 4 to 6 servings

Ingredients
8 ounces penne, rotini, or other small pasta
11/2 cups cooked or 1 (15.5-ounce) can chickpeas, drained and rinsed
1/2 cup pitted kalamata olives
1/2 cup minced oil-packed sun-dried tomatoes
1 (6-ounce) jar marinated artichoke hearts, drained
2 jarred roasted red peppers, chopped
Salt and freshly ground black pepper

1/2 cup frozen peas, thawed
1 tablespoon capers
2 teaspoons dried chives
1/2 cup olive oil
1/4 cup white wine vinegar
1/2 teaspoon dried basil
1 garlic clove, minced

Directions
1. In a pot of boiling salted water, cook the pasta, stirring occasionally, until al dente, about 10 minutes. Drain well and transfer to a large bowl. Add the chickpeas, olives, tomatoes, artichoke hearts, roasted peppers, peas, capers, and chives. Toss gently and set aside.
2. In a small bowl, combine the oil, vinegar, basil, garlic, sugar, and salt and black pepper to taste. Pour the dressing onto the pasta salad and toss to combine. Serve chilled or at room temperature.

Tabbouleh Salad
PREP: 15 MINUTES • COOK TIME: 10 MINUTES • TOTAL: 25 MINUTES • SERVES: 4

Ingredients
1 cup whole-wheat couscous
1 cup boiling water
Zest and juice of 1 lemon
1 garlic clove, pressed
Pinch sea salt

1 tablespoon olive oil, or flaxseed oil (optional)
½ cucumber, diced small
1 tomato, diced small
1 cup fresh parsley, chopped
¼ cup fresh mint, finely chopped

2 scallions, finely chopped | 4 tablespoons sunflower seeds (optional)

Directions
Preparing the Ingredients.
1. Put the couscous in a medium bowl, and cover with boiling water until all the grains are submerged. Cover the bowl with a plate or wrap. Set aside.
2. Put the lemon zest and juice in a large salad bowl, then stir in the garlic, salt, and the olive oil (if using). Put the cucumber, tomato, parsley, mint, and scallions in the bowl, and toss them to coat with the dressing. Take the plate off the couscous and fluff with a fork.
Add the cooked couscous to the vegetables, and toss to combine.
Serve topped with the sunflower seeds (if using).

Per Serving Calories: 304; Total fat: 11g; Carbs: 44g; Fiber: 6g; Protein: 10g

Tuscan White Bean Salad
PREP: 10 MINUTES • MARINATING TIME: 30 MINUTES • • SERVES: 2

Ingredients
FOR THE DRESSING
1 tablespoon olive oil
2 tablespoons balsamic vinegar
1 teaspoon minced fresh chives, or scallions
1 garlic clove, pressed or minced
1 tablespoon fresh rosemary, chopped, or 1 teaspoon dried
1 tablespoon fresh oregano, chopped, or 1 teaspoon dried

Pinch sea salt

FOR THE SALAD
1 (14-ounce) can cannellini beans, drained and rinsed, or 1½ cups cooked
6 mushrooms, thinly sliced
1 zucchini, diced
2 carrots, diced
2 tablespoons fresh basil, chopped

Directions
Preparing the Ingredients.
1. Make the dressing by whisking all the dressing ingredients together in a large bowl.
2. Toss all the salad ingredients with the dressing. For the best flavor, put the salad in a sealed container, shake it vigorously, and leave to marinate 15 to 30 minutes.

Per Serving Calories: 360; Total fat: 8g; Carbs: 68g; Fiber: 15g; Protein: 18g

Indonesian Green Bean Salad With Cabbage And Carrots
PREP: 15 MINUTES • COOK TIME: 0 MINUTES • TOTAL: 15 MINUTES • SERVES: 4 servings

Ingredients
2 cups green beans, trimmed and cut into 1-inch pieces
2 medium carrots, cut into 1/4-inch slices
2 cups finely shredded cabbage
1/3 cup golden raisins
1/4 cup unsalted roasted peanuts
1 garlic clove, minced
1 medium shallot, chopped

11/2 teaspoons grated fresh ginger
1/3 cup creamy peanut butter
2 tablespoons soy sauce
2 tablespoons fresh lemon juice
1 teaspoon sugar(optional)
1/4 teaspoon salt(optional)
1/8 teaspoon ground cayenne
¾ cup unsweetened coconut milk

Directions

1. Lightly steam the green beans, carrots, and cabbage for about 5 minutes, then place them in a large bowl. Add the raisins and peanuts and set aside to cool.
2. In a food processor or blender, puree the garlic, shallot, and ginger. Add the peanut butter, soy sauce, lemon juice, sugar, salt, and cayenne, and process until blended. Add the coconut milk and blend until smooth. Pour the dressing over the salad, toss gently to combine, and serve.

Cucumber And Onion Quinoa Salad
PREP: 15 MINUTES • COOK TIME: 20 MINUTES • TOTAL: 25 MINUTES • SERVES: 4

Ingredients

1½ cups dry quinoa, rinsed and drained
2¼ cups water
⅓ cup white wine vinegar
2 tablespoons extra-virgin olive oil
1 tablespoon chopped fresh dill
1½ teaspoons vegan sugar

2 pinches salt
¼ teaspoon freshly ground black pepper
2 cups sliced sweet onions
2 cups diced cucumber
4 cups shredded lettuce

Directions
Preparing the Ingredients.
1. In a medium pot, combine the quinoa and water. Bring to a boil.
   Cover, reduce the heat to medium-low, and simmer for 15 to 20 minutes, until the water is absorbed. Remove from the stove and let stand for 5 minutes. Fluff with a fork and set aside.
2. Meanwhile, in a small bowl, mix the vinegar, olive oil, dill, sugar, salt, and pepper. Set aside. Into each of 4 wide-mouth jars, add 2 tablespoons of dressing, ½ cup of onions, ½ cup of cucumber, 1 cup of cooked quinoa, and 1 cup of shredded lettuce. Seal the lids tightly.

Per Serving: Calories: 369; Fat: 11g; Protein: 10g; Carbohydrates: 58g; Fiber: 6g; Sugar: 12g; Sodium: 88mg

Moroccan Aubergine Salad
PREP: 30 MINUTES • COOK TIME: 15 MINUTES • TOTAL: 45 MINUTES • SERVES: 2

Ingredients

1 teaspoon olive oil
1 eggplant, diced
½ teaspoon ground cumin
½ teaspoon ground ginger
¼ teaspoon turmeric
¼ teaspoon ground nutmeg
Pinch sea salt

1 lemon, half zested and juiced, half cut into wedges
2 tablespoons capers
1 tablespoon chopped green olives
1 garlic clove, pressed
Handful fresh mint, finely chopped
2 cups spinach, chopped

Directions
Preparing the Ingredients.
1. Heat the oil in a large skillet on medium heat, then sauté the eggplant. Once it has softened slightly, about 5 minutes, stir in the cumin, ginger, turmeric, nutmeg, and salt. Cook until the eggplant is very soft, about 10 minutes.
2. Add the lemon zest and juice, capers, olives, garlic, and mint. Sauté for another minute or two, to blend the flavors. Put a handful of spinach on each plate, and spoon the eggplant mixture on top.
3. Serve with a wedge of lemon, to squeeze the fresh juice over the greens.

To tenderize the eggplant and reduce some of its naturally occurring bitter taste, you can sweat the eggplant by salting it. After dicing the eggplant, sprinkle it with salt and let it sit in a colander for about 30 minutes. Rinse the eggplant to remove the salt, then continue with the recipe as written.

Per Serving Calories: 97; Total fat: 4g; Carbs: 16g; Fiber: 8g; Protein: 4g

Potato Salad With Artichoke Hearts
PREP: 15 MINUTES • COOK TIME: 15 MINUTES • TOTAL: 15 MINUTES • SERVES: 4 to 6 servings

Ingredients
11/2 pounds Yukon Gold potatoes, peeled and cut into 1-inch dice

1 (10-ounce) package frozen artichoke hearts, cooked

2 cups halved ripe grape tomatoes

1/2 cup frozen peas, thawed

3 green onions, minced

1 tablespoon minced fresh parsley

1/3 cup olive oil

2 tablespoons fresh lemon juice

1 garlic clove, minced

Salt and freshly ground black pepper

Directions
1. In a large pot of boiling salted water, cook the potatoes until just tender but still firm, about 15 minutes. Drain well and transfer to a large bowl.
2. Quarter the artichokes and add them to the potatoes. Add the tomatoes, peas, green onions, and parsley and set aside.
3. In a small bowl, combine the oil, lemon juice, garlic, and salt and pepper to taste. Mix well, pour the dressing over potato salad, and toss gently to combine. Set aside at room temperature to allow flavors to blend, about 20 minutes. Taste, adjusting seasonings if necessary, and serve.

Giardiniera
PREP: 15 MINUTES • COOK TIME: 0 MINUTES • TOTAL: 15MINUTES • SERVES: 6 servings

Ingredients
1 medium carrot, cut into 1/4-inch rounds

1 medium red bell pepper, cut into 1/2-inch dice

1 cup small cauliflower florets

2 celery ribs, finely chopped

1/2 cup chopped onion

2 tablespoons salt (optional)

1/4 cup sliced pimiento-stuffed green olives

1 garlic clove, minced

1/2 teaspoon sugar (optional)

1/2 teaspoon crushed red pepper

1/4 teaspoon freshly ground black pepper

3 tablespoons white wine vinegar

1/3 cup olive oil

Directions
1. In a large bowl, combine the carrot, bell pepper, cauliflower, celery, and onion. Stir in the salt and add enough cold water to cover. Tightly cover the bowl and refrigerate for 4 to 6 hours.
2. Drain and rinse the vegetables and place them in a large bowl. Add the olives and set aside.
3. In a small bowl, combine the garlic, sugar, crushed red pepper, black pepper, vinegar, and oil, and mix well. Pour the dressing over the vegetables and toss gently to combine. Cover and refrigerate overnight before serving.

Creamy Avocado-Dressed Kale Salad
PREP: 10 MINUTES • COOK TIME: 20 MINUTES • TOTAL: 30 MINUTES • SERVES: 4

Ingredients
FOR THE DRESSING

1 avocado, peeled and pitted
1 tablespoon fresh lemon juice, or 1 teaspoon lemon juice concentrate and 2 teaspoons water
1 tablespoon fresh or dried dill1 small garlic clove, pressed
1 scallion, chopped
Pinch sea salt
¼ cup water

FOR THE SALAD

8 large kale leaves
½ cup chopped green beans, raw or lightly steamed
1 cup cherry tomatoes, halved
1 bell pepper, chopped
2 scallions, chopped
2 cups cooked millet, or other cooked whole grain, such as quinoa or brown rice
Hummus (optional)

Directions

1. **TO MAKE THE DRESSING**
   Put all the ingredients in a blender or food processor. Purée until smooth, then add water as necessary to get the consistency you're looking for in your dressing. Taste for seasoning, and add more salt if you need to.

2. **TO MAKE THE SALAD**
   Chop the kale, removing the stems if you want your salad less bitter, and then massage the leaves with your fingers until it wilts and gets a bit moist, about 2 minutes. You can use a pinch salt if you like to help it soften. Toss the kale with the green beans, cherry tomatoes, bell pepper, scallions, millet, and the dressing. Pile the salad onto plates, and top them off with a spoonful of hummus (if using).

Per Serving Calories: 225; Total fat: 7g; Carbs: 37g; Fiber: 7g; Protein: 7g

Indonesian-Style Potato Salad
PREP: 10 MINUTES • COOK TIME: 30 MINUTES • TOTAL: 40 MINUTES • SERVES: 4 to 6 servings

Ingredients

11/2 pounds small white potatoes, unpeeled
1 cup frozen peas, thawed
1/2 cup shredded carrot
4 green onions, chopped
1 tablespoon grapeseed oil
1 garlic clove, minced
1/3 cup creamy peanut butter

1/2 teaspoon Asian chili paste
2 tablespoons soy sauce
1 tablespoon rice vinegar
¾ cup unsweetened coconut milk
3 tablespoons chopped unsalted roasted peanuts, for garnish

Directions

1. In a large pot of boiling salted water, cook the potatoes until tender, 20 to 30 minutes. Drain well and set aside to cool.
2. When cool enough to handle, cut the potatoes into 1-inch chunks and transfer to a large bowl. Add the peas, carrot, and green onions, and set aside.
3. In a small saucepan, heat the oil over medium heat. Add the garlic and cook until fragrant, about 30 seconds. Stir in the peanut butter, chili paste, soy sauce, vinegar, and about half of the coconut milk. Simmer over medium heat for 5 minutes, stirring frequently to make a smooth sauce. Add as much of the remaining coconut milk as needed for a creamy consistency. Pour the dressing over the salad and toss well to combine. Garnish with peanuts and serve.

Roasted Beet and Avocado Salad
PREP: 10 MINUTES • COOK TIME: 30MINUTES • TOTAL: 40 MINUTES • SERVES: 2

Ingredients

2 beets, peeled and thinly sliced
1 teaspoon olive oil
Pinch sea salt
2 tablespoons chopped almonds, pumpkin seeds, or sunflower seeds (raw or toasted)

1 avocado
2 cups mixed greens
3 to 4 tablespoons Creamy Balsamic Dressing

Directions
Preparing the Ingredients.
1. Preheat the oven to 400°F.
   Put the beets, oil, and salt in a large bowl, and toss the beets with your hands to coat. Lay them in a single layer in a large baking dish, and roast them in the oven 20 to 30 minutes, or until they're softened and slightly browned around the edges.
2. While the beets are roasting, cut the avocado in half and take the pit out. Scoop the flesh out, as intact as possible, and slice it into crescents.
   Once the beets are cooked, lay slices out on two plates and top each beet slice with a similar-size avocado slice.
   Top with a handful of mixed greens. Drizzle the dressing over everything, and sprinkle on a few chopped almonds.

Per Serving Calories: 167; Total fat: 13g; Carbs: 15g; Fiber: 5g; Protein: 4g

Creamy Coleslaw
PREP: 10 MINUTES • COOK TIME: 0 MINUTES • TOTAL: 10 MINUTES • SERVES: 4 servings

Ingredients
1 small head green cabbage, finely shredded
1 large carrot, shredded
¾ cup vegan mayonnaise, homemade or store-bought
1/4 cup soy milk

2 tablespoons cider vinegar
1/2 teaspoon dry mustard
1/4 teaspoon celery seeds
1/2 teaspoon salt (optional)
Freshly ground black pepper

Directions
1. In a large bowl, combine the cabbage and carrot and set aside.
2. In a small bowl, combine the mayonnaise, soy milk, vinegar, mustard, celery seeds, salt, and pepper to taste. Mix until smooth and well blended. Add the dressing to the slaw and mix well to combine. Taste, adjusting seasonings if necessary, and serve.

Sesame Cucumber Salad
PREP: 15 MINUTES • COOK TIME: 0 MINUTES • TOTAL: 15 MINUTES • SERVES: 4 to 6 servings

Ingredients
2 medium English cucumbers, peeled and cut into 1/4-inch slices
2 tablespoons chopped fresh parsley
3 tablespoons toasted sesame oil
2 tablespoons soy sauce

1 tablespoon mirin
2 teaspoons rice vinegar
1 teaspoon brown sugar (optional)
2 tablespoons toasted sesame seeds

Directions
1. In a small bowl, combine the cucumbers and parsley and set aside.

2. In a separate small bowl, combine the oil, soy sauce, mirin, vinegar, and sugar, stirring to blend. Pour the dressing over the cucumbers. Set aside for at least 10 minutes.
3. Spoon the cucumber salad into small bowls, sprinkle with sesame seeds, and serve.

Basil Mango Jicama Salad
PREP: 15 MINUTES • CHILL TIME: 60 MINUTES • • SERVES: 6

Ingredients
1 jicama, peeled and grated
1 mango, peeled and sliced
¼ cup non-dairy milk
2 tablespoons fresh basil, chopped
1 large scallion, chopped

⅛ teaspoon sea salt
1½ tablespoons tahini (optional)
Fresh greens (for serving)
Chopped cashews (optional, for serving)
Cheesy Sprinkle (optional, for serving)

Directions
Preparing the Ingredients.
1. Put the jicama in a large bowl.
   Purée the mango in a food processor or blender, with just enough non-dairy milk to make a thick sauce. Add the basil, scallions, and salt. Stir in the tahini if you want to make a thicker, creamier, and more filling sauce.
2. Pour the dressing over the jicama and marinate, covered in the fridge, for 1 hour or more to break down some of the starch. Serve over a bed of greens, topped with chopped cashews and/or Cheesy Sprinkle (if using).
Per Serving Calories: 76; Total fat: 2g; Carbs: 14g; Fiber: 5g; Protein: 1g

Red Cabbage Slaw With Black-Vinegar Dressing
PREP: 15 MINUTES • COOK TIME: 0 MINUTES • TOTAL: 15 MINUTES • SERVES: 6 servings

Ingredients
4 cups shredded red cabbage
2 cups thinly sliced napa cabbage
1 cup shredded daikon radish
1/4 cup fresh orange juice
2 tablespoons Chinese black vinegar
1 tablespoon soy sauce

1 tablespoon grapeseed oil
1 tablespoon toasted sesame oil
1 teaspoon grated fresh ginger
1/2 teaspoon ground Szechuan peppercorns
1 tablespoon black sesame seeds, for garnish

Directions
1. In a large bowl, combine the red cabbage, napa, and daikon and set aside.
2. In a small bowl, combine the orange juice, vinegar, soy sauce, grapeseed oil, sesame oil, ginger, and peppercorns. Blend well. Pour the dressing onto the slaw, stirring to coat. Taste, adjusting seasonings if necessary. Cover and refrigerate to allow flavors to blend, about 2 hours. Sprinkle with sesame seeds and serve.

Corn And Red Bean Salad
PREP: 10 MINUTES • COOK TIME: 0 MINUTES • TOTAL: 10 MINUTES • SERVES: 4 servings

Ingredients
1 (10-ounce) package frozen corn kernels, cooked
11/2 cups cooked or 1 (15.5-ounce) can dark red kidney beans, drained and rinsed
1 celery rib, cut into 1/4-inch slices

2 green onions, minced
2 tablespoons chopped fresh cilantro or parsley
1/4 cup olive oil
2 tablespoons white wine vinegar

1/2 teaspoon ground cumin
1/4 teaspoon sugar (optional)

1/2 teaspoon salt (optional)
1/8 teaspoon freshly ground black pepper

Directions
1. In a large bowl, combine the corn, beans, celery, green onions, and cilantro, and set aside.
2. In a small bowl, combine the oil, vinegar, cumin, sugar, salt, and pepper. Mix well and pour the dressing over the vegetables. Toss gently to combine and serve.

Greek Potato Salad
PREP: 10 MINUTES • COOK TIME: 20 MINUTES • TOTAL: 30 MINUTES • SERVES: 4

Ingredients
6 potatoes, scrubbed or peeled and chopped
Salt
¼ cup olive oil
2 tablespoons apple cider vinegar
2 tablespoons freshly squeezed lemon juice

1 teaspoon dried herbs
½ cucumber, chopped
¼ red onion, diced
¼ cup chopped pitted black olives
Freshly ground black pepper

Directions
Preparing the Ingredients.
1. Put the potatoes in a large pot, add a pinch of salt, and pour in enough water to cover. Bring the water to a boil over high heat. Cook the potatoes for 15 to 20 minutes, until soft. Drain and set aside to cool. (Alternatively, put the potatoes in a large microwave-safe dish with a bit of water. Cover and heat on high power for 10 minutes.)
2. In a large bowl, whisk together the olive oil, vinegar, lemon juice, and dried herbs. Toss the cucumber, red onion, and olives with the dressing. Add the cooked, cooled potatoes, and toss to combine. Taste and season with salt and pepper as needed. Store leftovers in an airtight container in the refrigerator for up to 1 week.

Per Serving Calories: 358; Protein: 5g; Total fat: 16g; Saturated fat: 2g; Carbohydrates: 52g; Fiber: 5g

Rainbow Quinoa Salad
PREP: 51 MINUTES • COOK TIME: 0 MINUTES • TOTAL: 15 MINUTES • SERVES: 6-8

Ingredients
3 tablespoons olive oil
Juice of 1½ lemons
1 teaspoon garlic powder
½ teaspoon dried oregano
1 bunch curly kale, stemmed and roughly chopped
2 cups cooked tricolor quinoa

1 cup canned mandarin oranges in juice, drained
1 cup diced yellow summer squash
1 red bell pepper, seeded and diced
½ red onion, thinly sliced
½ cup dried cranberries or cherries
½ cup slivered almonds

Directions
Preparing the Ingredients.
1. In a small bowl, whisk together the oil, lemon juice, garlic powder, and oregano.
2. In a large bowl, toss the kale with the oil-lemon mixture until well coated. Add the quinoa, oranges, squash, bell pepper, and red onion and toss until all the ingredients are well combined. Divide among bowls or transfer to a large serving platter. Top with the cranberries and almonds.

Yellow Mung Bean Salad With Broccoli And Mango
PREP: 5 MINUTES • COOK TIME: 20 MINUTES • TOTAL: 25 MINUTES • SERVES: 4 servings

Ingredients

1/2 cup yellow mung beans, picked over, rinsed, and drained
3 cups small broccoli florets, blanched
1 ripe mango, peeled, pitted, and chopped
1 small red bell pepper, chopped
1 jalapeño or other hot green chile, seeded and minced

2 tablespoons chopped fresh cilantro
1 teaspoon grated fresh ginger
2 tablespoons fresh lemon juice
3 tablespoons grapeseed oil
1/3 cup unsalted roasted cashews, for garnish

Directions

1. In a saucepan of boiling salted water, cook the mung beans until just tender, 18 to 20 minutes. Drain and run under cold water to cool. Transfer the beans to a large bowl. Add the broccoli, mango, bell pepper, chile, and cilantro. Set aside.
2. In a small bowl, combine the ginger, lemon juice, oil. Stir to mix well, then pour the dressing over the vegetables and toss to combine. Sprinkle with cashews and serve.

Asian Slaw
PREP: 15 MINUTES • COOK TIME: 0 MINUTES • TOTAL: 15 MINUTES • SERVES: 4 servings

Ingredients

8 ounces napa cabbage, cut crosswise into 1/4-inch strips
1 cup grated carrot
1 cup grated daikon radish
2 green onions, minced
2 tablespoons chopped fresh parsley
2 tablespoons rice vinegar
1 tablespoon grapeseed oil

2 teaspoons toasted sesame oil
1 tablespoon soy sauce
1 teaspoon grated fresh ginger
1/2 teaspoon dry mustard
Salt and freshly ground black pepper
2 tablespoons chopped unsalted roasted peanuts, for garnish (optional)

Directions

1. In a large bowl, combine the napa cabbage, carrot, daikon, green onions, and parsley. Set aside.
2. In a small bowl, combine the vinegar, grapeseed oil, sesame oil, soy sauce, ginger, mustard, and salt and pepper to taste. Stir until well blended. Pour the dressing over the vegetables and toss gently to coat. Taste, adjusting seasonings if necessary. Cover and refrigerate to allow flavors to blend, about 2 hours. Sprinkle with peanuts, if using, and serve.

The Great Green Salad
PREP: 10 MINUTES • COOK TIME: 0 MINUTES • TOTAL: 10 MINUTES • SERVES:

Ingredients

1 head Boston or Bibb lettuce
8 asparagus spears, trimmed and cut into 2-inch pieces
2 mini seedless cucumbers, sliced
1 small zucchini, cut into ribbons with potato peeler

1 avocado, peeled, pitted, and sliced
½ cup store-bought vegan green goddess dressing
2 scallions, thinly sliced

Directions
Preparing the Ingredients.

Divide the lettuce leaves among 4 plates. Top each with some of the asparagus, cucumber, zucchini, and avocado. Drizzle each bowl with 2 tablespoons of dressing and sprinkle with scallions.

Summer Berries With Fresh Mint
PREP: 15 MINUTES • COOK TIME: 0 MINUTES • TOTAL: 15 MINUTES • SERVES: 4 to 6 servings

Ingredients
2 tablespoons fresh orange or pineapple juice
1 tablespoon fresh lime juice
1 tablespoon agave nectar
2 teaspoons minced fresh mint

2 cups pitted fresh cherries
1 cup fresh blueberries
1 cup fresh strawberries, hulled and halved
1/2 cup fresh blackberries or raspberries

Directions
1. In a small bowl, combine the orange juice, lime juice, agave nectar, and mint. Set aside.
2. In a large bowl, combine the cherries, blueberries, strawberries, and blackberries. Add the dressing and toss gently to combine. Serve immediately.

Curried Fruit Salad
PREP: 15 MINUTES • COOK TIME: 0 MINUTES • TOTAL: 15 MINUTES • SERVES: 4 to 6 servings

Ingredients
¾ cup vegan vanilla yogurt
1/4 cup finely chopped mango chutney
1 tablespoon fresh lime juice
1 teaspoon mild curry powder
1 Fuji or Gala apple, cored and cut into 1/2-inch dice
2 ripe peaches, halved, pitted, and cut into 1/2-inch dice

4 ripe black plums, halved and cut into 1/4-inch slices
1 ripe mango, peeled, pitted, and cut into 1/2-inch dice
1 cup red seedless grapes, halved
1/4 cup unsweetened toasted shredded coconut
1/4 cup toasted slivered almonds

Directions
1. In a small bowl, combine the yogurt, chutney, lime juice, and curry powder and stir until well blended. Set aside.
2. In a large bowl, combine the apple, peaches, plums, mango, grapes, coconut, and almonds. Add the dressing, toss gently to coat, and serve.

Stuffed Avocado
PREP: 10 MINUTES • COOK TIME: 0 MINUTES • TOTAL: 10 MINUTES • SERVES: 4

Ingredients
2 avocados, halved and pitted
1 (15-ounce) can black beans, rinsed and drained
1 cup frozen (and thawed) or fresh corn kernels
½ cup seeded and diced tomato
Juice of ½ lime

1 tablespoon maple syrup
1 teaspoon olive oil
2 pinches sea salt
2 pinches black pepper
1 tablespoon chopped fresh cilantro

Directions
Preparing the Ingredients.

1. Scoop some avocado flesh from each half with a spoon, leaving a ¼- to ½-inch wall of avocado in the shell.
2. In a large bowl, mix together the scooped-out avocado, beans, corn, tomato, lime juice, maple syrup, oil, salt, pepper, and cilantro until well incorporated.
   Spoon the filling into the avocado shells and enjoy.

Cranberry-Carrot Salad
PREP: 15 MINUTES • COOK TIME: 0 MINUTES • TOTAL: 15 MINUTES • SERVES: 4 servings

Ingredients
1 pound carrots, shredded
1 cup sweetened dried cranberries
1/2 cup toasted walnut pieces

2 tablespoons fresh lemon juice
3 tablespoons toasted walnut oil
1/8 teaspoon freshly ground black pepper

Directions
1. In a large bowl, combine the carrots, cranberries, and walnuts. Set aside.
2. In a small bowl, whisk together the lemon juice, walnut oil and pepper. Pour the dressing over the salad, toss gently to combine and serve.

Almond Crunch Chopped Kale Salad
PREP: 10 MINUTES • COOK TIME: 10 MINUTES • TOTAL: 20 MINUTES • SERVES: 4

Ingredients

FOR THE DRESSING
¼ cup tahini
2 tablespoons Dijon mustard
2 tablespoons maple syrup
1 tablespoon lemon juice
¼ teaspoon salt
FOR THE ALMOND CRUNCH
½ cup finely chopped raw almonds

2 teaspoons soy sauce or gluten-free tamari
1 teaspoon maple syrup
¼ teaspoon sea salt
FOR THE SALAD
1 bunch lacinato kale, stemmed and roughly chopped
1 green apple, cored and thinly sliced

Directions
Preheat the oven to 325°F. Line a baking sheet with parchment paper.
To make the dressing: Whisk together all the dressing ingredients in a small bowl and set aside.
1. **To make the almond crunch:** Mix together all the almond crunch ingredients in a medium bowl and spread out evenly on the prepared baking sheet. Bake for 5 to 7 minutes, until slightly darker in color and crunchy. Let cool for 3 minutes.
2. **To make the salad:** In a large bowl, mix together the kale and apples. Toss with the dressing and top with the almond crunch.

Apple-Sunflower Spinach Salad
PREP: 5 MINUTES • COOK TIME: 0 MINUTES • TOTAL: 5 MINUTES • SERVES: 1

Ingredients
1 cup baby spinach
½ apple, cored and chopped
¼ red onion, thinly sliced (optional)

2 tablespoons sunflower seeds or Cinnamon-Lime Sunflower Seeds
2 tablespoons dried cranberries
2 tablespoons Raspberry Vinaigrette

Directions

Preparing the Ingredients.

Arrange the spinach on a plate. Top with the apple, red onion (if using), sunflower seeds, and cranberries, and drizzle with the vinaigrette.

Per Serving Calories: 444; Protein: 7g; Total fat: 28g; Saturated fat: 3g; Carbohydrates: 53g; Fiber: 8g

Ruby Grapefruit and Radicchio Salad
PREP: 10 MINUTES • COOK TIME: 0 MINUTES • TOTAL: 10 MINUTES • SERVES: 4

Ingredients

FOR THE SALAD
1 large ruby grapefruit
1 small head radicchio, torn into bite-size pieces
2 cups green leaf lettuce, torn into bite-size pieces
2 cups baby spinach
1 bunch watercress
4 to 6 radishes, sliced paper-thin

FOR THE DRESSING
juice of 1 lemon
2 teaspoons agave
1 teaspoon white wine vinegar
½ teaspoon sea salt
½ teaspoon freshly ground black pepper
¼ cup extra-virgin olive oil

Directions

1. **To make the salad:** Cut both ends off of the grapefruit, stand it on a cutting board on one of the flat sides, and, using a sharp knife, cut away the peel and all of the white pith. Remove the individual segments by slicing between the membrane and fruit on each side of each segment, dropping the fruit into a large salad bowl as you go. Add the radicchio, lettuce, spinach, watercress, and radishes to the bowl and toss well.
2. **To make the dressing:** Whisk together the lemon juice, agave, vinegar, salt, and pepper. Slowly whisk in the olive oil until the mixture is well combined and -emulsified. Toss the salad with the dressing and serve immediately.

Darn Good Caesar Salad
PREP: 10 MINUTES • COOK TIME: 0 MINUTES • TOTAL: 10 MINUTES • SERVES: 4

Ingredients

FOR THE DRESSING
½ cup walnuts
½ cup water
3 tablespoons olive oil
Juice of ½ lime
1 tablespoon white miso paste
1 teaspoon soy sauce or gluten-free tamari
1 teaspoon Dijon mustard

1 teaspoon garlic powder
¼ teaspoon sea salt
½ teaspoon black pepper
FOR THE SALAD
2 heads romaine lettuce, chopped
1 cup cherry tomatoes, halved
vegan Parmesan, for garnish
Vegan croutons, for garnish (optional)

Directions

1. **To make the dressing:** In a blender, combine all the dressing ingredients and blend until almost smooth, about 2 minutes. It's okay if this dressing is slightly chunky, which is more like a classic Caesar dressing texture.
2. **To make the salad:** In a large bowl, toss the lettuce with half of the dressing. Add more as desired. Divide among serving plates and top with the tomatoes and Parmesan. Finish the salad off with croutons, if desired.

Potato Salad Redux

PREP: 5 MINUTES • COOK TIME: 30 MINUTES • TOTAL: 35 MINUTES • SERVES: 4 to 6 servings

Ingredients

11/2 pounds small white potatoes, unpeeled
2 celery ribs, cut into 1/4-inch slices
1/4 cup sweet pickle relish
3 tablespoons minced green onions
1/2 to ¾ cup vegan mayonnaise, homemade or store-bought

1 tablespoon soy milk
1 tablespoon tarragon vinegar
1 teaspoon Dijon mustard
1/2 teaspoon salt (optional)
Freshly ground black pepper

Directions

1. In a large pot of salted boiling water, cook the potatoes until just tender, about 30 minutes. Drain and set aside to cool. When cool enough to handle, peel the potatoes and cut them into 1-inch dice. Transfer the potatoes to a large bowl and add the celery, pickle relish, and green onions. Set aside.
2. In a small bowl, combine the mayonnaise, soy milk, vinegar, mustard, salt, and pepper to taste. Mix until well blended. Pour the dressing onto the potato mixture, toss gently to combine, and serve.

Apple and Ginger Slaw

PREP: 10 MINUTES • COOK TIME: 0 MINUTES • TOTAL: 10 MINUTES • SERVES: 4

Ingredients

2 tablespoons olive oil
juice of 1 lemon, or 2 tablespoons prepared lemon juice
1 teaspoon grated fresh ginger

pinch of sea salt
2 apples, peeled and julienned
4 cups shredded red cabbage

Directions

Preparing the Ingredients.
In a small bowl, whisk together the olive oil, lemon juice, ginger, and salt and set aside.
In a large bowl, combine the apples and cabbage.
Toss with the vinaigrette and serve immediately. Store leftovers in an airtight container in the refrigerator for up to 3 days.

Sunshine Fiesta Salad

PREP: 15 MINUTES • COOK TIME: 0 MINUTES • TOTAL: 15 MINUTES • SERVES: 4

Ingredients

FOR THE VINAIGRETTE
Juice of 2 limes
1 tablespoon olive oil
1 tablespoon maple syrup or agave
¼ teaspoon sea salt
FOR THE SALAD
2 cups cooked quinoa

1 tablespoon *Taco Seasoning* or store-bought taco seasoning
2 heads romaine lettuce, roughly chopped
1 (15-ounce) can black beans, rinsed and drained
1 cup cherry tomatoes, halved
1 cup frozen (and thawed) or fresh corn kernels
1 avocado, peeled, pitted, and diced
4 scallions, thinly sliced
12 tortilla chips, crushed

Directions

1. **To make the vinaigrette:** In a small bowl, whisk together all the vinaigrette ingredients.

2. **To make the salad:** In a medium bowl, mix together the quinoa and taco seasoning. In a large bowl, toss the romaine with the vinaigrette. Divide among 4 bowls. Top each bowl with equal amounts quinoa, beans, tomatoes, corn, avocado, scallions, and crushed tortillas chips.

French-Style Potato Salad

PREP: 5 MINUTES • COOK TIME: 30 MINUTES • TOTAL: 15 MINUTES • SERVES: 4 to 6 servings

Ingredients

11/2 pounds small white potatoes, unpeeled
2 tablespoons minced fresh parsley
1 tablespoon minced fresh chives
1 teaspoon minced fresh tarragon or 1/2 teaspoon dried

1/3 cup olive oil
2 tablespoons white wine or tarragon vinegar
1/8 teaspoon freshly ground black pepper

Directions

1. In a large pot of boiling salted water, cook the potatoes until tender but still firm, about 30 minutes. Drain and cut into 1/4-inch slices. Transfer to a large bowl and add the parsley, chives, and tarragon. Set aside.
2. In a small bowl, combine the oil, vinegar, pepper. Pour the dressing onto the potato mixture and toss gently to combine.
   Taste, adjusting seasonings if necessary. Chill for 1 to 2 hours before serving.

Roasted Carrot Salad

PREP: 10 MINUTES • COOK TIME: 30 MINUTES • TOTAL: 40 MINUTES • SERVES: 3

Ingredients

4 carrots, peeled and sliced
1 to 2 teaspoons olive oil or coconut oil
½ teaspoon ground cinnamon or pumpkin pie spice
Salt
1 (15-ounce) can cannellini beans or navy beans, drained and rinsed
3 cups chopped hearty greens, such as spinach, kale, chard, or collards

⅓ cup dried cranberries or pomegranate seeds
⅓ cup slivered almonds or Cinnamon-Lime Sunflower Seeds
¼ cup Raspberry Vinaigrette or Cilantro-Lime *Dressing*, or 2 tablespoons freshly squeezed orange or lemon juice whisked with 2 tablespoons olive oil and a pinch of salt

Directions

Preparing the Ingredients.

Preheat the oven or toaster oven to 400°F.

1. In a medium bowl, toss the carrots with the olive oil and cinnamon and season to taste with salt. Transfer to a small tray, and roast for 15 minutes or until browned around the edges. Toss the carrots, add the beans, and roast for 15 minutes more. Let cool while you prep the salad. Divide the greens among three plates or containers, top with the cranberries and almonds, and add the roasted carrots and beans.
2. Drizzle with the dressing of your choice. Store leftovers in an airtight container in the refrigerator for up to 1 week.

Roasted Potato Salad

With Chickpeas And Tomatoes

Ingredients

11/2 pounds Yukon Gold potatoes, cut into 1/2-inch dice
1 medium shallot, halved lengthwise and cut into 1/4-inch slices
1/4 cup olive oil
Salt and freshly ground black pepper
3 tablespoons white wine vinegar

11/2 cups cooked or 1 (15.5-ounce) can chickpeas, drained and rinsed
1/3 cup chopped drained oil-packed sun-dried tomatoes
1/4 cup green olives, pitted and halved
1/4 cup chopped fresh parsley

Directions

1. Preheat the oven to 425°F. In a large bowl, combine the potatoes, shallot, and 1 tablespoon of the oil. Season with salt and pepper to taste and toss to coat. Transfer the potatoes and shallot to a baking sheet and roast, turning once, until tender and golden brown, about 20 minutes. Transfer to a large bowl and set aside to cool.
2. In a small bowl, combine the remaining 3 tablespoons oil with the vinegar and pepper to taste. Add the chickpeas, tomatoes, olives, and parsley to the cooked potatoes and shallots. Drizzle with the dressing and toss gently to combine. Taste, adjusting seasonings if necessary. Serve warm or at room temperature.

Spinach and Pomegranate Salad
PREP: 10 MINUTES • COOK TIME: 0 MINUTES • TOTAL: 10 MINUTES • SERVES: 4

Ingredients

10 ounces baby spinach
seeds from 1 pomegranate
1 cup fresh blackberries
¼ red onion, thinly sliced
½ cup chopped pecans

¼ cup balsamic vinegar
¾ cup olive oil
½ teaspoon sea salt
½ teaspoon freshly ground black pepper

Directions
Preparing the Ingredients.
1. In a large bowl, combine the spinach, pomegranate seeds, blackberries, red onion, and pecans.
2. In a small bowl, whisk together the vinegar, olive oil, salt, and pepper. Toss with the salad and serve immediately.

Cobb Salad with Portobello Bacon
PREP: 15 MINUTES • COOK TIME: 0 MINUTES • TOTAL: 15 MINUTES • SERVES: 4

Ingredients

2 heads romaine lettuce, finely chopped
1 pint cherry tomatoes, halved
1 avocado, peeled, pitted, and diced
1 cup frozen (and thawed) or fresh corn kernels
1 large cucumber, peeled and diced

Portobello Bacon or store-bought vegan bacon
4 scallions, thinly sliced
Unhidden Valley Ranch Dressing or store-bought vegan ranch dressing

Directions
Preparing the Ingredients.

1. Scatter a layer of romaine in the bottom of each of 4 salad bowls. With the following ingredients, create lines that cross the top of the romaine, in this order: tomatoes, avocado, corn, cucumber, and portobello bacon.
2. Sprinkle with the scallions and drizzle with ranch dressing.

German-Style Potato Salad
PREP: 15 MINUTES • COOK TIME: 0 MINUTES • TOTAL: 15 MINUTES • SERVES: 4 to 6 servings

Ingredients
11/2 pounds white potatoes, unpeeled
1/2 cup olive oil
4 slices tempeh bacon, homemade or store-bought
1 medium bunch green onions, chopped
1 tablespoon whole-wheat flour

2 tablespoons sugar
1/3 cup white wine vinegar
1/4 cup water
1/2 teaspoon salt
1/8 teaspoon freshly ground black pepper

Directions
1. In a large pot of boiling salted water, cook the potatoes until just tender, about 30 minutes. Drain well and set aside to cool.
2. In a large skillet, heat the oil over medium heat. Add the tempeh bacon and cook until browned on both sides, about 5 minutes total. Remove from skillet, and set aside to cool.
3. Cut the cooled potatoes into 1-inch chunks and place in a large bowl. Crumble or chop the cooked tempeh bacon and add to the potatoes.
4. Reheat the skillet over medium heat. Add the green onions and cook for 1 minute to soften. Stir in the flour, sugar, vinegar, water, salt, and pepper, and bring to a boil, stirring until smooth. Pour the hot dressing onto the potatoes. Stir gently to combine and serve.

Sweet Pearl Couscous Salad with Pear & Cranberries
PREP: 5 MINUTES • COOK TIME: 10 MINUTES • TOTAL: 15 MINUTES • SERVES: 4

Ingredients
1 cup pearl couscous
1½ cups water
Salt
¼ cup olive oil
¼ cup freshly squeezed orange juice

1 tablespoon sugar, maple syrup, or *Simple Syrup*
1 pear, cored and diced
½ cucumber, diced
¼ cup dried cranberries or raisins

Directions
Preparing the Ingredients.
1. In a small pot, combine the couscous, water, and a pinch of salt. Bring to a boil over high heat, turn the heat to low, and cover the pot. Simmer for about 10 minutes, until the couscous is al dente.
2. Meanwhile, in a large bowl, whisk together the olive oil, orange juice, and sugar. Season to taste with salt and whisk again to combine.
3. Add the pear, cucumber, cranberries, and cooked couscous. Toss to combine. Store leftovers in an airtight container in the refrigerator for up to 1 week.
Per Serving Calories: 365; Protein: 6g; Total fat: 14g; Saturated fat: 2g; Carbohydrates: 55g; Fiber: 4g

Pear and Arugula Salad
PREP: 10 MINUTES • COOK TIME: 8 MINUTES • TOTAL: 18 MINUTES • SERVES: 4

Ingredients

¼ cup chopped pecans
10 ounces arugula
2 pears, thinly sliced
1 tablespoon finely minced shallot
2 tablespoons champagne vinegar

2 tablespoons olive oil
¼ teaspoon sea salt
¼ teaspoon freshly ground black pepper
¼ teaspoon dijon mustard

Directions

Preparing the Ingredients.
   Preheat the oven to 350°F.
1. Spread the pecans in a single layer on a baking sheet. Toast in the preheated oven until fragrant, about 6 minutes. Remove from the oven and let cool. In a large bowl, toss the pecans, arugula, and pears. In a small bowl, whisk together the shallot, vinegar, olive oil, salt, pepper, and -mustard. Toss with the salad and serve immediately.

Quinoa Salad With Black Beans And Tomatoes
PREP: 5 MINUTES • COOK TIME: 20 MINUTES • TOTAL: 25 MINUTES • SERVES: 4 servings

Ingredients

3 cups water
11/2 cups quinoa, well rinsed
Salt
11/2 cups cooked or 1 (15.5-ounce) can black beans, drained and rinsed
4 ripe plum tomatoes, cut into 1/4-inch dice

1/3 cup minced red onion
1/4 cup chopped fresh parsley
1/4 cup olive oil
2 tablespoons sherry vinegar
1/4 teaspoon freshly ground black pepper

Directions

1. In a large saucepan, bring the water to boil over high heat. Add the quinoa, salt the water, and return to a boil. Reduce heat to low, cover, and simmer until the water is absorbed, about 20 minutes.
2. Transfer the cooked quinoa to a large bowl. Add the black beans, tomatoes, onion, and parsley.
3. In a small bowl, combine the olive oil, vinegar, salt to taste, and pepper. Pour the dressing over the salad and toss well to combine. Cover and set aside for 20 minutes before serving.

Mediterranean Quinoa Salad
PREP: 5 MINUTES • COOK TIME: 20 MINUTES • TOTAL: 25 MINUTES • SERVES: 4 servings

Ingredients

2 cups water
1 cup quinoa, well rinsed
Salt
11/2 cups cooked or 1 (15.5-ounce) can chickpeas, drained and rinsed
1 cup ripe grape or cherry tomatoes, halved
2 green onions, minced
1/2 medium English cucumber, peeled and chopped

1/4 cup pitted brine-cured black olives
2 tablespoons toasted pine nuts
1/4 cup small fresh basil leaves
1 medium shallot, chopped
1 garlic clove, chopped
1 teaspoon Dijon mustard
2 tablespoons white wine vinegar
1/4 cup olive oil
Freshly ground black pepper

Directions

1. In a large saucepan, bring the water to boil over high heat. Add the quinoa, salt the water, and return to a boil. Reduce heat to low, cover, and simmer until water is absorbed, about 20 minutes.
2. Transfer the cooked quinoa to a large bowl. Add the chickpeas, tomatoes, green onions, cucumber, olives, pine nuts, and basil. Set aside.
3. In a blender or food processor, combine the shallot, garlic, mustard, vinegar, oil, and salt and pepper to taste. Process until well blended. Pour the dressing over the salad, toss gently to combine, and serve.

Apple, Pecan, and Arugula Salad
PREP: 10 MINUTES • COOK TIME: 0 MINUTES • TOTAL: 10 MINUTES • SERVES: 4

Ingredients
Juice of 1 lemon
2 tablespoons olive oil
1 tablespoon maple syrup
2 pinches sea salt
1 (5-ounce) package arugula
1 cup frozen (and thawed) or fresh corn kernels

½ red onion, thinly sliced
2 apples (preferably Gala or Fuji), cored and sliced
½ cup chopped pecans
¼ cup dried cranberries

Directions
Preparing the Ingredients.
1. In a small bowl, whisk together the lemon juice, oil, maple syrup, and salt. In a large bowl, combine the arugula, corn, red onion, and apples. Add the lemon-juice mixture and toss to combine.
2. Divide evenly among 4 plates and top with the pecans and cranberries.

Caesar Salad
PREP: 10 MINUTES • COOK TIME: 0 MINUTES • TOTAL: 10 MINUTES • SERVES: 1

Ingredients
FOR THE CAESAR SALAD
2 cups chopped romaine lettuce
2 tablespoons Caesar Dressing
1 serving Herbed Croutons or store-bought croutons

Vegan cheese, grated (optional)
MAKE IT A MEAL
½ cup cooked pasta
½ cup canned chickpeas, drained and rinsed
2 additional tablespoons Caesar Dressing

Directions
1. **To Make The Caesar Salad.** In a large bowl, toss together the lettuce, dressing, croutons, and cheese (if using).
2. **To Make It A Meal.** Add the pasta, chickpeas, and additional dressing. Toss to coat.

Per Serving (in a meal) Calories: 415; Protein: 19g; Total fat: 8g; Saturated fat: 1g; Carbohydrates: 72g; Fiber: 13g

Classic Potato Salad
PREP: 10 MINUTES • COOK TIME: 15 MINUTES • TOTAL: 25 MINUTES • SERVES: 4

Ingredients
6 potatoes, scrubbed or peeled and chopped
Pinch salt
½ cup Creamy Tahini Dressing or vegan mayo

1 teaspoon dried dill (optional)
1 teaspoon Dijon mustard (optional)
4 celery stalks, chopped

2 scallions, white and light green parts only, chopped

Directions
Preparing the Ingredients.
1. Put the potatoes in a large pot, add the salt, and pour in enough water to cover. Bring the water to a boil over high heat. Cook the potatoes for 15 to 20 minutes, until soft. Drain and set aside to cool. (Alternatively, put the potatoes in a large microwave-safe dish with a bit of water. Cover and heat on high power for 10 minutes.)
2. In a large bowl, whisk together the dressing, dill (if using), and mustard (if using). Toss the celery and scallions with the dressing. Add the cooked, cooled potatoes and toss to combine. Store leftovers in an airtight container in the refrigerator for up to 1 week.

Per Serving Calories: 269; Protein: 6g; Total fat: 5g; Saturated fat: 1g; Carbohydrates: 51g; Fiber: 6g

Brown Rice and Pepper Salad
PREP: 15 MINUTES • COOK TIME: 0 MINUTES • TOTAL: 15 MINUTES • SERVES: 4

Ingredients
2 cups prepared brown rice
½ red onion, diced
1 red bell pepper, diced
1 orange bell pepper, diced
1 carrot, diced
¼ cup olive oil
¼ teaspoon freshly ground black pepper

2 tablespoons unseasoned rice vinegar
1 tablespoon soy sauce
1 garlic clove, minced
1 tablespoon grated fresh ginger
¼ teaspoon sea salt

Directions
Preparing the Ingredients.
In a large bowl, combine the rice, onion, bell peppers, and carrot. In a small bowl, whisk together the olive oil, rice vinegar, soy sauce, garlic, ginger, salt, and pepper. Toss with the rice mixture and serve immediately.

Mediterranean Orzo & Chickpea Salad
PREP: 15 MINUTES • COOK TIME: 8 MINUTES • TOTAL: 23 MINUTES • SERVES: 4

Ingredients
¼ cup olive oil
2 tablespoons freshly squeezed lemon juice
Pinch salt
1½ cups canned chickpeas, drained and rinsed

2 cups orzo or other small pasta shape, cooked according to the package directions, drained, and rinsed with cold water to cool
2 cups raw spinach, finely chopped
1 cup chopped cucumber
¼ red onion, finely diced

Directions
Preparing the Ingredients.
In a large bowl, whisk together the olive oil, lemon juice, and salt. Add the chickpeas and cooked orzo, and toss to coat.
Stir in the spinach, cucumber, and red onion. Store leftovers in an airtight container in the refrigerator for up to 5 days.

Per Serving Calories: 233; Protein: 6g; Total fat: 15g; Saturated fat: 2g; Carbohydrates: 20g; Fiber: 5g

Nori Snack Rolls
PREP: 5 MINUTES • COOK TIME: 10 MINUTES • TOTAL: 15 MINUTES • SERVES: 4 ROLLS

Ingredients
2 tablespoons almond, cashew, peanut, or other nut butter
2 tablespoons tamari, or soy sauce
4 standard nori sheets

1 mushroom, sliced
1 tablespoon pickled ginger
½ cup grated carrots

Directions
Preparing the Ingredients.
1. Preheat the oven to 350°F.
   Mix together the nut butter and tamari until smooth and very thick. Lay out a nori sheet, rough side up, the long way.
   Spread a thin line of the tamari mixture on the far end of the nori sheet, from side to side. Lay the mushroom slices, ginger, and carrots in a line at the other end (the end closest to you).
2. Fold the vegetables inside the nori, rolling toward the tahini mixture, which will seal the roll. Repeat to make 4 rolls.
   Put on a baking sheet and bake for 8 to 10 minutes, or until the rolls are slightly browned and crispy at the ends. Let the rolls cool for a few minutes, then slice each roll into 3 smaller pieces.

Per Serving (1 roll) Calories: 79; Total fat: 5g; Carbs: 6g; Fiber: 2g; Protein: 4g

Risotto Bites
PREP: 15 MINUTES • COOK TIME: 20 MINUTES • TOTAL: 35 MINUTES • SERVES: 12 BITES

Ingredients
½ cup panko bread crumbs
1 teaspoon paprika
1 teaspoon chipotle powder or ground cayenne pepper

1½ cups cold Green Pea Risotto
Nonstick cooking spray

Directions
Preparing the Ingredients.
1. Preheat the oven to 425ºF.
   Line a baking sheet with parchment paper.
2. On a large plate, combine the panko, paprika, and chipotle powder. Set aside.
   Roll 2 tablespoons of the risotto into a ball.
   Gently roll in the bread crumbs, and place on the prepared baking sheet. Repeat to make a total of 12 balls.
   Spritz the tops of the risotto bites with nonstick cooking spray and bake for 15 to 20 minutes, until they begin to brown. Cool completely before storing in a large airtight container in a single layer (add a piece of parchment paper for a second layer) or in a plastic freezer bag.

Per Serving (6 bites): Calories: 100; Fat: 2g; Protein: 6g; Carbohydrates: 17g; Fiber: 5g; Sugar: 2g; Sodium: 165mg

Jicama and Guacamole

Ingredients

juice of 1 lime, or 1 tablespoon prepared lime juice

2 hass avocados, peeled, pits removed, and cut into cubes

½ teaspoon sea salt

½ red onion, minced

1 garlic clove, minced

¼ cup chopped cilantro (optional)

1 jicama bulb, peeled and cut into matchsticks

Directions

Preparing the Ingredients.

1. In a medium bowl, squeeze the lime juice over the top of the avocado and sprinkle with salt.
2. Lightly mash the avocado with a fork. Stir in the onion, garlic, and cilantro, if using.

   Serve with slices of jicama to dip in guacamole.

   To store, place plastic wrap over the bowl of guacamole and refrigerate. The guacamole will keep for about 2 days.

Garden Patch Sandwiches On Multigrain Bread

PREP: 15 MINUTES • COOK TIME: 0 MINUTES • TOTAL: 15 MINUTES • SERVES: 4 sandwiches

Ingredients

1 pound extra-firm tofu, drained and patted dry

1 medium red bell pepper, finely chopped

1 celery rib, finely chopped

3 green onions, minced

1/4 cup shelled sunflower seeds

1/2 cup vegan mayonnaise, homemade or store-bought

1/2 teaspoon salt

1/2 teaspoon celery salt

1/4 teaspoon freshly ground black pepper

8 slices whole grain bread

4 (1/4-inch) slices ripe tomato

4 lettuce leaves

Directions

1. Crumble the tofu and place it in a large bowl. Add the bell pepper, celery, green onions, and sunflower seeds. Stir in the mayonnaise, salt, celery salt, and pepper and mix until well combined.
2. Toast the bread, if desired. Spread the mixture evenly onto 4 slices of the bread. Top each with a tomato slice, lettuce leaf, and the remaining bread. Cut the sandwiches diagonally in half and serve.

Garden Salad Wraps

PREP: 15 MINUTES • COOK TIME: 10 MINUTES • TOTAL: 15 MINUTES • SERVES: 4 wraps

Ingredients

6 tablespoons olive oil

1 pound extra-firm tofu, drained, patted dry, and cut into 1/2-inch strips

1 tablespoon soy sauce

1/4 cup apple cider vinegar

1 teaspoon yellow or spicy brown mustard

1/2 teaspoon salt

1/4 teaspoon freshly ground black pepper

3 cups shredded romaine lettuce

3 ripe Roma tomatoes, finely chopped

1 large carrot, shredded

1 medium English cucumber, peeled and chopped

1/3 cup minced red onion

1/4 cup sliced pitted green olives

4 (10-inch) whole-grain flour tortillas or lavash flatbread

Directions

1. In a large skillet, heat 2 tablespoons of the oil over medium heat. Add the tofu and cook until golden brown, about 10 minutes. Sprinkle with soy sauce and set aside to cool.

2. In a small bowl, combine the vinegar, mustard, salt, and pepper with the remaining 4 tablespoons oil, stirring to blend well. Set aside.
3. In a large bowl, combine the lettuce, tomatoes, carrot, cucumber, onion, and olives. Pour on the dressing and toss to coat.

  To assemble wraps, place 1 tortilla on a work surface and spread with about one-quarter of the salad. Place a few strips of tofu on the tortilla and roll up tightly. Slice in half

Black Sesame Wonton Chips
PREP: 5 MINUTES • COOK TIME: 5 MINUTES • TOTAL: 10 MINUTES • SERVES: 24 chips

Ingredients

12 Vegan Wonton Wrappers
Toasted sesame oil

1/3 cup black sesame seeds
Salt

Directions

1. Preheat the oven to 450°F. Lightly oil a baking sheet and set aside. Cut the wonton wrappers in half crosswise, brush them with sesame oil, and arrange them in a single layer on the prepared baking sheet.
2. Sprinkle wonton wrappers with the sesame seeds and salt to taste, and bake until crisp and golden brown, 5 to 7 minutes. Cool completely before serving. These are best eaten on the day they are made but, once cooled, they can be covered and stored at room temperature for 1 to 2 days.

Marinated Mushroom Wraps
PREP: 15 MINUTES • COOK TIME: 0 MINUTES • TOTAL: 15 MINUTES • SERVES: 2 wraps

Ingredients

3 tablespoons soy sauce
3 tablespoons fresh lemon juice
11/2 tablespoons toasted sesame oil
2 portobello mushroom caps, cut into 1/4-inch strips
1 ripe Hass avocado, pitted and peeled

2 (10-inch) whole-grain flour tortillas
2 cups fresh baby spinach leaves
1 medium red bell pepper, cut into 1/4-inch strips
1 ripe tomato, chopped
Salt and freshly ground black pepper

Directions

1. In a medium bowl, combine the soy sauce, 2 tablespoons of the lemon juice, and the oil. Add the portobello strips, toss to combine, and marinate for 1 hour or overnight. Drain the mushrooms and set aside.

  Mash the avocado with the remaining 1 tablespoon of lemon juice.
2. To assemble wraps, place 1 tortilla on a work surface and spread with some of the mashed avocado. Top with a layer of baby spinach leaves. In the lower third of each tortilla, arrange strips of the soaked mushrooms and some of the bell pepper strips. Sprinkle with the tomato and salt and black pepper to taste. Roll up tightly and cut in half diagonally. Repeat with the remaining Ingredients and serve.

Tamari Toasted Almonds
PREP: 2 MINUTES • COOK TIME: 8 MINUTES • TOTAL: 10 MINUTES • SERVES: ½ CUP

Ingredients

½ cup raw almonds, or sunflower seeds
2 tablespoons tamari, or soy sauce

1 teaspoon toasted sesame oil

Directions

Preparing the Ingredients.

Heat a dry skillet to medium-high heat, then add the almonds, stirring very frequently to keep them from burning. Once the almonds are toasted, 7 to 8 minutes for almonds, or 3 to 4 minutes for sunflower seeds, pour the tamari and sesame oil into the hot skillet and stir to coat.

You can turn off the heat, and as the almonds cool the tamari mixture will stick to and dry on the nuts.

Per Serving (1 tablespoon) Calories: 89; Total fat: 8g; Carbs: 3g; Fiber: 2g; Protein: 4g

---

Avocado And Tempeh Bacon Wraps
PREP: 10 MINUTES • COOK TIME: 8 MINUTES • TOTAL: 18 MINUTES • SERVES: 4 wraps

Ingredients

2 tablespoons olive oil

8 ounces tempeh bacon, homemade or store-bought

4 (10-inch) soft flour tortillas or lavash flat bread

1/4 cup vegan mayonnaise, homemade or store-bought

4 large lettuce leaves

2 ripe Hass avocados, pitted, peeled, and cut into 1/4-inch slices

1 large ripe tomato, cut into 1/4-inch slices

Directions

1. In a large skillet, heat the oil over medium heat. Add the tempeh bacon and cook until browned on both sides, about 8 minutes. Remove from the heat and set aside.
2. Place 1 tortilla on a work surface. Spread with some of the mayonnaise and one-fourth of the lettuce and tomatoes.
3. Pit, peel, and thinly slice the avocado and place the slices on top of the tomato. Add the reserved tempeh bacon and roll up tightly. Repeat with remaining Ingredients and serve.

Kale Chips
PREP: 5 MINUTES • COOK TIME: 25 MINUTES • TOTAL: 30 MINUTES • SERVES: 2

Ingredients

1 large bunch kale

1 tablespoon extra-virgin olive oil

½ teaspoon chipotle powder

½ teaspoon smoked paprika

¼ teaspoon salt

Directions

Preparing the Ingredients.

1. Preheat the oven to 275ºF.
   Line a large baking sheet with parchment paper. In a large bowl, stem the kale and tear it into bite-size pieces. Add the olive oil, chipotle powder, smoked paprika, and salt.
2. Toss the kale with tongs or your hands, coating each piece well.
   Spread the kale over the parchment paper in a single layer.
   Bake for 25 minutes, turning halfway through, until crisp.
   Cool for 10 to 15 minutes before dividing and storing in 2 airtight containers.

Per Serving: Calories: 144; Fat: 7g; Protein: 5g; Carbohydrates: 18g; Fiber: 3g; Sugar: 0g; Sodium: 363mg

Tempeh-Pimiento Cheeze Ball

Ingredients

8 ounces tempeh, cut into 1/2-inch pieces
1 (2-ounce) jar chopped pimientos, drained
1/4 cup nutritional yeast

1/4 cup vegan mayonnaise, homemade or store-bought
2 tablespoons soy sauce
¾ cup chopped pecans

Directions

1. In a medium saucepan of simmering water, cook the tempeh for 30 minutes. Set aside to cool. In a food processor, combine the cooled tempeh, pimientos, nutritional yeast, mayo, and soy sauce. Process until smooth.
   Transfer the tempeh mixture to a bowl and refrigerate until firm and chilled, at least 2 hours or overnight.
2. In a dry skillet, toast the pecans over medium heat until lightly toasted, about 5 minutes. Set aside to cool.
3. Shape the tempeh mixture into a ball, and roll it in the pecans, pressing the nuts slightly into the tempeh mixture so they stick. Refrigerate for at least 1 hour before serving. If not using right away, cover and keep refrigerated until needed. Properly stored, it will keep for 2 to 3 days.

Peppers and Hummus
PREP: 15 MINUTES • COOK TIME: 0 MINUTES • TOTAL: 15 MINUTES • SERVES: 4

Ingredients

one 15-ounce can chickpeas, drained and rinsed
juice of 1 lemon, or 1 tablespoon prepared lemon juice
¼ cup tahini
3 tablespoons olive oil
½ teaspoon ground cumin

1 tablespoon water
¼ teaspoon paprika
1 red bell pepper, sliced
1 green bell pepper, sliced
1 orange bell pepper, sliced

Directions
Preparing the Ingredients.
1. In a food processor, combine chickpeas, lemon juice, tahini, 2 tablespoons of the olive oil, the cumin, and water.
2. Process on high speed until blended, about 30 seconds. Scoop the hummus into a bowl and drizzle with the remaining tablespoon of olive oil. Sprinkle with paprika and serve with sliced bell peppers.

Savory Roasted Chickpeas
PREP: 5 MINUTES • COOK TIME: 25 MINUTES • TOTAL: 30 MINUTES • SERVES: 1 CUP

Ingredients

1 (14-ounce) can chickpeas, rinsed and drained, or 1½ cups cooked
2 tablespoons tamari, or soy sauce
1 tablespoon nutritional yeast

1 teaspoon smoked paprika, or regular paprika
1 teaspoon onion powder
½ teaspoon garlic powder

Directions
Preparing the Ingredients.
1. Preheat the oven to 400°F.

2. Toss the chickpeas with all the other ingredients, and spread them out on a baking sheet. Bake for 20 to 25 minutes, tossing halfway through.

    Bake these at a lower temperature, until fully dried and crispy, if you want to keep them longer.

    You can easily double the batch, and if you dry them out they will keep about a week in an airtight container.

Per Serving (¼ cup) Calories: 121; Total fat: 2g; Carbs: 20g; Fiber: 6g; Protein: 8g

Savory Seed Crackers
PREP: 5 MINUTES • COOK TIME: 50 MINUTES • TOTAL: 55 MINUTES • SERVES: 20 CRACKERS

Ingredients
¾ cup pumpkin seeds (pepitas)

½ cup sunflower seeds

½ cup sesame seeds

¼ cup chia seeds

1 teaspoon minced garlic (about 1 clove)

1 teaspoon tamari or soy sauce

1 teaspoon vegan Worcestershire sauce

½ teaspoon ground cayenne pepper

½ teaspoon dried oregano

½ cup water

Directions
Preparing the Ingredients.
1. Preheat the oven to 325°F.

    Line a rimmed baking sheet with parchment paper.
2. In a large bowl, combine the pumpkin seeds, sunflower seeds, sesame seeds, chia seeds, garlic, tamari, Worcestershire sauce, cayenne, oregano, and water.

    Transfer to the prepared baking sheet, spreading out to all sides.
3. Bake for 25 minutes. Remove the pan from the oven, and flip the seed "dough" over so the wet side is up. Bake for another 20 to 25 minutes, until the sides are browned.

    Cool completely before breaking up into 20 pieces. Divide evenly among 4 glass jars and close tightly with lids.

Per Serving (5 crackers): Calories: 339; Fat: 29g; Protein: 14g; Carbohydrates: 17g; Fiber: 8g; Sugar: 1g; Sodium: 96mg

Tomato and Basil Bruschetta
PREP: 10 MINUTES • COOK TIME: 6 MINUTES • TOTAL: 16 MINUTES • SERVES: 12 BRUSCHETTA

Ingredients
3 tomatoes, chopped

¼ cup chopped fresh basil

1 tablespoon olive oil

pinch of sea salt

1 baguette, cut into 12 slices

1 garlic clove, sliced in half

Directions
Preparing the Ingredients.
1. In a small bowl, combine the tomatoes, basil, olive oil, and salt and stir to mix. Set aside. Preheat the oven to 425°F.
2. Place the baguette slices in a single layer on a baking sheet and toast in the oven until brown, about 6 minutes.

    Flip the bread slices over once during cooking. Remove from the oven and rub the bread on both sides with the sliced clove of -garlic.

    Top with the tomato-basil mixture and serve immediately.

Refried Bean And Salsa Quesadillas

PREP: 5 MINUTES • COOK TIME: 6 MINUTES • TOTAL: 11 MINUTES • SERVES: 4 quesadillas

Ingredients

1 tablespoon canola oil, plus more for frying
11/2 cups cooked or 1 (15.5-ounce) can pinto beans, drained and mashed
1 teaspoon chili powder

4 (10-inch) whole-wheat flour tortillas
1 cup tomato salsa, homemade or store-bought
1/2 cup minced red onion (optional)

Directions

1. In a medium saucepan, heat the oil over medium heat. Add the mashed beans and chili powder and cook, stirring, until hot, about 5 minutes. Set aside.
2. To assemble, place 1 tortilla on a work surface and spoon about 1/4 cup of the beans across the bottom half. Top the beans with the salsa and onion, if using. Fold top half of the tortilla over the filling and press slightly.
3. In large skillet heat a thin layer of oil over medium heat. Place folded quesadillas, 1 or 2 at a time, into the hot skillet and heat until hot, turning once, about 1 minute per side.
   Cut quesadillas into 3 or 4 wedges and arrange on plates. Serve immediately.

Tempeh Tantrum Burgers

PREP: 15 MINUTES • COOK TIME: 14 MINUTES • TOTAL: 19 MINUTES • SERVES: 4 burgers

Ingredients

8 ounces tempeh, cut into 1/2-inch dice
¾ cup chopped onion
2 garlic cloves, chopped
¾ cup chopped walnuts
1/2 cup old-fashioned or quick-cooking oats
1 tablespoon minced fresh parsley
1/2 teaspoon dried oregano

1/2 teaspoon dried thyme
1/2 teaspoon salt
1/4 teaspoon freshly ground black pepper
3 tablespoons olive oil
Dijon mustard
4 whole grain burger rolls
Sliced red onion, tomato, lettuce, and avocado

Directions

1. In a medium saucepan of simmering water, cook the tempeh for 30 minutes. Drain and set aside to cool. In a food processor, combine the onion and garlic and process until minced. Add the cooled tempeh, the walnuts, oats, parsley, oregano, thyme, salt, and pepper. Process until well blended. Shape the mixture into 4 equal patties.
2. In a large skillet, heat the oil over medium heat. Add the burgers and cook until cooked thoroughly and browned on both sides, about 7 minutes per side.
3. Spread desired amount of mustard onto each half of the rolls and layer each roll with lettuce, tomato, red onion, and avocado, as desired. Serve immediately.

Sesame- Wonton Crisps

PREP: 10 MINUTES • COOK TIME: 10 MINUTES • TOTAL: 20 MINUTES • SERVES: 12 crisps

Ingredients

12 Vegan Wonton Wrappers
2 tablespoons toasted sesame oil
12 shiitake mushrooms, lightly rinsed, patted dry, stemmed, and cut into 1/4-inch slices

4 snow peas, trimmed and cut crosswise into thin slivers
1 teaspoon soy sauce
1 tablespoon fresh lime juice

1/2 teaspoon brown sugar
1 medium carrot, shredded

Toasted sesame seeds or black sesame seeds, if available

Directions

1. Preheat the oven to 350°F. Lightly oil a baking sheet and set aside. Brush the wonton wrappers with 1 tablespoon of the sesame oil and arrange on the baking sheet. Bake until golden brown and crisp, about 5 minutes. Set aside to cool. (Alternately, you can tuck the wonton wrappers into mini-muffin tins to create cups for the filling. Brush with sesame oil and bake them until crisp.)
2. In a large skillet, heat the extra olive oil over medium heat. Add the mushrooms and cook until softened, 3 to 5 minutes. Stir in the snow peas and the soy sauce and cook 30 seconds. Set aside to cool.
3. In a large bowl, combine the lime juice, sugar, and remaining 1 tablespoon sesame oil. Stir in the carrot and cooled shiitake mixture. Top each wonton crisp with a spoonful of the shiitake mixture. Sprinkle with sesame seeds and arrange on a platter to serve.

Macadamia-Cashew Patties
PREP: 10 MINUTES • COOK TIME: 10 MINUTES • TOTAL: 20 MINUTES • SERVES: 4 patties

Ingredients

¾ cup chopped macadamia nuts
¾ cup chopped cashews
1 medium carrot, grated
1 small onion, chopped
1 garlic clove, minced
1 jalapeño or other green chile, seeded and minced
¾ cup old-fashioned oats

¾ cup dry unseasoned bread crumbs
2 tablespoons minced fresh cilantro
1/2 teaspoon ground coriander
Salt and freshly ground black pepper
2 teaspoons fresh lime juice
Canola or grapeseed oil, for frying
4 sandwich rolls
Lettuce leaves and condiment of choice

Directions

1. In a food processor, combine the macadamia nuts, cashews, carrot, onion, garlic, chile, oats, bread crumbs, cilantro, coriander, and salt and pepper to taste. Process until well mixed. Add the lime juice and process until well blended. Taste, adjusting seasonings if necessary. Shape the mixture into 4 equal patties.
2. In a large skillet, heat a thin layer of oil over medium heat. Add the patties and cook until golden brown on both sides, turning once, about 10 minutes total. Serve on sandwich rolls with lettuce and condiments of choice.

Lemon Coconut Cilantro Rolls
PREP: 30 MINUTES • CHILL TIME: 30 MINUTES • TOTAL: 60 MINUTES • SERVES: 16 PIECES

Ingredients

½ cup fresh cilantro, chopped
1 cup sprouts (clover, alfalfa)
1 garlic clove, pressed
2 tablespoons ground Brazil nuts or almonds
2 tablespoons flaked coconut
1 tablespoon coconut oil
Pinch cayenne pepper

Pinch sea salt
Pinch freshly ground black pepper
Zest and juice of 1 lemon
2 tablespoons ground flaxseed
1 to 2 tablespoons water
2 whole-wheat wraps, or corn wraps

Directions

Preparing the Ingredients.
1. Put everything but the wraps in a food processor and pulse to combine. Or combine the ingredients in a large bowl. Add the water, if needed, to help the mix come together.
2. Spread the mixture out over each wrap, roll it up, and place it in the fridge for 30 minutes to set. Remove the rolls from the fridge and slice each into 8 pieces to serve as appetizers or sides with a soup or stew.
   Get the best flavor by buying whole raw Brazil nuts or almonds, toasting them lightly in a dry skillet or toaster oven, and then grinding them in a coffee grinder.

Per Serving (1 piece) Calories: 66; Total fat: 4g; Carbs: 6g; Fiber: 1g; Protein: 2g

Tamari Almonds
PREP: 5 MINUTES • COOK TIME: 15 MINUTES • TOTAL: 20 MINUTES • SERVES: 8

Ingredients
1 pound raw almonds
3 tablespoons tamari or soy sauce
2 tablespoons extra-virgin olive oil

1 tablespoon nutritional yeast
1 to 2 teaspoons chili powder, to taste

Directions
Preparing the Ingredients.
1. Preheat the oven to 400ºF.
   Line a baking sheet with parchment paper.
2. In a medium bowl, combine the almonds, tamari, and olive oil until well coated.
   Spread the almonds on the prepared baking sheet and roast for 10 to 15 minutes, until browned.
   Cool for 10 minutes, then season with the nutritional yeast and chili powder.
   Transfer to a glass jar and close tightly with a lid.

Per Serving: Calories: 364; Fat: 32g; Protein: 13g; Carbohydrates: 13g; Fiber: 7g; Sugar: 3g; Sodium: 381mg

Tempeh Taco Bites
PREP: 5 MINUTES • COOK TIME: 45 MINUTES • TOTAL: 50 MINUTES • SERVES: 3 dozen

Ingredients
8 ounces tempeh
3 tablespoons soy sauce
2 teaspoons ground cumin
1 teaspoon chili powder
1 teaspoon dried oregano
1 tablespoon olive oil
1/2 cup finely minced onion
2 garlic cloves, minced
Salt and freshly ground black pepper

2 tablespoons tomato paste
1 chipotle chile in adobo, finely minced
1/4 cup hot water or vegetable broth, homemade or store-bought, plus more if needed
36 phyllo pastry cups, thawed
1/2 cup basic guacamole, homemade or store-bought
18 ripe cherry tomatoes, halved

Directions
1. In a medium saucepan of simmering water, cook the tempeh for 30 minutes. Drain well, then finely mince and place it in a bowl. Add the soy sauce, cumin, chili powder, and oregano. Mix well and set aside.

2. In a medium skillet, heat the oil over medium heat. Add the onion, cover, and cook for 5 minutes. Stir in the garlic, then add the tempeh mixture and cook, stirring, for 2 to 3 minutes. Season with salt and pepper to taste. Set aside.

3. In a small bowl, combine the tomato paste, chipotle, and the hot water or broth. Return tempeh mixture to heat and in stir tomato-chile mixture and cook for 10 to 15 minutes, stirring occasionally, until the liquid is absorbed.

   The mixture should be fairly dry, but if it begins to stick to the pan, add a little more hot water, 1 tablespoon at a time. Taste, adjusting seasonings if necessary. Remove from the heat.

4. To assemble, fill the phyllo cups to the top with the tempeh filling, using about 2 teaspoons of filling in each. Top with a dollop of guacamole and a cherry tomato half and serve.

Stuffed Cherry Tomatoes
PREP: 15 MINUTES • COOK TIME: 0 MINUTES • TOTAL: 15 MINUTES • SERVES: 6

Ingredients
2 pints cherry tomatoes, tops removed and centers scooped out
2 avocados, mashed
juice of 1 lemon
½ red bell pepper, minced

4 green onions (white and green parts), finely minced
1 tablespoon minced fresh tarragon
pinch of sea salt

Directions
Preparing the Ingredients.
1. Place the cherry tomatoes open-side up on a platter.
2. In a small bowl, -combine the avocado, lemon juice, bell pepper, scallions, tarragon, and salt.
3. Stir until well -combined. Scoop into the cherry tomatoes and serve immediately.

Spicy Black Bean Dip
PREP: 10 MINUTES • COOK TIME: 0 MINUTES • TOTAL: 10 MINUTES • SERVES: 2 CUPS

Ingredients
1 (14-ounce) can black beans, drained and rinsed, or 1½ cups cooked
Zest and juice of 1 lime
1 tablespoon tamari, or soy sauce

¼ cup water
¼ cup fresh cilantro, chopped
1 teaspoon ground cumin
Pinch cayenne pepper

Directions
Preparing the Ingredients.
1. Put the beans in a food processor (best choice) or blender, along with the lime zest and juice, tamari, and about ¼ cup of water.
2. Blend until smooth, then blend in the cilantro, cumin, and cayenne.
   If you don't have a blender or prefer a different consistency, simply transfer it to a bowl once the beans have been puréed and stir in the spices, instead of forcing the blender.
Per Serving (1 cup) Calories: 190; Total fat: 1g; Carbs: 35g; Fiber: 12g; Protein: 13g

French Onion Pastry Puffs

PREP: 10 MINUTES • COOK TIME: 35 MINUTES • TOTAL: 45 MINUTES - Makes 24 puffs

Ingredients
2 tablespoons olive oil
2 medium sweet yellow onions, thinly sliced
1 garlic clove, minced
1 teaspoon chopped fresh rosemary

Salt and freshly ground black pepper
1 tablespoon capers
1 sheet frozen vegan puff pastry, thawed
18 pitted black olives, quartered

Directions
1. In a medium skillet, heat the oil over medium heat. Add the onions and garlic, season with rosemary and salt and pepper to taste. Cover and cook until very soft, stirring occasionally, about 20 minutes. Stir in the capers and set aside.
Preheat the oven to 400°F. Roll out the puff pastry and cut into 2- to 3-inch circles using a lightly floured pastry cutter or drinking glass. You should get about 2 dozen circles.
2. Arrange the pastry circles on baking sheets and top each with a heaping teaspoon of onion mixture, patting down to smooth the top.
Top with 3 olive quarters, arranged decoratively—either like flower petals emanating from the center or parallel to each other like 3 bars.
3. Bake until pastry is puffed and golden brown, about 15 minutes. Serve hot.

Cheezy Cashew–Roasted Red Pepper Toasts
PREP: 15 MINUTES • COOK TIME: 0 MINUTES • TOTAL: 15 MINUTES • SERVES: 16 to 24 toasts

Ingredients
2 jarred roasted red peppers
1 cup unsalted cashews
1/4 cup water
1 tablespoon soy sauce

2 tablespoons chopped green onions
1/4 cup nutritional yeast
2 tablespoons balsamic vinegar
2 tablespoons olive oil

Directions
1. Use canapé or cookie cutters to cut the bread into desired shapes about 2 inches wide. If you don't have a cutter, use a knife to cut the bread into squares, triangles, or rectangles. You should get 2 to 4 pieces out of each slice of bread. Toast the bread and set aside to cool.
Coarsely chop 1 red pepper and set aside. Cut the remaining pepper into thin strips or decorative shapes and set aside for garnish.
2. In a blender or food processor, grind the cashews to a fine powder. Add the water and soy sauce and process until smooth. Add the chopped red pepper and puree. Add the green onions, nutritional yeast, vinegar, and oil and process until smooth and well blended.
3. Spread a spoonful of the pepper mixture onto each of the toasted bread pieces and top decoratively with the reserved pepper strips. Arrange on a platter or tray and serve.

Baked Potato Chips
PREP: 10 MINUTES • COOK TIME: 30 MINUTES • TOTAL: 40 MINUTES • SERVES: 4

Ingredients
1 large Russet potato
1 teaspoon paprika
½ teaspoon garlic salt
¼ teaspoon vegan sugar

¼ teaspoon onion powder
¼ teaspoon chipotle powder or chili powder
⅛ teaspoon salt
⅛ teaspoon ground mustard

⅛ teaspoon ground cayenne pepper
1 teaspoon canola oil

⅛ teaspoon liquid smoke

Directions

Preparing the Ingredients.

1. Wash and peel the potato. Cut into thin, 1/10-inch slices (a mandoline slicer or the slicer blade in a food processor is helpful for consistently sized slices).
   Fill a large bowl with enough very cold water to cover the potato. Transfer the potato slices to the bowl and soak for 20 minutes.
   Preheat the oven to 400ºF. Line a baking sheet with parchment paper.
2. In a small bowl, combine the paprika, garlic salt, sugar, onion powder, chipotle powder, salt, mustard, and cayenne.
   Drain and rinse the potato slices and pat dry with a paper towel.
   Transfer to a large bowl.
3. Add the canola oil, liquid smoke, and spice mixture to the bowl. Toss to coat.
   Transfer the potatoes to the prepared baking sheet.
4. Bake for 15 minutes. Flip the chips over and bake for 15 minutes longer, until browned. Transfer the chips to 4 storage containers or large glass jars.
   Let cool before closing the lids tightly.

Per Serving: Calories: 89; Fat: 1g; Protein: 2g; Carbohydrates: 18g; Fiber: 2g; Sugar: 1g; Sodium: 65mg

Mushrooms Stuffed With Spinach And Walnuts

PREP: 10 MINUTES • COOK TIME: 6 MINUTES • TOTAL: 16 MINUTES • SERVES: 4 to 6 servings

Ingredients

2 tablespoons olive oil
8 ounces white mushroom, lightly rinsed, patted dry, and stems reserved
1 garlic clove, minced

1 cup cooked spinach
1 cup finely chopped walnuts
1/2 cup unseasoned dry bread crumbs
Salt and freshly ground black pepper

Directions

1. Preheat the oven to 400°F. Lightly oil a large baking pan and set aside. In a large skillet, heat the oil over medium heat. Add the mushroom caps and cook for 2 minutes to soften slightly. Remove from the skillet and set aside.
2. Chop the mushroom stems and add to the same skillet. Add the garlic and cook over medium heat until softened, about 2 minutes. Stir in the spinach, walnuts, bread crumbs, and salt and pepper to taste. Cook for 2 minutes, stirring well to combine.
3. Fill the reserved mushroom caps with the stuffing mixture and arrange in the baking pan. Bake until the mushrooms are tender and the filling is hot, about 10 minutes. Serve hot.

Salsa Fresca

PREP: 15 MINUTES • COOK TIME: 0 MINUTES • TOTAL: 15 MINUTES • SERVES: 4

Ingredients

3 large heirloom tomatoes or other fresh tomatoes, chopped
½ red onion, finely chopped

½ bunch cilantro, chopped
2 garlic cloves, minced
1 jalapeño, minced

Juice of 1 lime, or 1 tablespoon prepared lime juice

¼ cup olive oil

Sea salt

Whole-grain tortilla chips, for serving

Directions

Preparing the Ingredients.

1. In a small bowl, combine the tomatoes, onion, cilantro, garlic, jalapeño, lime juice, and olive oil and mix well. Allow to sit at room temperature for 15 minutes. Season with salt.
2. Serve with tortilla chips.
   The salsa can be stored in an airtight container in the refrigerator for up to 1 week.

Guacamole
PREP: 10 MINUTES • COOK TIME: 0 MINUTES • TOTAL: 10 MINUTES • SERVES: 2

Ingredients

2 ripe avocados

2 garlic cloves, pressed

Zest and juice of 1 lime

1 teaspoon ground cumin

Pinch sea salt

Pinch freshly ground black pepper

Pinch cayenne pepper (optional)

Directions

Preparing the Ingredients.

1. Mash the avocados in a large bowl. Add the rest of the ingredients and stir to combine.
2. Try adding diced tomatoes (cherry are divine), chopped scallions or chives, chopped fresh cilantro or basil, lemon rather than lime, paprika, or whatever you think would taste good!

Per Serving (1 cup) Calories: 258; Total fat: 22g; Carbs: 18g; Fiber: 11g; Protein: 4g

Veggie Hummus Pinwheels
PREP: 10 MINUTES • COOK TIME: 0 MINUTES • TOTAL: 10 MINUTES • SERVES: 3

Ingredients

3 whole-grain, spinach, flour, or gluten-free tortillas

3 large Swiss chard leaves

¾ cup Edamame Hummus or prepared hummus

¾ cup shredded carrots

Directions

Preparing the Ingredients.

1. Lay 1 tortilla flat on a cutting board.
2. Place 1 Swiss chard leaf over the tortilla. Spread ¼ cup of hummus over the Swiss chard. Spread ¼ cup of carrots over the hummus. Starting at one end of the tortilla, roll tightly toward the opposite side.
3. Slice each roll up into 6 pieces. Place in a single-serving storage container.
   Repeat with the remaining tortillas and filling and seal the lids.

Per Serving: Calories: 254; Fat: 8g; Protein: 10g; Carbohydrates: 39g; Fiber: 8g; Sugar: 4g; Sodium: 488mg

Asian Lettuce Rolls
PREP: 15 MINUTES • COOK TIME: 5 MINUTES • TOTAL: 20 MINUTES • SERVES: 4

Ingredients

2 ounces rice noodles

2 tablespoons chopped thai basil

2 tablespoons chopped cilantro
1 garlic clove, minced
1 tablespoon minced fresh ginger
juice of ½ lime, or 2 teaspoons prepared lime juice

2 tablespoons soy sauce
1 cucumber, julienned
2 carrots, peeled and julienned
8 leaves butter lettuce

Directions

Preparing the Ingredients.

1. Cook the rice noodles according to package directions.
2. In a small bowl, whisk together the basil, cilantro, garlic, ginger, lime juice, and soy sauce. Toss with the cooked noodles, cucumber, and carrots.
   Divide the mixture evenly among lettuce leaves and roll.
   Secure with a toothpick and serve immediately.

Pinto-Pecan Fireballs
PREP: 5 MINUTES • COOK TIME: 30 MINUTES • TOTAL: 35 MINUTES • SERVES: about 20 pieces

Ingredients
1-1/2 cups cooked or 1 (15.5-ounce) can pinto beans, drained and rinsed
1/2 cup chopped pecans
1/4 cup minced green onions
1 garlic clove, minced
3 tablespoons wheat gluten flour (vital wheat gluten)

3 tablespoons unseasoned dry bread crumbs
4 tablespoons Tabasco or other hot sauce
1/4 teaspoon salt
1/8 teaspoon ground cayenne
1/4 cup vegan margarine

Directions

1. Preheat the oven to 350°F. Lightly oil a 9 x 13-inch baking pan and set aside. Blot the drained beans well with a paper towel, pressing out any excess liquid. In a food processor, combine the pinto beans, pecans, green onions, garlic, flour, bread crumbs, 2 tablespoons of the Tabasco, salt, and cayenne. Pulse until well combined, leaving some texture. Use your hands to roll the mixture firmly into 1-inch balls.
2. Place the balls in the prepared baking pan and bake until nicely browned, about 25 to 30 minutes, turning halfway through.
3. Meanwhile, in small saucepan, combine the remaining 2 tablespoons Tabasco and the margarine and melt over low heat. Pour the sauce over the fireballs and bake 10 minutes longer. Serve immediately.

Sweet Potato Biscuits
PREP: 60 MINUTES • COOK TIME: 10 MINUTES • TOTAL: 70 MINUTES • SERVES: 12 BISCUITS

Ingredients
1 medium sweet potato
3 tablespoons melted coconut oil, divided
1 tablespoon maple syrup

1 cup whole-wheat flour
2 teaspoons baking powder
Pinch sea salt

Directions

Preparing the Ingredients.

1. Bake the sweet potato at 350°F for about 45 minutes, until tender.
   Allow it to cool, then remove the flesh and mash.

2. Turn the oven up to 375°F and line a baking sheet with parchment paper or lightly grease it. Measure out 1 cup potato flesh.
3. In a medium bowl, combine the mashed sweet potato with 1½ tablespoons of the coconut oil and the maple syrup. Mix together the flour and baking powder in a separate medium bowl, then add the flour mixture to the potato mixture and blend well with a fork.
   On a floured board, pat the mixture out into a ½-inch-thick circle and cut out 1-inch rounds, or simply drop spoonfuls of dough and pat them into rounds.
4. Put the rounds onto the prepared baking sheet. Brush the top of each with some of the remaining 1½ tablespoons melted coconut oil. Bake 10 minutes, or until lightly golden on top. Serve hot.

Per Serving (1 biscuit) Calories: 116; Total fat: 4g; Carbs: 19g; Fiber: 3g; Protein: 3g

Lemon And Garlic Marinated Mushrooms
PREP: 15 MINUTES • COOK TIME: 0 MINUTES • TOTAL: 15 MINUTES • SERVES: 4 servings

Ingredients
3 tablespoons olive oil
2 tablespoons fresh lemon juice
2 garlic cloves, crushed
1 teaspoon dried marjoram
1/2 teaspoon coarsely ground fennel seed

1/2 teaspoon salt
1/4 teaspoon freshly ground black pepper
8 ounces small white mushrooms, lightly rinsed, patted dry, and stemmed
1 tablespoon minced fresh parsley

Directions
1. In a medium bowl, whisk together the oil, lemon juice, garlic, marjoram, fennel seed, salt, and pepper. Add the mushrooms and parsley and stir gently until coated.
2. Cover and refrigerate for at least 2 hours or overnight. Stir well before serving.

Garlic Toast
PREP: 5 MINUTES • COOK TIME: 5 MINUTES • TOTAL: 10 MINUTES • SERVES: 1 SLICE

Ingredients
1 teaspoon coconut oil, or olive oil
Pinch sea salt
1 to 2 teaspoons nutritional yeast

1 small garlic clove, pressed, or ¼ teaspoon garlic powder
1 slice whole-grain bread

Directions
Preparing the Ingredients.
1. In a small bowl, mix together the oil, salt, nutritional yeast, and garlic.
   You can either toast the bread and then spread it with the seasoned oil, or brush the oil on the bread and put it in a toaster oven to bake for 5 minutes.
   If you're using fresh garlic, it's best to spread it onto the bread and then bake it.

Per Serving (1 slice) Calories: 138; Total fat: 6g; Carbs: 16g; Fiber: 4g; Protein: 7g

Vietnamese-Style Lettuce Rolls
PREP: 15 MINUTES • COOK TIME: 0 MINUTES • TOTAL: 15 MINUTES • SERVES: 4 servings

Ingredients
2 green onions
2 tablespoons soy sauce

2 tablespoons rice vinegar
1 teaspoon sugar

1/8 teaspoon crushed red pepper
3 tablespoons water
3 ounces rice vermicelli
4 to 6 soft green leaf lettuce leaves
1 medium carrot, shredded

1/2 medium English cucumber, peeled, seeded, and cut lengthwise into 1/4-inch strips
1/2 medium red bell pepper, cut into 1/4-inch strips
1 cup loosely packed fresh cilantro or basil leaves

Directions

1. Cut the green part off the green onions and cut them lengthwise into thin slices and set aside. Mince the white part of the green onions and transfer to a small bowl. Add the soy sauce, rice vinegar, sugar, crushed red pepper, and water. Stir to blend and set aside.
2. Soak the vermicelli in medium bowl of hot water until softened, about 1 minute. Drain the noodles well and cut them into 3-inch lengths. Set aside.
3. Place a lettuce leaf on a work surface and arrange a row of noodles in the center of the leaf, followed by a few strips of scallion greens, carrot, cucumber, bell pepper, and cilantro. Bring the bottom edge of the leaf over the filling and fold in the two short sides. Roll up gently but tightly. Place the roll seam side down on a serving platter. Repeat with
4. remaining Ingredients. Serve with the dipping sauce.

Maple-Walnut Oatmeal Cookies
PREP: 5 MINUTES • COOK TIME: 10 MINUTES • TOTAL: 15 MINUTES • SERVES: about 2 dozen cookies

Ingredients
11/2 cups whole-grain flour
1 teaspoon baking powder
1/8 teaspoon salt
1 teaspoon ground cinnamon
1/4 teaspoon ground nutmeg
11/2 cups old-fashioned oats

1 cup chopped walnuts
1/2 cup vegan margarine, melted
1/2 cup pure maple syrup
1/4 cup light brown sugar
2 teaspoons pure vanilla extract

Directions
1. Preheat the oven to 375°F. In a large bowl, sift together the flour, baking powder, salt, cinnamon, and nutmeg. Stir in the oats and walnuts.
2. In a medium bowl, combine the margarine, maple syrup, sugar, and vanilla and mix well. Add the wet Ingredients to the dry Ingredients, stirring to mix well.
3. Drop the cookie dough by the tablespoonful onto an ungreased baking sheet and press down slightly with a fork. Bake until browned, 10 to 12 minutes. Cool the cookies slightly before transferring to a wire rack to cool completely. Store in an airtight container.

Banana-Nut Bread Bars
PREP: 5 MINUTES • COOK TIME: 30 MINUTES • TOTAL: 5 MINUTES • SERVES: 9 BARS

Ingredients
Nonstick cooking spray (optional)
2 large ripe bananas
1 tablespoon maple syrup
½ teaspoon vanilla extract

2 cups old-fashioned rolled oats
½ teaspoons salt
¼ cup chopped walnuts

Directions
Preparing the Ingredients.
1. Preheat the oven to 350ºF. Lightly coat a 9-by-9-inch baking pan with nonstick cooking spray (if using) or line with parchment paper for oil-free baking.
2. In a medium bowl, mash the bananas with a fork. Add the maple syrup and vanilla extract and mix well. Add the oats, salt, and walnuts, mixing well.
3. Transfer the batter to the baking pan and bake for 25 to 30 minutes, until the top is crispy. Cool completely before slicing into 9 bars. Transfer to an airtight storage container or a large plastic bag.

Per Serving (1 bar): Calories: 73; Fat: 1g; Protein: 2g; Carbohydrates: 15g; Fiber: 2g; Sugar: 5g; Sodium: 129mg

Apple Crumble
PREP: 20 MINUTES • COOK TIME: 25 MINUTES • TOTAL: 45 MINUTES • SERVES: 6

Ingredients
FOR THE FILLING
4 to 5 apples, cored and chopped (about 6 cups)

½ cup unsweetened applesauce, or ¼ cup water

2 to 3 tablespoons unrefined sugar (coconut, date, sucanat, maple syrup)
1 teaspoon ground cinnamon
Pinch sea salt

FOR THE CRUMBLE
2 tablespoons almond butter, or cashew or sunflower seed butter

2 tablespoons maple syrup
1½ cups rolled oats
½ cup walnuts, finely chopped
½ teaspoon ground cinnamon
2 to 3 tablespoons unrefined granular sugar (coconut, date, sucanat)

Directions
Preparing the Ingredients.
1. Preheat the oven to 350°F. Put the apples and applesauce in an 8-inch-square baking dish, and sprinkle with the sugar, cinnamon, and salt. Toss to combine.
2. In a medium bowl, mix together the nut butter and maple syrup until smooth and creamy. Add the oats, walnuts, cinnamon, and sugar and stir to coat, using your hands if necessary. (If you have a small food processor, pulse the oats and walnuts together before adding them to the mix.)
3. Sprinkle the topping over the apples, and put the dish in the oven.
Bake for 20 to 25 minutes, or until the fruit is soft and the topping is lightly browned.

Per Serving Calories: 356; Total fat: 17g; Carbs: 49g; Fiber: 7g; Protein: 7g

Chocolate-Cranberry Oatmeal Cookies
PREP: 5 MINUTES • COOK TIME: 15 MINUTES • TOTAL: 20 MINUTES • SERVES: about 2 dozen cookies

Ingredients
1/2 cup vegan margarine
1 cup sugar
1/4 cup apple juice
1 cup whole-grain flour
1 teaspoon baking powder

1/2 teaspoon salt
1 teaspoon pure vanilla extract
1 cup old-fashioned oats
1/2 cup vegan semisweet chocolate chips
1/2 cup sweetened dried cranberries

Directions
1. Preheat the oven to 375°F. In a large bowl, cream together the margarine and the sugar until light and fluffy. Blend in the juice.
Add the flour, baking powder, salt, and vanilla, blending well. Stir in the oats, chocolate chips, and cranberries and mix well.
2. Drop the dough from a teaspoon onto an ungreased baking sheet. Bake until nicely browned, about 15 minutes. Cool the cookies slightly before transferring to a wire rack to cool completely. Store in an airtight container.

Cashew-Chocolate Truffles
PREP: 15 MINUTES • COOK TIME: 0 MINUTES • PLUS 1 HOUR TO SET• SERVES: 12 TRUFFLES

Ingredients
1 cup raw cashews, soaked in water overnight
¾ cup pitted dates
2 tablespoons coconut oil

1 cup unsweetened shredded coconut, divided
1 to 2 tablespoons cocoa powder, to taste

Directions
Preparing the Ingredients.

1. In a food processor, combine the cashews, dates, coconut oil, ½ cup of shredded coconut, and cocoa powder. Pulse until fully incorporated; it will resemble chunky cookie dough. Spread the remaining ½ cup of shredded coconut on a plate.
2. Form the mixture into tablespoon-size balls and roll on the plate to cover with the shredded coconut. Transfer to a parchment paper–lined plate or baking sheet. Repeat to make 12 truffles.
   Place the truffles in the refrigerator for 1 hour to set. Transfer the truffles to a storage container or freezer-safe bag and seal.

Per Serving (1 truffle): Calories 238: Fat: 18g; Protein: 3g; Carbohydrates: 16g; Fiber: 4g; Sugar: 9g; Sodium: 9mg

Banana Chocolate Cupcakes
PREP: 20 MINUTES • COOK TIME: 20 MINUTES • TOTAL: 40 MINUTES • SERVES: 12 CUPCAKES

Ingredients
3 medium bananas
1 cup non-dairy milk
2 tablespoons almond butter
1 teaspoon apple cider vinegar
1 teaspoon pure vanilla extract
1¼ cups whole-wheat flour
½ cup rolled oats
¼ cup coconut sugar (optional)

1 teaspoon baking powder
½ teaspoon baking soda
½ cup unsweetened cocoa powder
¼ cup chia seeds, or sesame seeds
Pinch sea salt
¼ cup dark chocolate chips, dried cranberries, or raisins (optional)

Directions
Preparing the Ingredients.
1. Preheat the oven to 350°F. Lightly grease the cups of two 6-cup muffin tins or line with paper muffin cups.
2. Put the bananas, milk, almond butter, vinegar, and vanilla in a blender and purée until smooth. Or stir together in a large bowl until smooth and creamy.
   Put the flour, oats, sugar (if using), baking powder, baking soda, cocoa powder, chia seeds, salt, and chocolate chips in another large bowl, and stir to combine. Mix together the wet and dry ingredients, stirring as little as possible. Spoon into muffin cups, and bake for 20 to 25 minutes. Take the cupcakes out of the oven and let them cool fully before taking out of the muffin tins, since they'll be very moist.

Per Serving (1 cupcake) Calories: 215; Total fat: 6g; Carbs: 39g; Fiber: 9g; Protein: 6g

Minty Fruit Salad
PREP: 15 MINUTES • COOK TIME: 5 MINUTES • TOTAL: 20 MINUTES • SERVES: 4

Ingredients
¼ cup lemon juice (about 2 small lemons)
4 teaspoons maple syrup or agave syrup
2 cups chopped pineapple
2 cups chopped strawberries

2 cups raspberries
1 cup blueberries
8 fresh mint leaves

Directions
Preparing the Ingredients.
1. Beginning with 1 mason jar, add the ingredients in this order:
   1 tablespoon of lemon juice, 1 teaspoon of maple syrup, ½ cup of pineapple, ½ cup of strawberries, ½ cup of raspberries, ¼ cup of blueberries, and 2 mint leaves.

2. Repeat to fill 3 more jars. Close the jars tightly with lids.
   Place the airtight jars in the refrigerator for up to 3 days.

Per Serving: Calories: 138; Fat: 1g; Protein: 2g; Carbohydrates: 34g; Fiber: 8g; Sugar: 22g; Sodium: 6mg

Sesame Cookies
PREP: 15 MINUTES • COOK TIME: 0 MINUTES • TOTAL: 15 MINUTES • SERVES: 3 dozen cookies

Ingredients
¾ cup vegan margarine, softened
1/2 cup light brown sugar
1 teaspoon pure vanilla extract
2 tablespoons pure maple syrup

1/4 teaspoon salt
2 cups whole-grain flour
¾ cup sesame seeds, lightly toasted

Directions
1. In a large bowl, cream together the margarine and sugar until light and fluffy. Blend in the vanilla, maple syrup, and salt. Stir in the flour and sesame seeds and mix well.
2. Roll the dough into a cylinder about 2 inches in diameter. Wrap it in plastic wrap and refrigerate for 1 hour or longer. Preheat the oven to 325°F.
3. Slice the cookie dough into 1/8-inch-thick rounds and arrange on an ungreased baking sheet about 2 inches apart. Bake until light brown, about 12 minutes. When completely cool, store in an airtight container.

Mango Coconut Cream Pie
PREP: 20 MINUTES • CHILL TIME: 30 MINUTES • TOTAL: 50 MINUTES • SERVES: 8

Ingredients
FOR THE CRUST
½ cup rolled oats
1 cup cashews
1 cup soft pitted dates
FOR THE FILLING

1 cup canned coconut milk
½ cup water
2 large mangos, peeled and chopped, or about 2 cups frozen chunks
½ cup unsweetened shredded coconut

Directions
Preparing the Ingredients.
1. Put all the crust ingredients in a food processor and pulse until it holds together. If you don't have a food processor, chop everything as finely as possible and use ½ cup cashew or almond butter in place of half the cashews. Press the mixture down firmly into an 8-inch pie or springform pan.
2. Put the all filling ingredients in a blender and purée until smooth (about 1 minute). It should be very thick, so you may have to stop and stir until it's smooth.
3. Pour the filling into the crust, use a rubber spatula to smooth the top, and put the pie in the freezer until set, about 30 minutes. Once frozen, it should be set out for about 15 minutes to soften before serving.
4. Top with a batch of *Coconut Whipped Cream* scooped on top of the pie once it's set. Finish it off with a sprinkling of toasted shredded coconut.

Per Serving (1 slice) Calories: 427; Total fat: 28g; Carbs: 45g; Fiber: 6g; Protein: 8g

Cherry-Vanilla Rice Pudding (Pressure cooker)
PREP: 5 MINUTES • PRESSURE: 30 MINUTES • TOTAL: 1 HOUR, MINUTES • PRESSURE LEVEL: HIGH • RELEASE: NATURAL• SERVES 4-6

Ingredients

1 cup short-grain brown rice
1¾ cups nondairy milk, plus more as needed
1½ cups water
4 tablespoons unrefined sugar or pure maple syrup (use 2 tablespoons if you use a sweetened milk), plus more as needed

1 teaspoon vanilla extract (use ½ teaspoon if you use vanilla milk)
Pinch salt
¼ cup dried cherries *or* ½ cup fresh or frozen pitted cherries

Directions

1. **Preparing the Ingredients.** In your electric pressure cooker's cooking pot, combine the rice, milk, water, sugar, vanilla, and salt.
2. **High pressure for 30 minutes.** Close and lock the lid and ensure the pressure valve is sealed, then select High Pressure and set the time for 30 minutes.
3. **Pressure Release.** Once the cook time is complete, let the pressure release naturally, about 20 minutes. Once all the pressure has released, carefully unlock and remove the lid. Stir in the cherries and put the lid back on loosely for about 10 minutes. Serve, adding more milk or sugar, as desired.

PER SERVING Calories: 177; Total fat: 1g; Protein: 3g; Sodium: 27mg; Fiber: 2g

Chocolate Coconut Brownies
PREP: 5 MINUTES • COOK TIME: 35 MINUTES • TOTAL: 40 MINUTES • SERVES: 12 brownies

Ingredients

1 cup whole-grain flour
1/2 cup unsweetened cocoa powder
1 teaspoon baking powder
1/2 teaspoon salt
1 cup light brown sugar
1/2 cup canola oil

¾ cup unsweetened coconut milk
1 teaspoon pure vanilla extract
1 teaspoon coconut extract
1/2 cup vegan semisweet chocolate chips
1/2 cup sweetened shredded coconut

Directions

1. Preheat the oven to 350°F. Grease an 8-inch square baking pan and set aside. In a large bowl, combine the flour, cocoa, baking powder, and salt. Set aside.
   In a medium bowl, mix together the sugar and oil until blended. Stir in the coconut milk
2. and the extracts and blend until smooth. Add the wet Ingredients to the dry Ingredients, stirring to blend. Fold in the chocolate chips and coconut.
3. Scrape the batter into the prepared baking pan and bake until the center is set and a toothpick inserted in the center comes out clean, 35 to 40 minutes. Let the brownies cool 30 minutes before serving. Store in an airtight container.

Lime in the Coconut Chia Pudding
PREP: 10 MINUTES • CHILL TIME: 20 MINUTES • TOTAL: 30 MINUTES • SERVES: 4

Ingredients

Zest and juice of 1 lime
1 (14-ounce) can coconut milk
1 to 2 dates, or 1 tablespoon coconut or other unrefined sugar, or 1 tablespoon maple syrup, or 10 to 15 drops pure liquid stevia

2 tablespoons chia seeds, whole or ground
2 teaspoons matcha green tea powder (optional)

Directions
Preparing the Ingredients.
1. Blend all the ingredients in a blender until smooth. Chill in the fridge for about 20 minutes, then serve topped with one or more of the topping ideas.
2. Try blueberries, blackberries, sliced strawberries, Coconut Whipped Cream, or toasted unsweetened coconut.

Per Serving Calories: 226; Total fat: 20g; Carbs: 13g; Fiber: 5g; Protein: 3g

Strawberry Parfaits With Cashew Crème
PREP: 10 MINUTES • CHILL TIME: 50 MINUTES • • SERVES: 4 servings

Ingredients
1/2 cup unsalted raw cashews
4 tablespoons light brown sugar
1/2 cup plain or vanilla soy milk
¾ cup firm silken tofu, drained

1 teaspoon pure vanilla extract
2 cups sliced strawberries
1 teaspoon fresh lemon juice
Fresh mint leaves, for garnish

Directions
1. In a blender, grind the cashews and 3 tablespoons of the sugar to a fine powder. Add the soy milk and blend until smooth. Add the tofu and vanilla and continue to blend until smooth and creamy. Scrape the cashew mixture into a medium bowl, cover, and refrigerate for 30 minutes.
2. In a large bowl, combine the strawberries, lemon juice, and remaining 1 tablespoon sugar. Stir gently to combine and set aside at room temperature for 20 minutes.
3. Spoon alternating layers of the strawberries and cashew crème into parfait glasses or wineglasses, ending with a dollop of the cashew crème. Garnish with mint leaves and serve.

Mint Chocolate Chip Sorbet
PREP: 5 MINUTES • COOK TIME: 0 MINUTES • TOTAL: 5 MINUTES • SERVES: 1

Ingredients
1 frozen banana
1 tablespoon almond butter, or peanut butter, or other nut or seed butter
2 tablespoons fresh mint, minced

¼ cup or less non-dairy milk (only if needed)
2 to 3 tablespoons non-dairy chocolate chips, or cocoa nibs
2 to 3 tablespoons goji berries (optional)

Directions
Preparing the Ingredients.
1. Put the banana, almond butter, and mint in a food processor or blender and purée until smooth.
2. Add the non-dairy milk if needed to keep blending (but only if needed, as this will make the texture less solid). Pulse the chocolate chips and goji berries (if using) into the mix so they're roughly chopped up.

Per Serving Calories: 212; Total fat: 10g; Carbs: 31g; Fiber: 4g; Protein: 3g

Peach-Mango Crumble (Pressure cooker)
PREP: 10 MINUTES • PRESSURE: 6 MINUTES • TOTAL: 21 MINUTES • PRESSURE LEVEL: HIGH • RELEASE: QUICK• SERVES 4-6

Ingredients
3 cups chopped fresh or frozen peaches

3 cups chopped fresh or frozen mangos

4 tablespoons unrefined sugar or pure maple syrup, divided

1 cup gluten-free rolled oats

½ cup shredded coconut, sweetened or unsweetened

2 tablespoons coconut oil or vegan margarine

Directions

1. **Preparing the Ingredients.** In a 6- to 7-inch round baking dish, toss together the peaches, mangos, and 2 tablespoons of sugar. In a food processor, combine the oats, coconut, coconut oil, and remaining 2 tablespoons of sugar. Pulse until combined. (If you use maple syrup, you'll need less coconut oil. Start with just the syrup and add oil if the mixture isn't sticking together.) Sprinkle the oat mixture over the fruit mixture.

    Cover the dish with aluminum foil. Put a trivet in the bottom of your electric pressure cooker's cooking pot and pour in a cup or two of water. Using a foil sling or silicone helper handles, lower the pan onto the trivet.

2. **High pressure for 6 minutes.** Close and lock the lid and ensure the pressure valve is sealed, then select High Pressure and set the time for 6 minutes.

3. **Pressure Release.** Once the cook time is complete, quick release the pressure, being careful not to get your fingers or face near the steam release. Once all the pressure has released, carefully unlock and remove the lid.

    Let cool for a few minutes before carefully lifting out the dish with oven mitts or tongs. Scoop out portions to serve.

PER SERVING Calories: 321; Total fat: 18g; Protein: 4g; Sodium: 2mg; Fiber: 7g

Ginger-Spice Brownies
PREP: 5 MINUTES • COOK TIME: 35 MINUTES • TOTAL: 45 MINUTES • SERVES: 12 brownies

Ingredients

1¾ cups whole-grain flour
1 teaspoon baking powder
1 teaspoon baking soda
1/2 teaspoon salt
1 tablespoon ground ginger
1/2 teaspoon ground cinnamon
1/2 teaspoon ground allspice

3 tablespoons unsweetened cocoa powder
1/2 cup vegan semisweet chocolate chips
1/2 cup chopped walnuts
1/4 cup canola oil
1/2 cup dark molasses
1/2 cup water
1/3 cup light brown sugar
2 teaspoons grated fresh ginger

Directions

1. Preheat the oven to 350°F. Grease an 8-inch square baking pan and set aside. In a large bowl, combine the flour, baking powder, baking soda, salt, ground ginger, cinnamon, allspice, and cocoa. Stir in the chocolate chips and walnuts and set aside.

    In medium bowl, combine the oil, molasses, water, sugar, and fresh ginger and mix well.

    Pour the wet Ingredients into the dry Ingredients and mix well.

2. Scrape the dough into the prepared baking pan. The dough will be sticky, so wet your hands to press it evenly into the pan. Bake until a toothpick inserted in the center comes out clean, 30 to 35 minutes. Cool on a wire rack 30 minutes before cutting. Store in an airtight container.

Zesty Orange-Cranberry Energy Bites
PREP: 10 MINUTES • CHILL TIME: 15 MINUTES • TOTAL: 25 MINUTES • SERVES: 12 BITES

Ingredients

2 tablespoons almond butter, or cashew or sunflower seed butter
2 tablespoons maple syrup, or brown rice syrup
¾ cup cooked quinoa
¼ cup sesame seeds, toasted

1 tablespoon chia seeds
½ teaspoon almond extract, or vanilla extract
Zest of 1 orange
1 tablespoon dried cranberries
¼ cup ground almonds

Directions

Preparing the Ingredients.

1. In a medium bowl, mix together the nut or seed butter and syrup until smooth and creamy. Stir in the rest of the ingredients, and mix to make sure the consistency is holding together in a ball. Form the mix into 12 balls.
    Place them on a baking sheet lined with parchment or waxed paper and put in the fridge to set for about 15 minutes.
2. If your balls aren't holding together, it's likely because of the moisture content of your cooked quinoa. Add more nut or seed butter mixed with syrup until it all sticks together.

Per Serving (1 bite) Calories: 109; Total fat: 7g; Carbs: 11g; Fiber: 3g; Protein: 3g

Chocolate And Walnut Farfalle

PREP: 10 MINUTES • COOK TIME: 0 MINUTES • TOTAL: 10 MINUTES • SERVES: 4 servings

Ingredients

1/2 cup chopped toasted walnuts
1/4 cup vegan semisweet chocolate pieces
8 ounces farfalle

3 tablespoons vegan margarine
1/4 cup ight brown sugar

Directions

1. In a food processor or blender, grind the walnuts and chocolate pieces until crumbly. Do not overprocess. Set aside.
2. In a pot of boiling salted water, cook the farfalle, stirring occasionally, until al dente, about 8 minutes. Drain well and return to the pot.
3. Add the margarine and sugar and toss to combine and melt the margarine.
    Transfer the noodle mixture to a serving

Almond-Date Energy Bites

PREP: 5 MINUTES • CHILL TIME: 15 MINUTES • TOTAL: 20 MINUTES • SERVES: 24 BITES

Ingredients

1 cup dates, pitted
1 cup unsweetened shredded coconut
¼ cup chia seeds

¾ cup ground almonds
¼ cup cocoa nibs, or non-dairy chocolate chips

Directions

Preparing the Ingredients.

1. Purée everything in a food processor until crumbly and sticking together, pushing down the sides whenever necessary to keep it blending. If you don't have a food processor, you can mash soft Medjool dates. But if you're using harder baking dates, you'll have to soak them and then try to purée them in a blender.

2. Form the mix into 24 balls and place them on a baking sheet lined with parchment or waxed paper. Put in the fridge to set for about 15 minutes. Use the softest dates you can find. Medjool dates are the best for this purpose. The hard dates you see in the baking aisle of your supermarket are going to take a long time to blend up. If you use those, try soaking them in water for at least an hour before you start, and then draining.

Per Serving (1 bite) Calories: 152; Total fat: 11g; Carbs: 13g; Fiber: 5g; Protein: 3g

Pumpkin Pie Cups (Pressure cooker)
PREP: 5 MINUTES • PRESSURE: 6 MINUTES • TOTAL: 20 MINUTES • PRESSURE LEVEL: HIGH • RELEASE: QUICK• SERVES 4-6

Ingredients
1 cup canned pumpkin purée
1 cup nondairy milk
6 tablespoons unrefined sugar or pure maple syrup (less if using sweetened milk), plus more for sprinkling
¼ cup spelt flour or all-purpose flour
½ teaspoon pumpkin pie spice
Pinch salt

Directions
1. **Preparing the Ingredients.** In a medium bowl, stir together the pumpkin, milk, sugar, flour, pumpkin pie spice, and salt. Pour the mixture into 4 heat-proof ramekins. Sprinkle a bit more sugar on the top of each, if you like. Put a trivet in the bottom of your electric pressure cooker's cooking pot and pour in a cup or two of water. Place the ramekins onto the trivet, stacking them if needed (3 on the bottom, 1 on top).
2. **High pressure for 6 minutes.** Close and lock the lid and ensure the pressure valve is sealed, then select High Pressure and set the time for 6 minutes.
3. **Pressure Release.** Once the cook time is complete, quick release the pressure. Once all the pressure has released, carefully unlock and remove the lid. Let cool for a few minutes before carefully lifting out the ramekins with oven mitts or tongs. Let cool for at least 10 minutes before serving.

PER SERVING Calories: 129; Total fat: 1g; Protein: 3g; Sodium: 39mg; Fiber: 3g

Coconut and Almond Truffles
PREP: 15 MINUTES • COOK TIME: 0 MINUTES • TOTAL: 15 MINUTES • SERVES: 8 TRUFFLES

Ingredients
1 cup pitted dates
1 cup almonds
½ cup sweetened cocoa powder, plus extra for coating
½ cup unsweetened shredded coconut

¼ cup pure maple syrup
1 teaspoon vanilla extract
1 teaspoon almond extract
¼ teaspoon sea salt

Directions
Preparing the Ingredients.
1. In the bowl of a food processor, combine all the ingredients and process until smooth. Chill the mixture for about 1 hour.
2. Roll the mixture into balls and then roll the balls in cocoa powder to coat.
Serve immediately or keep chilled until ready to serve.

Pecan And Date-Stuffed Roasted Pears

PREP: 10 MINUTES • COOK TIME: 30 MINUTES • TOTAL: 40 MINUTES • SERVES: 4 servings

Ingredients

4 firm ripe pears, cored
1 tablespoon fresh lemon juice
1/2 cup finely chopped pecans
4 dates, pitted and chopped
1 tablespoon vegan margarine

1 tablespoon pure maple syrup
1/4 teaspoon ground cinnamon
1/8 teaspoon ground ginger
1/2 cup pear, white grape, or apple juice

Directions

1. Preheat the oven to 350°F. Grease a shallow baking dish and set aside. Halve the pears lengthwise and use a melon baller to scoop out the cores. Rub the exposed part of the pears with the lemon juice to avoid discoloration.
2. In a medium bowl, combine the pecans, dates, margarine, maple syrup, cinnamon, and ginger and mix well.
3. Stuff the mixture into the centers of the pear halves and arrange them in the prepared baking pan. Pour the juice over the pears. Bake until tender, 30 to 40 minutes. Serve warm.

Lime-Macerated Mangos

PREP: 10 MINUTES • COOLING TIME: 6 HOURS • • SERVES: 4 to 6 servings

Ingredients

3 ripe mangos
1/3 cup light brown sugar
2 tablespoons fresh lime juice

1/2 cup dry white wine
Fresh mint sprigs

Directions

1. Peel, pit, and cut the mangos into 1/2-inch dice. Layer the diced mango in a large bowl, sprinkling each layer with about 1 tablespoon of the sugar. Cover with plastic wrap and refrigerate 2 hours.
2. Pour in the lime juice and wine, mixing gently to combine with the mango. Cover and refrigerate for 4 hours.
3. About 30 minutes before serving time, bring the fruit to room temperature. To serve, spoon the mango and the liquid into serving glasses and garnish with mint.

Fudgy Brownies (Pressure cooker)

PREP: 10 MINUTES • PRESSURE: 5 MINUTES • TOTAL: 20 MINUTES • PRESSURE LEVEL: HIGH • RELEASE: QUICK • SERVES 4-6

Ingredients

3 ounces dairy-free dark chocolate
1 tablespoon coconut oil or vegan margarine
½ cup applesauce
2 tablespoons unrefined sugar

⅓ cup all-purpose flour
½ teaspoon baking powder
Pinch salt

Directions

1. **Preparing the Ingredients.** Put a trivet in your electric pressure cooker's cooking pot and pour in a cup or two of two of water. Select Sauté or Simmer. In a large heat-proof glass or ceramic bowl, combine the chocolate and coconut oil. Place the bowl over the top of your pressure cooker, as you would a double boiler. Stir occasionally until the chocolate is melted, then turn off the pressure cooker. Stir the

applesauce and sugar into the chocolate mixture. Add the flour, baking powder, and salt and stir just until combined. Pour the batter into 3 heat-proof ramekins. Put them in a heat-proof dish and cover with aluminum foil. Using a foil sling or silicone helper handles, lower the dish onto the trivet. (Alternately, cover each ramekin with foil and place them directly on the trivet, without the dish.)

2. **High pressure for 6 minutes.** Close and lock the lid and ensure the pressure valve is sealed, then select High Pressure and set the time for 5 minutes.

3. **Pressure Release.** Once the cook time is complete, quick release the pressure. Once all the pressure has released, carefully unlock and remove the lid.

   Let cool for a few minutes before carefully lifting out the dish, or ramekins, with oven mitts or tongs. Let cool for a few minutes more before serving.

   Top with fresh raspberries and an extra drizzle of melted chocolate.

PER SERVING Calories: 316; Total fat: 14g; Protein: 5g; Sodium: 68mg; Fiber: 5g

Chocolate-Banana Fudge
PREP: 10 MINUTES • CHILL TIME: 2 HOURS • • SERVES: about 36 pieces

Ingredients
1 ripe banana

¾ cup vegan semisweet chocolate chips

4 cups confectioners' sugar

1 teaspoon pure vanilla extract

Directions
1. Line an 8-inch square baking pan with enough waxed paper or aluminum foil so that the ends hang over the edge of the pan. (This will help you get the fudge out of the pan later.) Set aside. Place the banana in a food processor and blend until smooth.
   9Melt the chocolate chips in a double boiler or microwave, then add to the pureed banana along with the sugar and vanilla and process until smooth.
2. Scrape the mixture into the prepared pan. Smooth the top and refrigerate until firm, at least 2 hours.
3. Once chilled, grip the waxed paper, lift the fudge from the pan, and transfer it to a cutting board. Remove and discard the waxed paper. Cut the fudge into small pieces and serve. Cover and refrigerate any leftovers.

Chocolate–Almond Butter Truffles
PREP: 15 MINUTES • CHILL TIME: 45 MINUTES • • SERVES: about 24 truffles

Ingredients
1 cup vegan semisweet chocolate chips

1/2 cup almond butter

2 tablespoons plain or vanilla soy milk

1 tablespoon pure vanilla extract

1 cup confectioners' sugar

2 tablespoons unsweetened cocoa powder

1/2 cup finely chopped toasted almonds

Directions
1. Melt the chocolate in a double boiler or microwave.
   In a food processor, combine the almond butter, soy milk, and vanilla and blend until smooth. Add the sugar, cocoa, and the melted chocolate and blend until smooth and creamy.
2. Transfer the mixture to a bowl and refrigerate until chilled, at least 45 minutes.
3. Roll the chilled mixture into 1-inch balls and place them on an ungreased baking sheet.
4. Place the ground almonds in a shallow bowl and roll the balls in them, turning to coat. Place the truffles on a serving platter, refrigerate for 30 minutes, and serve.

Chocolate Macaroons

PREP: 10 MINUTES • COOK TIME: 15 MINUTES • TOTAL: 25 MINUTES • SERVES: 8 MACAROONS

Ingredients

1 cup unsweetened shredded coconut
2 tablespoons cocoa powder
⅔ cup coconut milk

¼ cup agave
pinch of sea salt

Directions

Preparing the Ingredients.

1. Preheat the oven to 350°F. Line a baking sheet with parchment paper. In a medium saucepan, cook all the ingredients over -medium-high heat until a firm dough is formed. Scoop the dough into balls and place on the baking sheet.
2. Bake for 15 minutes, remove from the oven, and let cool on the baking sheet. Serve cooled macaroons or store in a tightly sealed container for up to

Chocolate Pudding

PREP: 5 MINUTES • COOK TIME: 0 MINUTES • TOTAL: 5 MINUTES • SERVES: 1

Ingredients

1 banana
2 to 4 tablespoons nondairy milk
2 tablespoons unsweetened cocoa powder

2 tablespoons sugar (optional)
½ ripe avocado or 1 cup silken tofu (optional)

Directions

Preparing the Ingredients.

In a small blender, combine the banana, milk, cocoa powder, sugar (if using), and avocado (if using). Purée until smooth. Alternatively, in a small bowl, mash the banana very well, and stir in the remaining ingredients.

Per Serving Calories: 244; Protein: 4g; Total fat: 3g; Saturated fat: 1g; Carbohydrates: 59g; Fiber: 8g

Lime and Watermelon Granita

PREP: 15 MINUTES • CHILLING TIME: 6 HOURS • • SERVES: 4

Ingredients

8 cups seedless -watermelon chunks
juice of 2 limes, or 2 tablespoons prepared lime juice

½ cup sugar
strips of lime zest, for garnish

Directions

Preparing the Ingredients.

1. In a blender or food processor, combine the watermelon, lime juice, and sugar and process until smooth. You may have to do this in two batches. After processing, stir well to combine both batches.
2. Pour the mixture into a 9-by-13-inch glass dish. Freeze for 2 to 3 hours. Remove from the freezer and use a fork to scrape the top layer of ice. Leave the shaved ice on top and return to the freezer.
3. In another hour, remove from the freezer and repeat. Do this a few more times until all the ice is scraped up. Serve frozen, garnished with strips of lime zest.

Chocolate-Covered Peanut Butter–Granola Balls

PREP: 15 MINUTES • CHILL TIME: 30 MINUTES •• SERVES: about 3 dozen pieces

Ingredients

1/2 cup granola, homemade or store-bought
1/4 cup light brown sugar
1/2 cup golden raisins
1/2 cup unsalted shelled sunflower seeds

1/4 cup sesame seeds
11/2 cups creamy peanut butter
2 cups vegan semisweet chocolate chips

Directions

1. In a food processor, pulse together the granola, sugar, raisins, sunflower seeds, and sesame seeds. Blend in the peanut butter a little at a time to form a smooth dough. Refrigerate until chilled, for several hours or overnight.
2. Form the mixture into 1-inch balls and set aside. Melt the chocolate in a double boiler or microwave.
3. Dip the balls into the melted chocolate and arrange on an ungreased baking sheet. Refrigerate until firm, about 30 minutes, and serve.

Coconut-Banana Pudding

PREP: 4 MINUTES • COOK TIME: 5 MINUTES • OVERNIGHT TO SET • SERVES: 4

Ingredients

3 bananas, divided
1 (13.5-ounce) can full-fat coconut milk
¼ cup organic cane sugar
1 tablespoon cornstarch

1 teaspoon vanilla extract
2 pinches sea salt
6 drops natural yellow food coloring (optional)
Ground cinnamon, for garnish

Directions

Preparing the Ingredients.

1. Combine 1 banana, the coconut milk, sugar, cornstarch, vanilla, and salt in a blender. Blend until smooth and creamy. If you're using the food coloring, add it to the blender now and blend until the color is evenly dispersed.
2. Transfer to a saucepot and bring to a boil over medium-high heat. Immediately reduce to a simmer and whisk for 3 minutes, or until the mixture thickens to a thin pudding and sticks to a spoon.
3. Transfer the mixture to a container and allow to cool for 1 hour. Cover and refrigerate overnight to set. When you're ready to serve, slice the remaining 2 bananas and build individual servings as follows: pudding, banana slices, pudding, and so on until a single-serving dish is filled to the desired level. Sprinkle with ground cinnamon.

Spiced Apple Chia Pudding

PREP: 5 MINUTES • CHILL TIME: 30 MINUTES • TOTAL: 35 MINUTES • SERVES: 1

Ingredients

½ cup unsweetened applesauce
¼ cup nondairy milk or canned coconut milk
1 tablespoon chia seeds

1½ teaspoons sugar
Pinch ground cinnamon or pumpkin pie spice

Directions

Preparing the Ingredients.

In a small bowl, stir together the applesauce, milk, chia seeds, sugar, and cinnamon. Enjoy as is, or let sit for 30 minutes so the chia seeds soften and expand.

Per Serving Calories: 153; Protein: 3g; Total fat: 5g; Saturated fat: 1g; Carbohydrates: 26g; Fiber: 10g

Caramelized Pears with Balsamic Glaze
PREP: 5 MINUTES • COOK TIME: 15 MINUTES • TOTAL: 20 MINUTES • SERVES: 4

Ingredients
1 cup balsamic vinegar
¼ cup plus 3 tablespoons brown sugar
¼ teaspoon grated nutmeg

pinch of sea salt
¼ cup coconut oil
4 pears, cored and cut into slices

Directions
Preparing the Ingredients.

1. In a medium saucepan, heat the balsamic vinegar, ¼ cup of the brown sugar, the nutmeg, and salt over medium-high heat, stirring to thoroughly incorporate the sugar. Allow to simmer, stirring occasionally, until the glaze reduces by half, 10 to 15 minutes.
2. Meanwhile, heat the coconut oil in a large sauté pan over medium-high heat until it shimmers. Add the pears to the pan in a single layer. Cook until they turn golden, about 5 minutes. Add the remaining 3 tablespoons brown sugar and continue to cook, stirring occasionally, until the pears caramelize, about 5 minutes more.

   Place the pears on a plate. Drizzle with balsamic glaze and serve.

Spicy Chocolate Cake With Dark Chocolate Glaze
PREP: 15 MINUTES • COOK TIME:30 MINUTES • TOTAL: 45 MINUTES • SERVES: 8 servings

Ingredients
Cake
1¾ cups whole-grain flour
1 cup light brown sugar
1/4 cup unsweetened cocoa powder
1 teaspoon baking soda
1/2 teaspoon baking powder
11/2 teaspoons ground cinnamon
1/4 teaspoon ground cayenne
1/3 cup extra olive oil
1 tablespoon apple cider vinegar

11/2 teaspoons pure vanilla extract
1 cup cold water
Glaze
2 (1-ounce) squares unsweetened vegan chocolate
1/4 cup plain or vanilla soy milk
1/2 cup light brown sugar
2 tablespoons vegan margarine
1/2 teaspoon pure vanilla extract
Pinch ground cayenne

Directions
1. Make the cake: Preheat the oven to 350°F. Grease a 9-inch round cake pan and set aside.
   In a large bowl, combine the flour, sugar, cocoa, baking soda, baking powder, cinnamon, and cayenne. In a medium bowl, combine the oil, vinegar, vanilla, and water. Stir the wet Ingredients into the dry Ingredients, mixing until just combined.
2. Pour the batter into the prepared pan and bake until a toothpick inserted into the center comes out clean, about 30 minutes. Cool the cake in the pan for 10 to 15 minutes, then invert it onto a wire rack and let the cake cool completely while you make the glaze.
3. Make the glaze: In a double boiler, combine the chocolate and soy milk and cook, stirring constantly, until the chocolate is melted. Stir in the sugar and cook, stirring constantly, for 5 minutes. Remove from

the heat and stir in the margarine, vanilla, and cayenne. Drizzle the glaze over the cooled cake. Refrigerate the cake to let the glaze set before serving.

Blueberry-Peach Crisp
PREP: 15 MINUTES • COOK TIME: 30 MINUTES • TOTAL: 45 MINUTES • SERVES: 8 servings

Ingredients
4 fresh ripe peaches, peeled, pitted, and cut into 1/4-inch slices
2 cups fresh blueberries
1 tablespoon cornstarch
¾ cup light brown sugar

2 teaspoons fresh lemon juice
1 teaspoon ground cinnamon
1/2 cup whole-grain flour
1/2 cup old-fashioned oats
3 tablespoons vegan margarine

Directions
1. Preheat the oven to 375°F. Lightly oil a 9-inch square baking pan and set aside. In a large bowl, combine the peaches, blueberries, cornstarch, 1/4 cup of the sugar, lemon juice, and 1/2 teaspoon of the cinnamon. Mix gently and spoon into the prepared baking pan. Set aside.
2. In small bowl, combine the flour, oats, margarine, the remaining 1/2 cup sugar, and the remaining 1/2 teaspoon cinnamon. Use a pastry blender or fork to mix until crumbly.
3. Sprinkle the topping over the fruit mixture and bake until the top is browned and bubbly in the center, 30 to 40 minutes. Serve warm.

Salted Coconut-Almond Fudge
PREP: 5 MINUTES • SET TIME: 1 HOUR • • SERVES: 12

Ingredients
¾ cup creamy almond butter
½ cup maple syrup
⅓ cup coconut oil, softened or melted

6 tablespoons fair-trade unsweetened cocoa powder
1 teaspoon coarse or flaked sea salt

Directions
Preparing the Ingredients.
1. Line a loaf pan with a double layer of plastic wrap. Place one layer horizontally in the pan with a generous amount of overhang, and the second layer vertically with a generous amount of overhang.
2. In a medium bowl, gently mix together the almond butter, maple syrup, and coconut oil until well combined and smooth. Add the cocoa powder and gently stir it into the mixture until well combined and creamy.
3. Pour the mixture into the prepared pan and sprinkle with the sea salt. Bring the overflowing edges of the plastic wrap over the top of the fudge to completely cover it. Place the pan in the freezer for at least 1 hour or overnight, until the fudge is firm.
   Remove the pan from the freezer and lift the fudge out of the pan using the plastic-wrap overhangs to pull it out. Transfer to a cutting board and cut into 1-inch pieces.

Caramelized Bananas
PREP: 5 MINUTES • COOK TIME: 10 MINUTES • TOTAL: 15 MINUTES • SERVES: 2

Ingredients
2 tablespoons vegan margarine or coconut oil

2 bananas, peeled, halved crosswise and then lengthwise

2 tablespoons dark brown sugar, demerara sugar, or coconut sugar

2 tablespoons spiced apple cider

Chopped walnuts, for topping

Directions

Preparing the Ingredients.

1. Melt the margarine in a nonstick skillet over medium heat. Add the bananas, and cook for 2 minutes. Flip, and cook for 2 minutes more.
2. Sprinkle the sugar and cider into the oil around the bananas, and cook for 2 to 3 minutes, until the sauce thickens and caramelizes around the bananas. Carefully scoop the bananas into small bowls, and drizzle with any remaining liquid in the skillet. Sprinkle with walnuts.

Per Serving Calories: 384; Protein: 4g; Total fat: 24g; Saturated fat: 13g; Carbohydrates: 46g; Fiber: 5g

Quick Apple Crisp
PREP: 10 MINUTES • COOK TIME: 45 MINUTES • TOTAL: 55 MINUTES • SERVES: 6 servings

Ingredients

5 Granny Smith apples, peeled, cored, and cut into 1/4-inch slices

1/2 cup pure maple syrup

1 tablespoon fresh lemon juice

1 teaspoon ground cinnamon

1/2 cup whole-grain flour

1/2 cup old-fashioned oats

1/2 cup finely chopped walnuts or pecans

2/3 cup light brown sugar

1/2 cup vegan margarine, softened

Directions

1. Preheat the oven to 350°F. Lightly oil a 9-inch square baking pan. Place the apples in the prepared pan. Drizzle the maple syrup and lemon juice over the apples and sprinkle with 1/2 teaspoon of the cinnamon. Set aside.
2. In a medium bowl, mix the flour, oats, walnuts, sugar, and the remaining 1/2 teaspoon cinnamon. Use a pastry blender to cut in the margarine until the mixture resembles coarse crumbs. Spread the topping over the apples and bake until bubbly and lightly browned on top, about 45 minutes. Serve warm.

Mixed Berries and Cream
PREP: 10 MINUTES • COOK TIME: 0 MINUTES • TOTAL: 10 MINUTES • SERVES: 4

Ingredients

two 15-ounce cans full-fat coconut milk

3 tablespoons agave

½ teaspoon vanilla extract

1 pint fresh blueberries

1 pint fresh raspberries

1 pint fresh strawberries, sliced

Directions

Preparing the Ingredients.

1. Refrigerate the coconut milk overnight. When you open the can, the liquid will have separated from the solids. Spoon out the solids and reserve the liquid for another purpose.
2. In a medium bowl, whisk the agave and vanilla extract into the coconut solids. Divide the berries among four bowls. Top with the coconut cream. Serve immediately.

Peanut Butter Cups

PREP: 20 MINUTES • COOK TIME: 0 MINUTES • TOTAL: 20 MINUTES • SERVES: 12 CUPS

Ingredients

1½ cups vegan chocolate chips, divided
½ cup peanut butter, almond or cashew butter, or sunflower seed butter

¼ cup packed brown sugar
2 tablespoons nondairy milk

Directions

Preparing the Ingredients.

1. Line the cups of a muffin tin with paper liners or reusable silicone cups.
2. In a small microwave-safe bowl, heat ¾ cup of the chocolate chips on high power for 1 minute. Stir. Continue heating in 30-second increments, stirring after each, until the chocolate is melted.
3. Pour about 1½ teaspoons of melted chocolate into each prepared muffin cup. Set aside, and allow them to harden.
4. In a small bowl, stir together the peanut butter, brown sugar, and milk until smooth. Scoop about 1½ teaspoons of the mixture on top of the chocolate base in each cup. It's okay if the chocolate is not yet hardened.
5. Melt the remaining ¾ cup of chocolate chips using the directions in step 1. Pour another 1½ teaspoons of chocolate on top of the peanut butter in each cup, softly spreading it to cover. Let the cups sit until the chocolate hardens, about 15 minutes in the refrigerator or several hours on the counter. Leftovers will keep in the refrigerator for up to 2 weeks.

Per Serving (1 cup) Calories: 227; Protein: 4g; Total fat: 14g; Saturated fat: 6g; Carbohydrates: 22g; Fiber: 3g

Carrot Cake

PREP: 15 MINUTES • COOK TIME: 45 MINUTES • TOTAL: 60 MINUTES • SERVES: 8 servings

Ingredients

2 cups whole-grain flour
2 teaspoons baking powder
1 teaspoon baking soda
2 teaspoons ground cinnamon
1/2 teaspoon ground allspice
1 teaspoon salt
1 cup light brown sugar

1/2 cup plain or vanilla soy milk
1/2 cup canola or other neutral oil
1/4 cup pure maple syrup
2 teaspoons pure vanilla extract
2 cups finely shredded carrots
1/2 cup golden raisins
1 recipe "Cream Cheese" Frosting

Directions

1. Preheat the oven to 350°F. Grease a 9-inch square baking pan and set aside.
    In a medium bowl, mix the flour, baking powder, baking soda, cinnamon, allspice, and salt.
2. In a large bowl, combine the sugar, soy milk, oil, maple syrup, and vanilla, then add the wet Ingredients to the dry Ingredients. Stir in the carrots and raisins until just mixed.
    Scrape the batter into the prepared pan. Bake until a toothpick comes out clean, about 45 minutes.
3. Let the cake cool in pan for 15 minutes, then invert onto a wire rack to cool completely. When completely cool, frost the cake with "Cream Cheese" Frosting.

Spice Cake With Mango And Lime

PREP: 15 MINUTES • COOK TIME: 45 MINUTES • TOTAL: 60 MINUTES • SERVES: 8 servings

Ingredients

1 1/2 cups whole-grain flour
¾ cup light brown sugar
1/4 cup yellow cornmeal
1 teaspoon baking soda
1/2 teaspoon salt
1/2 teaspoon baking powder
1/2 teaspoon ground cinnamon

1/2 teaspoon ground allspice
1/2 teaspoon ground ginger
1 cup applesauce
1/3 cup canola or other neutral oil
2 teaspoons grated lime zest
2 tablespoons water
1 ripe mango, peeled, pitted, and chopped

Directions

1. Preheat the oven to 350°F. Lightly oil a 9-inch round cake pan and set aside.
2. In a large bowl, combine the flour, sugar, cornmeal, baking soda, salt, baking powder, cinnamon, allspice, and ginger and set aside.
3. In a medium bowl, combine the applesauce, oil, lime zest, and water, stirring to blend.
4. Fold in the mango. Add the wet Ingredients to the dry Ingredients and mix to combine.
5. Pour the batter into the prepared baking pan. Bake until a toothpick inserted in the center comes out clean, 45 to 50 minutes. Let the cake cool in the pan for 10 minutes then invert onto a wire rack to cool completely before slicing.

Dessert Crêpes
PREP: 5 MINUTES • COOK TIME: 10 MINUTES • TOTAL: 15 MINUTES • SERVES: 10 crêpes

Ingredients

1 1/3 cups plain or vanilla soy milk
1 cup whole-grain flour
1/3 cup firm tofu, drained and crumbled
3 tablespoons vegan margarine, melted
2 tablespoons light brown sugar

1 1/2 teaspoons pure vanilla extract
1/2 teaspoon baking powder
1/8 teaspoon salt
Canola or other neutral oil, for cooking

Directions

1. In a blender, combine all the Ingredients (except the oil for cooking) and blend until smooth.
2. Heat a nonstick medium skillet or crêpe pan over medium-high heat. Coat the pan with a small amount of oil. Pour about 3 tablespoons of the batter into the center of the skillet and tilt the pan to spread the batter out thinly. Cook until golden on both sides, flipping once. Transfer to a platter and repeat with the remaining batter, oiling the pan as needed.
3. The crêpes can now be used in the recipes below or topped with your favorite dessert sauce or sautéed fruit. These taste best if used on the same day that they are made.

Strawberry Sorbet
PREP: 15 MINUTES • COOK TIME: 0 MINUTES • TOTAL: 15 MINUTES • SERVES: about 1 pint

Ingredients

1/2 cup light brown sugar
1/2 cup water

2 cups hulled strawberries
2 teaspoons fresh lemon juice

Directions

1. In a medium saucepan, combine the sugar and water. Cook, stirring, over low heat until sugar is dissolved, about 3 minutes. Increase the heat to high and bring to a boil, then remove from the heat. Transfer to a heatproof bowl and refrigerate until chilled about 2 hours.
2. In a blender or food processor, combine the strawberries and lemon juice and blend until smooth. Add the cooled sugar syrup to the strawberry mixture and process until smooth.
3. Freeze the mixture in an ice cream maker according to the manufacturer's Directions. When the mixture is finished churning in the machine, it will be soft, but ready to eat. For a firmer sorbet, transfer to a freezer-safe container and freeze no more than 1 to 2 hours for best flavor and texture.

Orange Granita
PREP: 15 MINUTES • COOK TIME: 0 MINUTES • TOTAL: 15 MINUTES • SERVES: about 3 cups

Ingredients
1/2 cup lightbrown sugar
1/2 cup water

2 cups orange juice
1 teaspoon fresh lemon juice

Directions
1. In a medium saucepan, combine the sugar and water and bring to a boil. Cook, stirring, until the sugar dissolves. Remove from heat and set aside to cool, about 15 minutes. Stir in the orange juice and lemon juice, then pour the mixture into a shallow baking pan.
2. Cover and freeze until firm, stirring about once per hour, about 3 hours.
3. When firm, remove the mixture from the freezer and scrape it with the tines of a fork until fluffy. Spoon the granita into a container, cover, and freeze until serving time. The taste and texture of the granita is best if eaten within a few hours after it is made.

Spiced Rhubarb Sauce
PREP: 10 MINUTES • COOK TIME: 15 MINUTES • TOTAL: 25 MINUTES • SERVES: 4

Ingredients
½ cup water
½ cup sugar
¼ teaspoon grated nutmeg

¼ teaspoon ground ginger
¼ teaspoon ground cinnamon
1 pound rhubarb, cut into ½- to 1-inch pieces

Directions
Preparing the Ingredients.
In a large saucepan, bring the water, sugar, nutmeg, ginger, and cinnamon to a boil. Add the rhubarb and cook over medium-high heat, stirring frequently, until the rhubarb is soft and saucy, about 10 minutes. Chill for at least 30 minutes before serving.

Apple And Pear Cobbler
PREP: 15 MINUTES • COOK TIME: 30 MINUTES • TOTAL: 45 MINUTES • SERVES: 6 servings

Ingredients
3 Granny Smith apples, peeled, cored, and shredded
2 ripe pears, peeled, cored, and cut into 1/4-inch slices

2 teaspoons fresh lemon juice
1/2 cup plus 2 tablespoons light brown sugar
2 tablespoons cornstarch
1 teaspoon ground cinnamon

1/2 teaspoon ground allspice
1 cup whole-grain flour
11/2 teaspoons baking powder

1/4 teaspoon salt
2 tablespoons canola or other neutral oil
1/2 cup plain or vanilla soy milk

Directions

1. Preheat the oven to 400°F. Grease a 9-inch square baking pan. Spread the apples and pears in the prepared pan. Sprinkle with the lemon juice and toss to coat. Stir in 1/2 cup of the sugar, cornstarch, cinnamon, and allspice, stirring to mix.
2. In a medium bowl, combine the flour, the remaining 2 tablespoons sugar, the baking powder, and the salt. Add the oil and mix with a fork until the mixture resembles coarse crumbs. Mix in the soy milk. Spread the topping over the fruit. Bake until golden, about 30 minutes. Serve warm.

Winter Fruit Sauce
PREP: 15 MINUTES • COOK TIME: 20 MINUTES • TOTAL: 35 MINUTES • SERVES: about 2 cups

Ingredients
1 cup water
1 cup dried mixed fruit
1 teaspoon fresh lemon juice

1/2 teaspoon ground cinnamon
1/4 cup apple juice

Directions

1. In a large saucepan, combine the water, dried fruit, lemon juice, and cinnamon. Cover and bring to a boil over high heat. Reduce heat to medium and simmer for 20 minutes.
2. Remove from the heat and set aside to cool, 15 minutes, then transfer to a blender or food processor and process until smooth. Add the apple juice and process until blended. Return the sauce to the saucepan and heat on low until warm. Store leftover sauce covered in the refrigerator for up to 3 days.

Chocolate-Coconut Bars
PREP: 20 MINUTES • CHILL TIME: 20 MINUTES • • SERVES: 16 BARS

Ingredients
¼ cup coconut oil or unsalted vegan margarine, plus more for preparing the baking dish (optional)
2 cups unsweetened shredded coconut

¼ cup sugar
2 tablespoons maple syrup or Simple Syrup
1 cup vegan chocolate chips

Directions
Preparing the Ingredients.
1. Coat an 8-inch square baking dish with coconut oil or line it with parchment paper, set aside.
2. In a small bowl, stir together the coconut, sugar, maple syrup, and coconut oil. Transfer the mixture to the prepared baking dish, and press it down firmly with the back of a spoon.
3. In a small microwave-safe bowl, heat the chocolate chips on high power for 1 minute. Stir. Continue heating in 30-second increments, stirring after each, until the chocolate is melted. Pour the melted chocolate over the coconut base, and let it sit until the chocolate hardens, about 20 minutes. Cut into 16 bars. They will keep, covered and refrigerated, for up to 1 week.

Per Serving (1 bar) Calories: 305; Protein: 3g; Total fat: 26g; Saturated fat: 22g; Carbohydrates: 19g; Fiber: 6g

HERITAGE OF FOOD: A FAMILY GATHERING

To survive, we need to eat. As a result, food has turned into a symbol of loving, nurturing and sharing with one another. Recording, collecting, sharing and remembering the recipes that have been passed to you by your family is a great way to immortalize and honor your family. It is these traditions that carve out your individual personality. You will not just be honoring your family tradition by cooking these recipes, but they will also inspire you to create your own variations, which you can then pass on to your children's.

The recipes are just passed on to everyone, and nobody actually possesses them. I too love sharing recipes. The collection is vibrant and rich as a number of home cooks have offered their inputs to ensure that all of us can cook delicious meals at our home. I am thankful to each one of you who has contributed to this book and has allowed their traditions to pass on and grow with others. You guys are wonderful!

I am also thankful to the cooks who have evaluated all these recipes. You're, as well as, the comments that came from your family members and friends were invaluable.

If you have the time and inclination, please consider leaving a short review wherever you can, we would love to learn more about your opinion.

https://www.amazon.com/review/review-your-purchases/

About the Author

Jennifer is a New York-based food writer, experienced chef. She loves sharing Easy, Delicious and Healthy recipes, especially the delicious and healthy meals that can be prepared using her power air fryer XL. Jennifer is a passionate advocate for the health benefits of a low-carb lifestyle. When she's not cooking, Jennifer enjoys spending time with her husband and her kids, gardening and traveling.

Made in the USA
Coppell, TX
26 January 2020